# 9/11 DECEPTIONS

# 9/11 Deceptions

by

The Planners and Perpetrators of 9/11 who
were Enabled, Protected, and Concealed by
Officials in Government and Media

# M.P. Lelong

Library of Congress Control Number:         2010913557
ISBN:            Hardcover          978-1-4535-7562-8
                 Softcover          978-1-4535-7561-1
                 Ebook              978-1-4535-7563-5

**To order additional copies of this book, contact:**
Xlibris Corporation
1-888-795-4274
www.Xlibris.com
Orders@Xlibris.com
85887

# CONTENTS

## PART II—GOVERNMENT STORY FOR TWIN TOWER COLLAPSES AND REFUTING ARGUMENTS

**PART III—SUITABLE CUTTER CHARGES AND
EXPLOSIVES FOR DEMOLISHING WTC BUILDINGS**

## PART IV—SLIGHT-OF-HAND
## ATTACK UPON THE PENTAGON

## PART V—DISRUPTION OF AIRCRAFT ATTACKS AS PLANNED UPON THE PENTAGON AND WASHINGTON, D.C.

## PART VI—JOINT PLANNING AND EXECUTION OF 9/11 ATTACKS BY U.S. OFFICIALS AND A FOREIGN AGENCY

## PART VII—AIRCRAFT DEFENSE, AIRCRAFT CAPACITIES, AND PASSENGER COMPENSATION

# PART VIII—US GOVERNMENT ENABLING AND US GOVERNMENT COVERING UP OF 9/11 ATTACKS

## PART X—WHAT WAS PLANNED AND WHAT MIGHT HAVE BEEN

# PREFACE

This book is essentially a literature survey of published information. It is composed of paraphrases and quotations from numerous Internet articles and from more than a dozen excellent books about the events of 9/11. These articles and books were chosen to present a complete and reasonable story of the events on that tragic day. It does not include information from videos about 9/11, such as *Loose Change* and *911 Mysteries*, even though many of them are very good, because the author is hard of hearing.

In spite of the systematic government and media cover-up about 9/11, such as excluding people from the World Trade Center site, forbidding the use of cameras and even confiscating cameras at Ground Zero and carefully monitoring every truck load of steel being sent to a port before shipment to China and elsewhere, the dedicated "9/11 truthers" have produced a surprising amount of carefully developed information which can be printed. This book accordingly contains only secondary material, already published, which has been as accessible to such authorities as Glenn Beck and Bill O'Reilly as they have been to the present author. These two eminent TV personalities, like the rest of the media, seem to have no interest in solving the deceptive murder mysteries of

9/11. The present author has a very strong interest in knowing the truth about 9/11 and seeing justice done according to law. He believes that the contents of this book do generally identify the criminals.

At intervals of the story, the author has entered his comments. To distinguish such comments from the literature-derived story, each such paragraph is bracketed by "[AC]," for "Author's Comment," just as quotation marks bracket quotations.

Many potential readers will read no further because they have been "brainwashed" (a term used during the Cold War with the Soviet Union to describe the mind changing programs on POWs of the Communists). The 21$^{st}$ century brainwashing about 9/11 has been done by coordinated government and media stories and pictures (especially doctored videos) of 9/11 events, which were repeated countless times, until the government/media stories became imprinted in the public mind, thereby creating *faith* in 9/11-according-to-government. Any challenge to that faith tends to cause an emotional upset.

An incident illustrating such upset occurred when the author said to a retired airliner pilot, "9/11 was an inside job." He responded by intent eye-to-eye contact and saying, "I don't believe you, and *I don't want to know.*"

The means for bringing down the three huge and massively constructed buildings of the World Trade Center has been a puzzle. Solving this puzzle requires explaining how, within a time span of about ten seconds, (1) the top thirty floors of the South Tower separated from the floors below and then began to rotate while tilting about 22°; (2) those thirty top floors suddenly erupted upwardly and sideways within about three seconds; (3) all the 110 lightweight concrete floors in each twin tower were decomposed into very fine dust (the finer the dust, the more power needed); (4) nearly all people and all safes, computers, and other office equipment and furniture within each twin tower were burned, melted, or also reduced to such very fine dust; (5) hundreds of tons of steel were hurled sidewise for up to six hundred feet toward the Winter Gardens; (6) many of the two hundred thousand tons of steel beams and columns within each tower were bent without cracking (some into a pretzel shape) and some were cut into a length of about 30 feet; (7) some of the structural steel in the thick core columns was necessarily heated to a softening point in the neighborhood of 2,000°F, whereby this steel could be bent without cracking; (8) the 1,300-feet-tall Twin Towers were reduced to one story within ten seconds instead of a height of 35 stories after a customary demolition; (9) pools of molten steel were found in the resultant rubble and basement levels of all three buildings; and (10) a means for creating heat at high temperatures kept these pools molten and kept this rubble at elevated temperatures for at least three months, in spite of heavy rains and millions of gallons of water being pumped on to the rubble by firefighters.

The official story for the Twin Towers says that the impact of a Boeing 767 airliner upon each tower, followed by fires which were fed by its jet fuel, plus office furniture in about seven impacted floors, heated the steel in the burning floors to such high temperatures that those burning floors collapsed. Then the floors above the seven collapsed floors fell so heavily upon the floors below the collapsed floors that the entire building fell down as would a house of playing cards.

A careful study of this official story, painstakingly supported by print and TV media for nine years, indicates that it is surely a hoax supported by a web of deceptions. The *extremely high* temperatures required to heat massive steel beams (up to six inches thick) almost instantaneously to softening temperatures are so very much greater than the temperatures that a jet fuel fire or an office fire can provide that the official story is clearly impossible—indeed, it's an engineering absurdity and a major deception.

Even if heating time is ignored, the government story is impossible, for structural steel begins to soften at about 1,000°F but is soft enough to bend without cracking only at "yellow or white hot" temperatures, about 2,000°F. In contrast, the National Institute of Standards and Technology (NIST) "found no evidence that any of the steel samples, including those from the impact areas and fire-damaged floors, had reached temperatures exceeding 1,110°F (650°C)." NIST also found that none of the recovered core columns had reached even 482°F (250°C).

The government story totally rejects any use of explosives, thereby creating another major deception. As a matter of fact, the placing of a variety of carefully selected explosives within these three buildings and their expertly timed detonations are exactly the key to the whole WTC murder mystery. The same key explains most of the 9/11 damage to the Pentagon. This book explores explosive usage in some detail. Explosives which could have been used include thermite, thermate, and super thermite cutter charges and such super explosives as mini-atom bombs, micro-hydrogen bombs, and HAARP/beam weapons.

The nineteen Arabs, upon whom the crimes of 9/11 were blamed, never entered the four airliners according to flight records. Moreover, the alleged uses of cell phones, which provided evidence for Muslims being aboard the airliners, were technically impossible in 2001. So the Arab story and the cell phone stories were important deceptions, especially in combination.

—

Cell phone transmissions from a plane had to reach cell sites on the ground, requiring several seconds. Because the airliners had considerable mass and flew at high altitudes, more seconds were needed for transmission to the cell sites. Then the airliners' speeds made it impossible for even a single word to be received at the initial cell site before the transmission had to skip to the next cell site and then to a third one, etc.

Agents of Israel's Mossad were living close to the Arabs who were taking flight training. Some of the Arabs were even training at Pensacola Naval Air Station. The Mossad agents learned their plans, probably with the help of at least one female agent and pillow talk, and decided to use those plans and blame the consequences on the Arabs who would be made to disappear. With abundant money, they persuaded the Arabs to be very conspicuous late on September 10 and then to follow a carefully arranged plan that would take them out of the USA on September 11.

So if the Arabs were not aboard the planes, why did the four aircraft even change course? Many major deceptions are involved in answering that question. They are explored in several chapters.

Then if the Arabs were merely paid patsies, who were the actual criminals? The answer to this mystery can best be found by independent federal grand juries which can conduct investigations that are independent of judges and prosecutors and thereby able to investigate governmental corruption. To be independent, these grand juries must be unshackled from official control and have authority from the Fifth Amendment to the U.S. Constitution to issue *presentments* for action thereon by jurors in a federal district court.

Such independent federal grand juries, however, are now impractical because Rules 6 and 7 of the Federal Rules of Criminal

Procedure, written by a congressional committee in 1946, specify "indictment" and omit "presentment," contrary to the Fifth Amendment to the U.S. Constitution. Grand juries which issue indictments are controlled by a district attorney and consequently by the federal government so that certain corruptions and felonies can now be protected. Routine criminal court procedures have hardened this omission into nationwide habit. Nevertheless, the authority of the U.S. Constitution has the power to override all federal rules and laws.

It should be borne in mind that in addition to the 9/11 perpetrators who placed a variety of timed explosives in key places and later detonated them and were clearly guilty of murder, the planners were also guilty of murder as accessories before the fact, and the concealers were equally guilty of murder as accessories after the fact. Without a feeling of certainty that the concealers would be very effective (as indeed they have been for more than nine years), it is quite possible that the planners and perpetrators who were living in the United States would have been afraid to commit their evil deeds. These concealers include various officials in the Bush and Obama administrations and many U.S. media owners and officials, both print and television.

# PART I
## World Trade Center in Manhattan and Destruction of Buildings 1, 2, and 7

# CHAPTER 1

## The World Trade Center in Manhattan and Its History

### *Historical Background*

The seven WTC buildings were constructed at different times. Rockefeller, vice chairman of Chase Manhattan Bank, handled a project to plan "a world trade center" that would hopefully transform the southern tip of Manhattan from a flagging, stagnant backwater to a vital mainstream. The building project became the work of the New York Port Authority, which moved the site to 13.5 acres on the east side of Manhattan near the Brooklyn Bridge. The governor of New York State at that time was Nelson Rockefeller, David's brother. The project included twin towers, each having 110 floors, each including 4 million square feet of office space for about 20,000 occupants and merely three stairwells. This was possible because the fire code had been changed in 1968 to save building costs.[1]

In more detail, the New York City building code was revised by the New York Building Congress, a trade organization of

—

construction unions and real estate interests, who had long lobbied for revising the code, arguing that the 1938 code did not anticipate improvements in technology such as the availability of lightweight materials. They believed that these materials would serve just as well for many purposes as the much heavier steel skeletons wrapped in masonry to resist fire as required by the 1938 code. Another purpose was to reduce the amount of space required for escape ways. Turning over some of that precious floor space to seemingly outsized safety requirements was surely an imprudent and uneconomical regulation of business. The new code quietly changed some of that real estate used for evacuation routes into more office space and thus more money.

The previous generation of skyscrapers in New York had to have at least one "fire tower"—a masonry-enclosed stairwell, which was entered through a 107-square-foot vestibule. Any smoke entering with fleeing people would be captured and vented. Then the people had to pass through a second doorway, thereby enabling them to flee down the stairs without bringing along trails of smoke.[2]

## Construction Details

Towers 1, 2, and 7 were designed as framed tube structures. Twin Towers 1 and 2 comprised a frame of 240 closely spaced perimeter columns, tied together by 52-inch wide spandrel beams along the exterior perimeters of the buildings, and a core of forty-seven columns, which enclosed three stairways, numerous elevator shafts, conference rooms, and restrooms. Each core column had a rectangular cross section of approximately 36 inches by 14 inches at its base with 4 inches of steel all around, tapering to one-fourth-inch thickness at the top. The perimeter columns supported wind loads and shared the gravity loads with the core columns, all columns being attached to the bedrock, which was 65 feet below the surface. The floors consisted of 4-inch-thick lightweight concrete slabs laid on a fluted and galvanized steel deck. A grid of lightweight bridging trusses and main trusses supported the floors. The trusses had a span of 60 feet in the long-span areas and 35 feet in the short-span areas.[3]

Each tower was a box within a box, joined by horizontal trusses at each floor. The outer box, measuring 208 feet by 208 feet, was constructed of 14-inch (36-cm) wide steel columns. On every floor above the plaza level, the spaces between the columns were filled with 22-inch (56-cm) wide windows. The columns were covered with aluminum so that the towers had a distinctive silver color. The inner box at the core of each tower was about 135 feet by 85 feet (41 by 26 m). The design gave the building remarkable stability. This tube design created great real estate because the available space, about ¾ of an acre per floor, could be configured as each occupant desired.

When completed in 1970, the North Tower was 1,368 feet in height, 100 feet higher than the Empire State Building. The forty-seven core columns supported about 53 percent of the weight of each building and were massive, up to 52 inches wide and 7 inches thick at the base, where they weighed as much as 5,000 pounds per linear foot. The core columns began as box columns at the foot of each building and gradually changed to rolled wide-flange beams ("I" beams) higher up. The pinstripe (perimeter) columns carried 47 percent of the weight of the building, running it down to its foundation and the bedrock, and also resisted the force of the wind. These exterior columns were reinforced with broad steel plates known as spandrels, which girdled the building, like ribs, at every floor. The perimeter columns were connected to the core by means of steel bar-joist trusses bneath the concrete floors. The FEMA report said, "The floor framing system for the two towers was complex and substantially more redundant than typical bar joist floor systems."

Although the core columns gradually decreased in size from bottom to top, the external dimensions of the perimeter columns had to be uniform all the way up for aesthetic reasons. This appearance of outward uniformity required the use of heat-treated, that is, high-strength steel, which had become available in the 1960s. Prefabrication and a modular design were other innovations that reduced costs and enabled speedy construction.

Although lightweight, the floor design was so sound that it easily supported the weight of libraries, file rooms, and heavy safes without needing additional supports. The lightweight truss assembles were vulnerable to fire damage, however, because they consisted of rather thin steel members. For this reason, at the time of construction, the trusses were spray-coated with protective insulation, 0.75 inch thick, and this was later upgraded to an average thickness of more than 2 inches. (The technical term for the insulation is Spray-applied Fire Resistant Material: SFRM) The core columns had a fire-barrier of gypsum wallboard.[4]

The strength of each tower and its resistance to impact of an airliner were so great that each tower was able to absorb a plane's impact easily so that within a few dozen seconds after the plane crash, the North Tower was quiet, stable, and motionless.

Gravity was a lesser force to be withstood by the buildings than was the force of the wind. Each face could withstand a hurricane of 140 mph, and the wind load on an ordinary day was 30 times greater than the force of the airplane striking it on September 11. Moreover, the mass of each tower was 1,000 times greater than the mass of each airliner so that it was not surprising that the buildings continued to stand after the planes hit. The surviving pinstripe columns on the north face of the North Tower, for example, formed an arch around the wound, creating new paths for the weight of the building to travel along the unscathed columns.[5]

## *Lack of Profitability, Transfer of Operating Authority, and Insurance Moves*

However, because of its expensive elevator system (ninety-nine elevators in each tower), the project was not profitable. Many offices were vacant. Moreover, the buildings were considered to be an architectural white elephant and undesirable real estate partly because asbestos was used as insulation. Attempts by the Port Authority to get permits to demolish the buildings were turned down because of the known asbestos problem. Disassembling the Twin Towers floor by floor was estimated to cost $15 billion; even the scaffolding for the operation was estimated to cost $2.4 billion.

On July 24, 2001, Lewis M. Eisenberg, chairman of the Port Authority of New York and New Jersey agreed to lease the Twin Towers and other portions of the World Trade Center to Silverstein Properties, Inc., and Westfield America, Inc., for ninety-nine years in a deal worth $3.2 billion. Westfield America, Inc., was to be responsible for the retail space, and Silverstein Properties's lease was to cover the 10 million square feet of office space in the Twin Towers and Buildings 4 and 5. Silverstein already owned

Building 7. Building 6 was the U.S. Customs Building. The World Trade Center was thereby privatized. It was the first time in its thirty-three-year history that the complex had ever changed ownership.

A property risk assessment report was prepared for Silverstein Properties, Inc., before it obtained the lease for the World Trade Center. This report dealt with the scenario of an aircraft hitting one of the WTC towers as one of the "maximum foreseeable losses." The report said, "This scenario is within the realm of the possible, but highly unlikely."

Silverstein promptly insured the complex for $7 billion against "terrorist attacks." He paid an installment of $14 million. Silverstein immediately hired a new security company for the complex. It was Securacom (now Stratasec), having George W. Bush's brother, Marvin Bush, on its board of directors, and Marvin's cousin, Wirt Walker III, as its CEO. Securacom also provided electronic security for Dulles International and United Airlines—two key players in the 9/11 attacks. After September 11, 2001, the insurance company, Swiss Re, paid Mr. Silverstein $4.6 billion.[6]

[Author's Comment—AC] Damage to both of the Twin Towers by the impacts of two airplanes would have been extremely unlikely, for if one impact was "highly unlikely," damage to both towers would have been at least (highly unlikely)$^2$. Silverstein could not normally have expected the towers to be destroyed by such impacts, for they were planned to withstand them. He could have reasonably expected the impacts to have been only moderately damaging to those huge, massive, and overly built buildings and have known that steel framed buildings were routinely resistant to fires for many hours. Therefore, Silverstein must have *known*, when he leased the World Trade Center in which the Twin Towers were losing money, that *both* Twin Towers would be struck and that they would be *destroyed* after the impacts by some abnormally powerful means, thereby enabling him to avoid the $15 billion cost of dismantling them, floor by floor. When he insured the towers against terrorism, he was again demonstrating his foreknowledge of future events, at least to the extent of spending $14 million of his own money. [AC]

## Investigations of Chief Conspirator
## Osama bin Laden and al Qaeda

The history of the World Trade Center obviously involves the bomb attacks in 1993 and the disastrous attacks of September 11, 2001. As everyone knows, the latter have been blamed on nineteen individuals, most of them from Saudi Arabia. According to the official account, there was a conspiracy among radical Muslims against the United States, and Osama bin Laden was the chief conspirator.

In March 2001, the Russian Permanent Mission at the United Nations secretly submitted "an unprecedentedly detailed report" to the UN Security Council about bin Laden and his whereabouts, including "a listing of all bin Laden's bases, his government contacts and foreign advisors—enough information, they said, to kill him. But the Bush administration took no action." Alex Standish, the editor of *Jane's Intelligence Review* , would later conclude that the attacks of 9/11 were not an intelligence failure but the result of "a political decision not to act against bin Laden."

By the summer of 2001, Osama bin Laden was America's "most wanted" criminal for whom it was offering a $5 million bounty, and the U.S. government had supposedly tried to kill him. And yet in July 2001, according to reports by several of Europe's most respected news sources, bin Laden spent two weeks in the American hospital in Dubai (of the United Arab Emirates). Besides being treated by an American surgeon, Dr. Terry Callaway, he was also reportedly visited by the head of Saudi intelligence and, on July 12, by the local CIA agent, Larry Michell. Although the reports were denied by the CIA, the hospital, and bin Laden himself, Dr. Callaway reportedly simply refused comment, and the news agencies stood by their story.

The explosive story was "widely reported in Europe, but barely at all in the US." Secretary of Defense Rumsfeld commented that finding bin Laden would be like "searching for a needle in a stack of hay," but his interviewer wrote that the United States could have ordered his arrest and extradition in Dubai in July 2001 and added, "But then they would not have had a pretext for waging a war."[8]

It is interesting that the U.S. Federal Bureau of Investigation (FBI) has an online listing of Most Wanted Terrorists, which includes a web page about Osama bin Laden. He is "wanted by the FBI for the August 1998 attacks upon U.S. embassies in Dar es Salaam, Tanzania, and in Nairobi, Kenya, which killed over 200 people." Rewards of $27 million are offered for information leading to his apprehension or conviction. However, this FBI web page makes no reference to 9/11.[9]

The reason why this web page does not mention 9/11 in connection with bin Laden was explained by the FBI as follows:

The FBI gathers evidence. Once evidence is gathered, it is turned over to the Department of Justice. The Department of Justice then decides whether it has enough evidence to present to a federal grand jury. In the case of the 1998 United States Embassies being bombed, bin Laden has been formally indicted and charged by a grand jury. He has not been finally indicted and charged in connection with 9/11 *because the FBI has no hard evidence connecting bin Laden with 9/11.*[10]

# Chapter 1 Notes

1. The Port Authority of New York and New Jersey Press Release No. 101-2001. "GOVERNOR PATAKI, ACTING GOVERNOR DIFRANCESCO LAUD HISTORIC PORT AUTHORITY AGREEMENT TO PRIVATIZE WORLD TRADE CENTER. July 24, 2001. http:www.panynj.gov/abouttheportauthority/ presscenter/PressReleases/PressRelease/inde . . .

2. Dwyer, Jim and Kevin Flynn. *102 Minutes: the Untold Story of the Fight to Survive inside the Twin Towers.* 2005. New York, N.Y. Henry Holt and Company, 105- 107.

3. *HowStuffWorks* "The World Trade Center," *http://people. howstuffworks.com/wtc1.htm.*

4. Gaffney, Mark. *The 9/11 Mystery Plane and the Vanishing of America.* Walterville, OR 97489, Trine Day LLC, PO Box 577, 161, 162.

5. Dwyer, Jim and Kevin Flynn, 40.

6. History Commons. "Context of 'July 24, 2001: World Trade Center Ownership Changes Hands For the First Time.'" http://www. historycommons.org/context.jsp?item=a072401silverstein.

7. Marrs, Jim. *The Terror Conspiracy: Deception, 9/11 and the Loss of Liberty.* 2006. New York, N.Y. 10003. The Disinformation Company, Ltd., 163 Third Avenue. Suite 103, 50.

8. Griffin, David Ray. *The New Pearl Harbor: Disturbing Questions about the Bush Administration and 9/11.* 2005. Northampton, Massachusetts 01060. Interlink Publishing Group, Inc., 46 Crosby Street, 76, 77.

9. FBI. "Most Wanted Terrorists: Murder of U.S. Nationals Outside the United States; Conspiracy to Murder U.S. Nationals Outside the

United States; Attack on a Federal Facility Resulting in Death-Usama bin Laden." *http://www.fbi.gov/wanted/terrorists/terbinladen.htm.*
10. Gaffney, 115, 116.

# CHAPTER 2

## Alleged Hijackings of
## Four U.S. Commercial Airliners on
## September 11, 2001

### *Airliners, Fighter Jets, and Standard Operating Procedures*

Four passenger airplanes turned around after leaving Logan Airport near Boston, Newark Airport near New York City, and Dulles Airport in northern Virginia. Each should have been intercepted by two fighter jets within about ten minutes of turning around, according to standard operating procedures (SOP) so that no airliner should have been able to reach the World Trade Center or the Pentagon.

These standard operating procedures were completely and strangely canceled on September 11, something that had never occurred before. The cancelations created dangerous situations, for the SOP is needed to prevent midair collisions of both airliners and private planes in addition to confronting hijacked planes. The FAA reported in a news release on August 9, 2002, that it had scrambled fighters sixty-seven times between September 2000 and June 2001, and the *Calgary Herald* (October 13, 2001) reported that NORAD scrambled fighters 129 times in 2000. One explanation is that six or more war games were occurring that morning, which caused confusion; another explanation is that such routine protective systems were sabotaged when the supreme U.S. military command issued "stand down" orders; a third explanation is that this command included at least U.S. President George Bush, U.S. Secretary of Defense Donald Rumsfeld, and the then Acting Head of the Joint Chiefs of Staff, Air Force Gen. Richard Myers. Moreover, Vice President Richard Cheney had been placed by President Bush directly in charge of managing the "seamless integration" of all training exercises in May 2001.[1]

## Passenger Manifests

The official passenger manifests from American and United Airlines covering these four 9/11 flights contained no names identified as hijackers, and this fact has not been explained. However, several alleged hijackers were found to be alive overseas. On September 2, the *London Times* reported, "Five of the hijackers were using stolen identities, and investigators are studying the possibility that the entire suicide squad consisted of impostors."[2]

# Airliner Flights in Accordance with U.S. Government Story

## American Airlines Flight 11

American Airlines (AA) Flight 11 left Logan Airport at Boston at 7:59 a.m. At 8:14 this airliner failed to respond to an order to climb from the Federal Aviation Administration (FAA) ground control, and its radio and transponder went off, suggesting a possible hijacking. At 8:20, the plane went radically off course. At 8:28 the plane turned toward New York City.

At 8:46 a.m., Flight 11 crashed into the WTC's North Tower, WTC-1, thirty-two minutes after evidence of possible hijacking and twenty-five minutes after evidence of a definite hijacking. No fighter jets had been scrambled. If they had been scrambled, according to SOP, Flight 11 would have been intercepted by 8:24 a.m. in response to loss of radio and transponder signals and by 8:30 in response to changing its course.

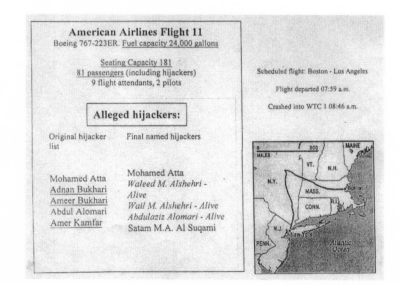

American Airlines Flight 11
Boeing 767-223ER. Fuel capacity 24,000 gallons

Seating Capacity 181
81 passengers (including hijackers)
9 flight attendants, 2 pilots

Scheduled flight: Boston - Los Angeles

Flight departed 07:59 a.m.

Crashed into WTC 1 08:46 a.m.

Alleged hijackers:

Original hijacker list — Final named hijackers

Mohamed Atta
Adnan Bukhari
Ameer Bukhari
Abdul Alomari
Amer Kamfar

Mohamed Atta
Waleed M. Alshehri - Alive
Wail M. Alshehri - Alive
Abdulaziz Alomari - Alive
Satam M.A. Al Suqami

## United Airlines Flight 175

United Airlines (UA) Flight 175 left Logan Airport at Boston at 8:14 a.m. At 8:42 its radio and transponder went off, and it veered off course so that it flew over New York City. FAA officials reportedly notifie1d NORAD at 8:43 a.m. Fighter jets should have intercepted Flight 175 at 8:53 and should have been ready to shoot down this "hijacked plane" if it did not immediately follow orders. However, no jets arrived, and the UA airliner crashed into a corner of WTC-2, the South Tower, at 9:03 a.m. Significantly, "no one associated with NORAD or the FAA has been punished."[3]

**United Airlines Flight 175**
Boeing 767-222. Fuel capacity 24,000 gallons

Seating Capacity 181
56 passengers (including hijackers)
7 flight attendants, 2 pilots

**Alleged hijackers:**

Marwan Al-Shehhi
Fayez Rashid Ahmed Hassan Al Qadi
Banihammad
Ahmed Alghamdi
Hamza Alghamdi
*Mohand Alshehri - Alive*

*Full details*

Scheduled flight: Boston - Los Angeles

Flight departed 08:14 a.m.

Crashed into WTC2 09:03 a.m.

## *American Airlines Flight 77*

American Airlines (AA) Flight 77 left Dulles Airport, southwest of Washington, D.C., at 8:20 a.m. At 8:46, it went significantly off course for several minutes but was back on course at 8:50 when radio contact was lost. At 8:56 the plane's transponder went off, and the plane disappeared from the air traffic controller's radar screen in Indianapolis. No fighter jets were scrambled even though Andrews AFB was only thirteen miles away. At 9:25, twenty-nine minutes after Flight 77 disappeared, air controllers at Dulles Airport reported that a fast-moving plane was heading toward the White House.

AA Flight 77 flew on an easterly course over Arlington. Then, beginning at about 7,000 feet above the ground, the aircraft made a difficult "downward spiral," turning almost a complete circle, and dropped the last 7,000 feet in two-and-a-half minutes.

At about 9:38, wedge 1 of the Pentagon was hit, killing 125 workers, primarily civilians. A huge fireball was created, which was seen by many people in the morning traffic. They believed they saw AA 77 flying above their heads and into the Pentagon.[4]

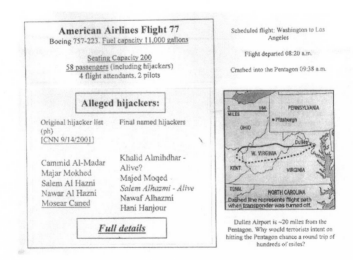

## *United Airlines Flight 93*

United Airlines (UA) Flight 93 left Newark Airport at 8:42 a.m., forty-one minutes late for takeoff. At 9:27 a passenger allegedly called his wife, telling her that the plane had been hijacked. At 9:28 ground flight controllers heard sounds of screaming and scuffling. The official story is that passengers decided to attack the hijackers with a "Let's roll" order and apparently were succeeding when there was "some sort of explosion" and "white smoke coming from the plane," suggesting that the plane had been "holed"—shot down by a missile—after it seemed that the passengers were gaining control of it.

The tape of the cockpit recording begins at 9:31 and ends at 10:02. At 9:56 fighter jets were finally given orders to intercept and shoot down any airplanes under the control of hijackers. The government claimed that Flight 93 crashed at 10:03. A seismic study concluded that the crash occurred slightly after 10:06. Shortly before the crash, CBS television reported that two F-16 fighters were closely tailing the airliner. As the fighters got nearer to Flight 93, Vice President Cheney was asked three times to confirm that the fighters should engage, and Cheney said, "Yes." Witnesses on the ground heard "a loud thump," "a loud bang," or "two loud bangs" before the plane headed downward. These accounts "virtually all support a missile strike."[5]

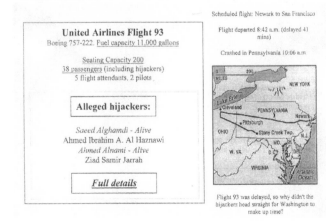

Scheduled flight: Newark to San Francisco

**United Airlines Flight 93**
Boeing 757-222. Fuel capacity 11,000 gallons

Seating Capacity 200
38 passengers (including hijackers)
5 flight attendants, 2 pilots

**Alleged hijackers:**

*Saeed Alghamdi - Alive*
Ahmed Ibrahim A. Al Haznawi
*Ahmed Alnami - Alive*
Ziad Samir Jarrah

*Full details*

Flight departed 8:42 a.m. (delayed 41 mins)

Crashed in Pennsylvania 10:06 a.m.

Flight 93 was delayed, so why didn't the hijackers head straight for Washington to make up time?

—

# Chapter 2 Notes

1. Zarembka, Paul. *The Hidden History of 9-11*. Second Edition. 2008. New York, NY 10013. Seven Stories Press, 140 Watts Street, 127-132.
2. Firmage, Joseph P. "30. Hijacker names missing from flight manifests" and "31. Several alleged hijackers discovered alive and well." *Journal of 9/11 Studies*, August 2006/Volume 2, 36.
3. Griffin, David Ray. Updated edition. *The New Pearl Harbor: Disturbing Questions about the Bush Administration and 9/11.* 2005. Northampton, Massachusetts: Olive Branch Press, 3-7.
4. Ibid., 25.
5. Ibid., 49-53.

# CHAPTER 3

## Detailed Discussions of Route Changes, Plane Swappings, and Other Deceptions Involving the Four 9/11 Commercial Flights

### *Plane Interceptions By Fighter Jets*

Dr. Griffin realized that in his earlier book he had written only of NORAD (the North American Aerospace Defense Command) and not specifically of NORAD's Northeast Air Defense Sector, known as NEADS, located in Rome, New York. Because all the 9/11 flights were in that sector, the FAA's contact with the military would have been with NEADS.

Dr. Griffin also realized that he had failed to distinguish between two different reasons for contacting the military: hijackings and in-flight emergencies, each having different protocols. The hijackings protocol was quite slow because it often takes time to establish whether a plane has really been hijacked and because it was assumed that the hijackers wanted to enter into negotiations, not to commit suicide, so that military planes would not intercept the hijacked plane but would follow several miles behind it, out of sight. In contrast, the in-flight emergency protocol was aimed at intercepting the plane as quickly as possible. The following procedure was typically used:

> [T]he interceptor "launch system" is sitting in waiting for immediate reaction and launch. Interceptors are located in open-ended hangars near the ends of runways, the flight crews are located within a few feet and few moments of climbing on board the fighter, the mechanics keep the aircraft mechanically fit and warm with power sources connected for immediate start-up . . . This is a highly skilled and highly practiced event . . . Everyone [concerned is] prepared to launch within a few minutes of the request . . . The "emergency scramble protocol" [then] calls for the fighter pilots to fly at top speed to intercept the emergency aircraft.

Although some people have claimed that the pilots would not have shot down the airliners, one expert, Robert Hordon, had a contrary opinion:

> [M]ake no mistake about this, should the "hijacked aircraft" appear to threaten major populations, or seem to be headed for important military or civilian targets, then the pilots can shoot them down on their own. Shootdown orders are authorized for the pilots to use under certain conditions, some of them pre-approved by higher ups, and some of them at a moment's notice . . . . If an Otis fighter . . . pilot saw the Boeing descend and head straight for NYC, he would already be considering shooting the aircraft down miles and miles away from NYC. And this

is regardless of it being an airliner full of passengers. If the pilot came to the conclusion that AA 11 was going to crash into NYC, or its nuclear plant, I will guarantee that AA 11 would have been shot down prior to hitting any buildings.[1]

The air defense network on September 11, 2001, had predictable and effective procedures for dealing with just such attacks. Nevertheless, response was delayed for more than an hour and a half after the attacks had started. "There are failures upon failures, in what might be described as a strategy of layered failures, or *failure in depth*," which can be divided into four types:

Failures to report: Based on the official timeline, the FAA response times for reporting the deviating aircraft were many times longer than the prescribed times.

Failures to scramble: NORAD, once notified of the off-course aircraft, failed to scramble jets from the nearest bases.

Failures to intercept: Once airborne, interceptors failed to reach their targets because they flew at small fractions of their top speeds.

Failures to redeploy: Fighters that were airborne and within interception range of the deviating aircraft did not redeploy to pursue them.[2]

Dr. Griffin concluded that if standard operating procedures had been followed, Flight 11 would have been intercepted before the North Tower was struck. NORAD's reason that it was not intercepted was that the FAA had not followed standard procedures. Instead of notifying the military at 8:21 when Flight 11 went off course or even at 8:25 when it learned that Flight 11 had been hijacked, the FAA only notified NEADS at 8:40. "But if FAA personnel at Boston Center had violated procedures so radically, with such disastrous consequences, they should have been fired and perhaps even charged with criminal dereliction of duty. But no one was even publicly reprimanded."

Dr. Griffin further concluded that the 9/11 Commission Report had only strengthened his earlier explanation for the military's failure to intercept Flight 11: a stand-down order had been issued.[3]

Confirmation of Dr. Griffin's conclusion comes from 9-11 Research.com:

> No plausible explanation has been provided for failing to scramble interceptors in a timely fashion from bases within easy range to protect the September 11th targets. Fighters that were dispatched were scrambled from distant bases. Early in the attack, when Flight 11 had turned directly south toward New York City, it was obvious that New York City and the World Trade Center, and Washington, D.C. would be likely targets. They were only scrambled from distant bases. Moreover there were no redundant or backup scrambles.[4]

Jim Tucker of *American Free Press* wrote that since the World Trade Center towers were erected, planes had flown into their restricted space over 1,000 times, and every time they were intercepted.[5]

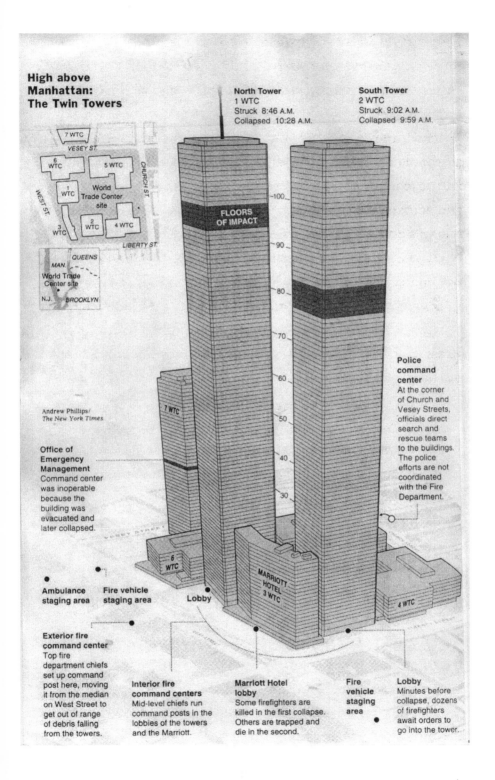

# High above Manhattan: The Twin Towers

**North Tower**
1 WTC
Struck 8:46 A.M.
Collapsed 10:28 A.M.

**South Tower**
2 WTC
Struck 9:02 A.M.
Collapsed 9:59 A.M.

7 WTC

VESEY ST.

6 WTC

5 WTC

CHURCH ST.

1 WTC

World Trade Center site

WEST ST.

3 WTC

2 WTC

4 WTC

LIBERTY ST.

QUEENS

MAN.

World Trade Center site

N.J.

BROOKLYN

FLOORS OF IMPACT

—100—

—90—

—80—

—70—

—60—

—50—

—40—

—30—

Andrew Phillips/
The New York Times.

7 WTC

**Police command center**
At the corner of Church and Vesey Streets, officials direct search and rescue teams to the buildings. The police efforts are not coordinated with the Fire Department.

**Office of Emergency Management**
Command center was inoperable because the building was evacuated and later collapsed.

6 WTC

MARRIOTT HOTEL 3 WTC

4 WTC

Lobby

**Ambulance staging area**

**Fire vehicle staging area**

**Exterior fire command center**
Top fire department chiefs set up command post here, moving it from the median on West Street to get out of range of debris falling from the towers.

**Interior fire command centers**
Mid-level chiefs run command posts in the lobbies of the towers and the Marriott.

**Marriott Hotel lobby**
Some firefighters are killed in the first collapse. Others are trapped and die in the second.

**Fire vehicle staging area**

**Lobby**
Minutes before collapse, dozens of firefighters await orders to go into the tower.

## Grounding of American Airlines Flight 11 and Take Off of United Airlines Flight 175 from Boston Logan International Airport as a Combined Flight

American Flight 11 did not take off from Boston Logan International Airport, as shown by the Bureau of Traffic Statistics (BTS). AA 0011 was scheduled to depart from Logan at 07 45 AM on 09/11/2001 for LAX as its Destination Airport with a Scheduled Elapsed Time (Minutes) of 0374, but its Actual Elapsed Time (Minutes) was 0000, its Departure Time was 0, its Wheels-off Time was 00 00, and its Taxi-out Time (Minutes) was 0000.

Passengers could have purchased a ticket for Flight 11, but they could not have left the airport on that flight on September 11, 2001. The "BTS database is accurate and also definite. Flight 11 did not depart on 911."

> Flights are canceled all the time and combined with other flights according to the dictates of the airlines and passenger loads any given day. Yet there are no records of any such occurrences on 9/11. The official story is set in stone. The people boarded Flight 11. They boarded AT (sic) Flight 11's gate.

Phil Jayhan pointed out, however, that the government has not produced a single video of the passengers boarding any of the four 9/11 flights. Doing so could have demonstrated that the passengers were in a different part of the airport than they were stated to be by official records.[6]

A deception was successfully used at Boston Logan International Airport when the passengers from both Flights 11 and 175 were

combined into one flight, identified as United Airlines Flight 175,
that apparently took off on schedule.

> Above Stuart air force base we are told that flight 11
> and 175 nearly collided they got so close. We were also
> given snippets of this through air traffic control tapes.
> The explanation for this is as plausible as it is logical.
> This is where the 2 military drones which were to strike
> to (sic) world trade centers took off from. They would
> replace the flight path of Flight 175 as well as the path
> of flight 11, which up to this point was provided for by
> an electronic warfare plane which was one of "4" such
> aircraft in the air for the War games which were taking
> place on 9/11/2001.

> Sometime shortly after this, Flight 175 NOW HAVING
> BEEN REPLACED BY A MILITARY DRONE ON
> RADAR will change its transponder to Delta 1989, and
> make an emergency landing at Cleveland, with reports
> of a bomb aboard. This plane would contain roughly 200
> people, and not only is it plausible that these people were
> the people from flights 11 & 175, it is highly probable
> and likely.

UA Flight 175 did land at the Cleveland Airport at 10:10
a.m., and at 12:30 the 69 passengers were taken into the FAA
headquarters, the I-X Exposition Center, at the south end of
Cleveland Hopkins International Airport. Because of the "bomb
aboard" story, the Cleveland Airport was closed and evacuated. The
sixty-nine passengers and nine crew members were interrogated

for three hours. UA Flight 93 landed at 10:45 in the Cleveland Airport. Its passengers were taken to the evacuated NASA Center in the north end of the airport.[7]

## *Swapping of Planes and Plane Courses*

A flight controller watching radar sees a plan view of a passing plane A, as if he were flying in the air directly over plane A. If another plane B that is at a lower or higher altitude crosses the course of plane A, the radar sees only one plane within a space of half a kilometer (1637 feet) as the blips merge. Then if plane A turns within that space to follow the course of plane B while plane B also turns to follow the course of plane A, the flight controller will be unaware that the planes have swapped.[8]

[AC]Both Flights175 and 93 probably swapped in the air with military drone planes after reaching Stuart Air Force base. They were thereby no longer involved with the WTC events.[AC]

## *Crashing of Alleged Flight 11 onto North Tower*

However, video evidence shows that the alleged Flight 11 crashed into the north face of the North Tower at 8:46 a.m. on September 11, 2001, but it also shows a bright flash at the tower's face just prior to impact. Substitution by a suitably painted military drone, capable of firing a missile before impact, provides a reasonable explanation for "bouncing back" of luggage, etc.[9]

## Crashing of Alleged Flight 175 onto South Tower

The alleged Flight 175 that struck a corner of the South Tower had a missile attached to its underside and was also clearly a suitably painted military drone. A bright flash also was visible on the south face of the South Tower immediately before impact. It should also be noted that an engine from the plane that hit WTC 2 landed at the corner of Chuck and Murray Streets. This engine "was a CFM-56 which is not utilized on a Boeing 767i+, confirming that the south tower was not hit by flight 175, but by another plane that had taken its place." It was identified by engine experts from photographs. A CFM-56 engine is installed in a Boeing 737 airliner. It does not have enough power to lift a Boeing 767 airliner. It is important, however, to note that it also "bounced" back from the south face of the South Tower with a force that overcame the momentum imparted by the aircraft.[10]

An article from Spain comments about a "thorough *digital image analysis*" done by a Spanish university about "these strange objects attached to the underside of the Flight 175" that concluded that "the objects were three-dimensional and could not have been caused by shadows or reflections.[11]

[AC] It is worthwhile to note that this heavy engine apparently did bounce back from the south face of the South Tower, but body parts, luggage, or clothing evidently did not. In other words, the military aircraft substituting for UA Flight 175 was an empty military drone.[AC]

—

# Official Government Story Was a Collossal Hoax

A lengthy article by Dr. Morgan Reynolds, dated March 5, 2006, concluded:

- 9/11 was a colossal hoax, an egregious example of false-flag terrorism
- Corporate media dutifully sold the scam
- Four reported airliners vanished as if by magic

September 11 was a well-planned psy-op, deceptive at every level, intended to manipulate public opinion, and wildly successful in the short run. Given this background, virtually everything the government and its media stenographers parrot to this day must be construed as deception until proven otherwise.[12]

Hoffman and like-minded defenders of the 767 theory want their cake and eat it too: supposedly powerful 767s easily penetrate steel walls and floors yet identically crumbled within a fraction of a second and vanished inside despite huge fuselage length and wingspan ¾ the length of a tower wall. Both 767s were never seen again from any side of either tower, a dazzling combination of imposing strength and fragility within a tenth of a second.

The two end points—easy tower penetration at high speed without visible deceleration and flight termination within 200 feet—are nonsense.

The official Hoffman theory is impossible to accept unless the plane was rigged to explode or disintegrate upon contact with the wall, enabling its thorough destruction inside. That might restore some plausibility to the 767 story but it is certainly not the government story. Such explosives would add considerable complexity for the perpetrators in an already-complex crime package, violating the KISS rule. The basic problem remains that a large commercial jetliner could not punch a clean, debris-free hole into a steel tower wall to begin with. The plane would need help, explosive help of its own and/or explosives from inside the building. Even the explosions that took place blew no aircraft parts out the tower gashes to settle below the impact walls.[13]

## Oral Histories of Plane Impacts and "Bounced Back" Evidence from North Tower Crash

From "more than 12,000 pages of oral histories rendered in the voices of 503 firefighters, paramedics, and emergency "medical technicians," all of whom were published by the *New York Times*, these comments are available:

PO James E Hall "I heard the sound of jet engines and observed an aircraft with a blue tail colour fly directly into the south face of tower 2"

Firefighter James Curran p2 (1st plane) "We heard the plane, we looked up. It was low enough that it

—

55

rattled the buildings we were staring at it. We saw it come out from behind the buildings and hit tower one"

Chief Albert Turi p4 "I heard something similar to the sound of a jet engine taking off, and when I looked up I saw the impact of the second plane hitting the south tower and immediately a huge fireball erupted that actually masked the upper half of the building and part of the of north tower. It was so enormous that even from that great distance (corner of Fulton and Church, east side of wtc) I could feel the radiant heat on my face.

Lieutenant Wayne Mera p5 "We were walking up Vessey and we saw parts of the plane on the ground still burning"

Paramedic Manuel Delgado p27near a little plaza close to West Boadway and west Vessey "Right there, there was like a big engine part. It seemed like the whole engine was right there, lying right in the middle of the street."

Firefighter Thomas Lynn p3 saw plane parts on West street

Captain Ray Goldback p4 Dey or Cortland St "littered with plane parts"

Firefighter John Moribito p7

After first hit, before second hit "I noticed in the courtyard there were valises, suitcases, strewn about the courtyard. There were wallets everywhere, broken glass, and then I noticed that there were *airplane tickets*"

Paramedic Manuel Delgado p27-27 "When we first got there, down Vessey towards West, there was a ton of body parts and like baggage, clothes and stuff. We saw lots of shoes, even some luggage"

Firefighter Frank Vaskis p7 saw a foot and other body parts on West Street.[14]

[AC] As shown in the accompanying sketch of the WTC and nearby streets, there was a bright and large flash on this north face, indicating an explosion at the exact place that the fuselage of the Flight 11 airliner would have struck the north face of WTC 1. Then several men saw evidence indicating that plane parts, people, luggage, baggage, tickets, shoes, and clothes had been hurled *backwards*, with respect to the airliner's course. Considering the momentum imparted by the airliner's speed of 450 miles per hour, only powerful explosives could have given so much *bounce* to these non-bouncy articles. (The engine described by Paramedic Manuel Delgado "near a little plaza close to West Broadway and west Vessey" has not been identified because of secrecy imposed by Mayor Giuliani and FEMA, but it would have also required a tremendous force to overcome its momentum and hurl it about 300 feet over Building 6 to that intersection.)[AC]

—

# *Typical Aircraft Maintenance and Wreckage Investigations*

George Nelson commented on his long experience as an aircraft accident investigator in the US Air Force, as follows:

> In all my years of direct and indirect participation, I never witnessed nor even heard of an aircraft loss, where the wreckage was accessible, that prevented investigators from finding enough hard evidence to positively identify the make, model, and specific registration number of the aircraft - and in most cases the precise cause of the accident. This is because every military and civilian passenger-carrying aircraft have many parts that are identified for safety of flight. That is, if any of the parts are to fail at any time during a flight, the failure would likely result in the catastrophic loss of aircraft and passengers. Consequently, these parts are individually controlled by a distinctive serial number and tracked by a records section of the maintenance operation and by another section called plans and scheduling.
>
> Following a certain number of flying hours or, in the case of landing gear, a certain number of takeoff-and-landing cycles, these critical parts are required to be changed, overhauled or inspected by specialist mechanics. When these parts are installed, their serial numbers are married to the aircraft registration numbers in the aircraft records and the plans and scheduling section will notify maintenance specialists when the parts must be replaced. If the parts are not replaced within

specified time or cycle limits, the airplane will normally be grounded until the maintenance action is completed. Most of these time-change parts, whether hydraulic flight surface actuators, pumps, landing gears, engines or engine components, are virtually indestructible. It would be impossible for an ordinary crash to destroy or obliterate all of those critical time-change parts or their serial numbers. I repeat, impossible.

Retired Colonel George Nelson concluded:

As painful and heartbreaking as was the loss of innocent lives and the lingering health problems of thousands more, a most troublesome and nightmarish possibility remains that so many Americans appear to be involved in the most heinous conspiracy in our country's history.[15]

## Software for Remote Control of Airplanes from a Ground Station or Another Plane in 2001

The U.S. military developed the technology to capture planes by remote control as far back as the mid-1970s because there had been a sharp upsurge in terrorist hijackings. This was done by taking absolute control of the plane's computerized flight control system through a remote channel, thereby cutting the hijackers out of the control loop and enabling ground control to listen in on cockpit conversations in a target aircraft and then take absolute control of the plane's computerized flight control system through a remote channel and finally return the hijacked plane to a chosen airport where police could arrest the hijackers. For this technology to perform best, however, it had to be built into a new aircraft design.

That's exactly what Boeing did by including a "back door" into the computer designs for its 767 and 757 commercial airliners. The late aeronautical engineer, Joe Vialls, contended that the Boeing system's secret computer code was acquired by evildoers within the Bush administration who used the remote channel on September 11, 2001, to activate the hidden channel built into the transponders. These evildoers thereby took over the flight controls without either the commercial pilots or the hijackers (if present) being able to do anything about it so that the airliners then became drones.

[AC] Neocons and other Zionists, such as Douglas Feith, Paul Wolfowitz, Dov Zakheim, and Richard Pearle, having top secret U.S. security clearance, were powerful men in the Pentagon and surely had enough authority to access that code from Boeing. [AC]

Vialls pointed out that not one of the eight commercial pilots and copilots aboard the four allegedly hijacked airliners on 9/11 sent the standard digital signal alerting FAA authorities that a plane had been hijacked. Sending this SOS merely required keying in a four-digit code that provides a unique "identity" for each aircraft, "essential in crowded airspace to avoid mid-air collisions." Another clue to remote-control takeover was the near total loss of radio contact. "The pilots lost the ability to transmit after the evildoers commandeered the transponders." Or, if there were no hijackers, the controllers were trying to lock onto the aircraft. "Technically, a transponder is a combined radio transmitter and receiver which operates automatically." [16]

Finally, as shown in a video of the last seconds of Flight 175, the airliner executed a steep diving maneuver during its final approach. This dive exceeded the flight control software that prevents a pilot from making steep turns that would create substantial and dangerous g-forces, which could cause heart attacks and other dangers to passengers with resultant lawsuits.

Vialls died in 2005. Critics have said that Boeing 767s and 757s, even though fully computerized, were not fly-by-wire designs like some newer planes such as the Global Hawk, which can fly thousands of miles without a pilot aboard. (Another example is the Predator, a drone widely used in Iraq and Afghanistan.) According to these critics, a pilot could have turned off the autopilot and flown the plane manually. To counter these critics, experts have suggested that a stupefying or deadly gas was released into each "hijacked" airliner cabin, causing pilots and passengers to become unconscious or dead.[17]

In a letter to General Peter Pace, USMC and Vice Chairman, JCS, retired Colonel Donn de Grand Pre on 23 January 2002 suggested that "in fact, all personnel on board were rendered instantly unconscious (within 18 minutes, at most) by controlled decompression."[18]

Another objection involves time delay or a latency period. The number of crashes of unmanned Predators, for example, would have caused any 9/11 perpetrators within the U.S. government to have instantly rejected ROV technology as unreliable. However, such a latency period involves a communications satellite. A more reliable method requires only direct line of sight and involves no latency period issue. An E-3, an AWACS, or one of the Nightwatch fleet's four E-4Bs could have been at high altitude over or near New York City, where it would have been in direct line of sight with both

Flight 11 and Flight 175 and thereby able to guide both planes to a position near the Twin Towers, where Giuliani's command post on the twenty-third floor of WTC-7 could have taken over. Guiding the planes into the Twin Towers would have then been a simple matter.

[AC] Such remote control also explains how the 9/11 planes could have exceeded their software limits and also how the plane identified by the government as Flight 77 performed its more than 270-degree spiraling descent of 7,000 feet in two and a half minutes preceding the Pentagon attack. [AC]

In 2003, von Buelow, a former minister of research and technology in the German government, wrote a book in German entitled *Die CIA und der 11. September. Internatinaler Terror Und die Rolle der Geheimdienste,* which is translated as *The CIA and September 11: International terrorism and the role of secret services,* Piper Verlag, Munich, in which he discussed Joe Vialls's remote control theory while calling for a new 9/11 investigation. In radio interviews, von Buelow argued that the "hijacked" planes were most likely guided by some form of remote control. He thought that 9/11 was a covert operation carried out by a small group within the U.S. intelligence community, numbering fewer than fifty people.

[AC] This information may indicate that the CIA carried out 9/11 as a covert operation. [AC]

The Boeing 757 and 767 passenger planes were equipped with fully autonomous flight capability and were the only two Boeing commuter aircraft capable of fully autonomous flight so that they could be programmed to take off, fly to a destination, and land, completely without a pilot at the controls.

A group of military and civilian U.S. pilots, under the chairmanship of Colonel Donn de Grand Pre, deliberated nonstop for seventy-two hours about such remote control and concluded that the flight crews of the four passenger airliners that were involved in the 9/11 tragedies had no control over their aircraft. Under such fully autonomous flight control, the pilots would have been helpless to perform a "barrel roll" or any other defense hijackers. "In an instant a pilot can commence a roll. A barrel roll would knock off their feet anyone standing and disorient them. (A barrel roll is a combination between a loop and a roll, which results in the aircraft tracing out a corkscrew path. This maneuver can produce high G-forces inside the plane.)"[19]

### *Grounding of American Airlines Flight 77, Transfer of Its Passengers to a Charter Flight That Landed in Newark Airport, Pedestrian Transfer of Its Passengers to United Airlines Flight 93, and Its Take-off, 41 Minutes Late*

Flight 93 received its small load of passengers at Newark Airport. It was 41 minutes late when it took off, but it was boarded twice. That lateness enabled a late-sleeping passenger, Mark Bingham, to be driven madly by his friend, Matthew Hall, from Manhattan to Newark where they "screeched to a halt outside Terminal A at 7:40 . . . . United attendants reopened the door to the boarding ramp and let him on the plane." Then Flight 93 taxied "around the corner to pick up another 'charter' for the day flight, a second group of people."

Flight 77 also never took off from Dulles Airport, as shown by BTS and as indicated by the lack of a surveillance video. The Flight 77 passengers were loaded onto a charter flight at Dulles for Newark Airport. It landed there in time to taxi on the tarmac to where Flight 93 was waiting. Triton Clayton White, a New York Giant football player, "had played a Monday night game in Denver and flew back home the next morning. We usually get off the plane on the tarmac and board a bus to get to our cars. I noticed another plane sitting next to ours because the people were walking to the plane across the tarmac instead of through the jetway. Two weeks later, as we're taking another plane to a game, one of the stewardesses informed us the plane that had been boarding next to us was Flight 93 that crashed in Pennsylvania on 9/11. That was a very eerie feeling."

Flight 93 took off from Newark Airport at 8:42 a.m."By 9:30, the FAA had grounded all flights out of Boston and New York." Flight 93 also landed at the Cleveland airport at 10:45 a.m., as both the mayor of Cleveland and United Airlines publicly acknowledged on September 11. The 200 people aboard Flight 93 were sequestered at the other end of the airport, at the NASA Glenn hangar. Delta 1989 and Flight 93 had roughly 260 people between them, the same number as Flights 11, 175, 77, and 93 combined. This theory, one of several alternative theories, solves the mystery about what happened to the passengers of the four flights who disappeared without a fuss, disturbance, or commotion of any kind in airports full of people.[20]

On the morning of 9/11 a little known Cincinnati television station ran a story saying Flight 93 landed at

Cleveland International Airport instead of crashing in
Pennsylvania as claimed in the official government story.
Reporters at WCPO Channel 9 quoted then Cleveland
Mayor Michael R. White as saying "a Boeing 767 out
of Boston made a emergency landing due to a bomb
threat," the airplane landing safely, moved to a secure
location and evacuated.

The early morning report went on to say United Airlines
verified the plane as Flight 93, but was also deeply
concerned about another jetliner in the vicinity, Flight
175, flying from Boston to Los Angeles.

An article by Greg Szymanski, a cyber space sleuth and an
independent investigative journalist whose articles could be seen
at www.LewisNews.com, notes that "the 9/11 Commission or
the FBI never thoroughly investigated the news report or former
Mayor White's statement." As of November 11, 2005, what was
currently posted on the website was, "This story has been removed
from WCPO.com. It was a preliminary AP story, and was factually
incorrect." However, the original posting said "nothing about being
an AP article," and it "continued to be posted for all dates through
June 2004, and disappeared only after that."

Szymanski was intrigued when "Phil Jayhan, a serious 9/11 fact
gatherer," who put together *www.letsroll911.org*, received a strange phone
call from Rep. Crane, the former head of the powerful House Ways and
Means Committee. Jayhan wrote on his website that Crane "didn't have
a problem with the missile and the pod or that the flight was switched, so
he was well acquainted with my web site when he called. But he, they (?)
were stumped as to the missing people, and where they went."[21]

## *The Federal Government's Story Being a Hoax, What Happened to the Four Aircraft and Their Passengers?*

To tantalize readers with a twinge of curiosity, what happened to the airliners if they were not destroyed while being used as projectiles? Two destinations, in which all four airliners received the same treatment, are given below in the Bumble Planes and Pearl theories. What if two of the airliners received an entirely different treatment than the other two?

## *Destruction of Both American Airlines Planes and Continued Existence for Both United Airlines Planes*

The following information was posted by RMNewsMailbag on 5 July 2006 "regarding the paper-fate of the four aircraft that went 'missing' on 9/11."

1. American Airlines Flight 11, Aircraft Serial No. 22332, Boeing Certificate Issue Date 01/06/2000, Model 767-200, tail number N334AA, Cancel Date 01/14/2002; reason for Cancellation: Destroyed.

2. American Airlines Flight 77, Aircraft Serial No. 24602, Boeing Certificate Issue Date 05/08/1991, Model 757-223, tail number N644AA, Cancel Date 01/14/2002; reason for Cancellation: Destroyed.

3. United Airlines Flight 175, Aircraft Serial No. 21873, Boeing Certificate Issue Date 01/18/1984, Model 767-222,

tail number N612UA, Cancel Date 09/28/2005; reason for
Cancellation: Cancelled.

4. United Airlines Flight 93, Aircraft Serial No. 28142, Boeing
   Certificate Issue Date 07/01/1996, Model 757-222, tail
   number N591UA, Cancel Date 09/28/2005; Reason for
   Cancellation: Cancelled.[22]

[AC] So the two airliners which did not take off from Boston
and Dulles Airports during the morning of September 11, 2001
were destroyed fairly promptly (within four months) whereas the
two airliners which did take off from Boston and Newark Airports
were merely cancelled four years later. As a speculation, the CIA
informed American Airlines during the afternoon of 9/11 that
its passenger airliners with tail numbers N334AA and N644AA
would take off from Boston and Dulles Airports at about dusk that
day as drones and would be destroyed during the night over the
Atlantic Ocean; adequate compensation would be paid but secrecy
would be required.

[AC] What happened to the two United Airliners aircraft will
be discussed after the Bumble Planes and Pearl theories.[AC]

It is interesting that various theories have been proposed as to
what happened to the passengers of some or all of these flights.
"The Flight of the Bumble Planes" by Snake Plissken, as told to
Carol A. Valentine in http://www.publi-action.com/911/bumble.
html, proposed in March 2002 that the passengers and crews of
Flights 11, 175, and 77 were loaded into Flight 93 at a military
base. When Flight 93 was shot down, it was the "easiest way to
dispose of 15,000 lbs of human flesh." The airliners which were
used for Flights 11, 175, and 77 were probably sent to the Aerospace

Maintenance and Regeneration Center (AMAARC) which is located outside Tuscon, Arizona; it is an Air Force aeroplane graveyard and a storehouse for spare parts.[23]

Another theory by Professor A. K. Dewdney in "Operation Pearl," August 2003, *http://www.serendipity.li/wot/operation.pearl.htm*, proposed that the passengers were loaded into Flight 93 and that the other planes were then flown eastwards over the Atlantic Ocean as drones and destroyed by bombs over the water.[24]

[Author's Comment - AC] The Bumble Planes and Operation Pearl theories require the Cleveland landings of Delta Flight 1989 and United Airlines Flight 93 to be relatively ignored and to be replaced by landings at or near Harrisburg, Pennsylvania for transfers of passengers. Both theories also require 15,000 pounds of human body parts, plus shoes and clothes, to be picked up by hand in a wooded area, the grisly stuff to be placed in bags, and the bags to be carried to trucks on the nearest road. It would have been a formidable task and would have been in addition to the job of picking up the luggage of 260 passengers plus the luggage of the pilots and flight attendants, probably scattered over an area of several square miles. If bones, rings, or wallets of the passengers, pilots, and flight attendants had been missed, they might have been found by local residents during subsequent months. These findings could have caused the identifications of passengers, pilots, and/or flight attendants who were supposedly on another flight than Flight 93 and thereby could have caused consequent questioning of the entire government story.

[AC]An alternative theory should take into account the apparent facts that body parts, shoes, clothing, and luggage were seen by several people at the intersection of Vesey Street and West

Broadway Street, at approximately the southeast corner of WTC 7 in Manhattan, and also by one man on West Street after "bouncing" backward from the north face of the North Tower where it was allegedly hit by Flight 11, and that a rib bone was found in Indian Lake, Pennsylvania over which the alleged Flight 93 received a missile or two.

[AC]This alternative theory includes Flight 175 landing at Stuart Air Force Base, discharging approximately 58 (or 169) passengers, and then taking off to land at the Cleveland Airport at 10:10 a.m. The 58 (or 169) unfortunate passengers were loaded aboard the drone military planes which substituted for Flights 11 and 93. As described in Chapter 33, only 58 passengers were dead according to the Social Security Death Index, whereas the relatives of 169 passengers accepted the Victims Compensation money, and one of these two groups are theorized as being the ones unloaded within Stuart Air Force Base.]

## *Airliner Passengers and Detention Camps*

[AC] Even though all flights had been grounded by FAA that morning, Delta 1989 and UA 93 could have taken off according to a planned governmental deception and headed west, just as a certain El Al flight had been assisted by military officials to leave JFK Airport that same afternoon for Israel, as described in chapter 19. About three hours later, Delta 1989 and UA 93 could have landed in Groom Lake Air Force Base, located in Nellis AFB, Nevada Desert, Area 51.

[AC] If that happened, were the passengers allowed to telephone their wives and other family members before leaving Cleveland?

Would such communications explain the small numbers of relatives who applied for compensation, as discussed in chapter 33?

[AC] Both of the airliners could have been repainted and used for routine passenger and cargo military flights within Area 51 for another four years until September 29, 2005.

[AC] The passengers in both airliners were probably brought to a detention camp in Nellis AFB where they may remain to this day. They may also be working on secret projects in the very secret Groom Lake Air Force Base. [AC]

[AC] Whatever happened, these passengers were removed from Delta 1989 and Flight 93 and were then brought to a detention camp in Nellis AFB where they may remain to this day.

AC] Nellis Air Force Base - Area 51 is a highly secret installation for testing new aircraft. It is possible that the 202 (260-58) passengers and four air crews were selected to live for years on Nellis AFB and to work there.]AC]

U2 pilot training in the 50's. The SR-71 was developed here. The Groom Dry Lake area of the Nellis Air Force Range and Nuclear Test Site in the Nevada desert, about 80 miles NNW of Las Vegas.

It is here that the US government is test-flying highly secret *Black Project* aircraft, including UFOs, for a number of years.

Every weekday morning, at least 500 people arrive at the guarded terminal owned by EG&G on the northwest side of McCarran Airport in Las Vegas, Nevada. Here they board one of a small fleet of unmarked Boeing 737-200s.

Using three digit numbers prefixed by the word "Janet" as their callsigns, the 737s fly off every half hour. Their destination is Groom Lake, an installation so secret, its existence is denied by the government agencies and contractors that have connections there.[25]

Victor Thorn has written about these detention camps called internment camps, which have been established and are ready to detain citizens if mass insurrections occur. Congressman Ron Paul wrote about them in his September 2008 newsletter as follows:

Even though we know that detention facilities are already in place, [the government] now wants to legalize the construction of FEMA camps on military installations using the ever popular excuse that the facilities are for the purposes of a national emergency.

Victor Thorn suggested that more likely targets for detainment than illegal immigrants are "anti-New World Order proponents, Second Amendment advocates, dissidents, people who refuse to participate in forced inoculation programs, Christians, tax protesters, and those deemed 'extremists' and 'enemies of the state' under a recent Department of Homeland Security report on 'homegrown right-wing terrorists.'"

As an indication of their seriousness in pushing this agenda, Bob Unruh revealed a disturbing development on August 7 for *World Net Daily*: "An ad campaign featured on a U.S. Army website seeking those who would be interested in being an 'internment/ resettlement' specialist is raising alarms across the country." What specifically would this position entail? The description is clear: "Internment/Resettlement (I/$) specialists in the Army are primarily responsible for day-to-day operations in a military confinement/ correctional facility or detention/internment facility."

HR 645 was introduced in Congress on January 22, 2010 "to direct the Secretary of Homeland Security to establish national emergency centers on military installations," as the bill actually states as its central purpose. Further, HR 645 would create a Guantánamo-style setting after martial law is declared. At that point, posse comitatus laws would be rendered nonexistent, replaced by military jurisdiction over all detainees. As a result, the incarcerated would find it much more difficult to enforce their Constitutional rights to a fair trial and/or legal representation.

These camps "could conceivably be geared toward creating what many Americans have feared in recent years - detention centers, or concentration camps, on American soil." Although HR 645 is very recent, there was nothing to prevent the powers-that-be from establishing an impromptu detention camp in the very large Nellis AFB Nevada Desert, Area 51.[26]

President Obama spoke of "prolonged detention" for all those who posed a threat to U.S. security when he spoke on May 21 at the National Archives in Washington, D.C.

James McCord, an Air Force Reserve colonel, was part of a national group in the Office of Emergency Preparedness (the predecessor to FEMA). This group was responsible for contingency plans "in the event of emergency . . . for imposing censorship [and] preventive detention of civilian 'security risks,' who would be placed in military 'camps.'"

Dick Cheney and Donald Rumsfeld, as part of the supersecret continuity of government planning that was partially implemented for the first time on September 11, 2001, secretly participated in developing these plans throughout the 1980s.[27]

# Chapter 3 Notes

1.  Griffin, David Ray. *The New Pearl Harbor Revisited: 9/11, The Cover-up, and the Expose.* 2008 Northampton, Massachusetts 01060. Olive Branch Press, 46 Crosby Street, 1, 2, 6.
2.  9-11 Research.wtc.net. NORAD Stand-down. "The Prevention of Interceptions of the Commandeered Planes." http://911research.wtc7.net/planes/analysis/norad/
3.  Griffin 2008, 3-5.
4.  9-Research. NORAD Stand-Down. "The Prevention of Interceptions of the Commandeered Planes." http://911Research.wtc7.net/planes/analysis/norad/
5.  Jayhan, Phil. "The '4' Flights of 9/11 - What Happened to the Passengers? *http://stevebeckow.com/2010/08/phil-jayhan-the-4-flights-of-911-what-hap* . . . , 2-6.
6.  Ibid., 10.
7.  Dewdney, A. K., "Operation Pearl." August 2003. http:www.serendipity.li/wot/operation_pearl.htm, 1, 4, 5.
8.  Hunter, Steve. "9/11 DVD Censored! Image of Strange Flash as Flight 11 Hit North Tower Missing From Footage." http://www.prisonplanet.com/150903dvdcensored.html.
9.  Carlson, Jon. "South Tower Flight UA175 Dropped WRONG Engine In NYC Street." http://groups.yahoo.com/group/TheNeuschwabenlandTimes/message/13946.
10. Ioli, Sali al and Luigi bin Liner. "Flight 175. Too Hot to Handle The Photo that Shook Spain. *http://www.amics21.com/911/flight175/*
11. Reynolds, Morgan. "We Have Some Holes in the Plane Stories." *http://www.gnosticliberationfront.com/we_have_some_holes_in_the_plane_stories.htm.*,3.

12. Ibid. 25.

13. PumpItOut.com Forum. Transcripts FDNY, Paramedics, EMT's." http://sl.zetaboards.com/pumpitout/topic/770325/1/.

14. Nelson, George. "Aircraft Parts and the Precautionary Principle; Impossible to Prove a Falsehood True: Aircraft Parts as a Clue to their Identity." http://www.physics911.net/georgenelson.

15. Vialls, Joe. "Electronically Hijacking the WTC Attack Aircraft." *http://www.the* truthseeker.co.uk/print.asp?ID=206.

16. Gaffney, Mark H. *The 9/11 Mystery Plane and the Vanishing of America,* Walterville, OR 97489. Trine Day LLC, PO Box 577, 218, 219.

17. de Grand Pre, *Barbarians Inside the Gates. Book III. The Rattler's Revenge.* Madison, Virginia 22727. Grand Pre Publishers, Ltd., PO Box 1124, 553.

18. Gaffney, Mark H., 220-222.

19. 9-11 Research.com. "Suicide Pilots. The Official Story of the Flight Takeovers." *Http://911research.wtc7.net/planes/analysis/pilots.html.*

20. Box, Woody. "The Cleveland Airport Mystery." *http://www.european911citizensjury.com/17.htm.*

21. Szymanski, Greg. "Flt 93 And Flt 175 Landed At Or Near Cleveland On 911 - Says Former Cleveland Mayor. Cincinnati WCPO TV Cover-Ups Why Account Removed From Web Site." *http://www.rense.com/general68/says.htm.*

22. RMNewsMailbag. "Very Strange 9.11 Aircraft Registrations." 5 July 2006. http://www.rumormillnews.com/cgi-bin/forum.cgi?read=90306.

23. Plissken, Snake as told to Carol A. Valentine "9-11: The Flight of the Bumble Planes." *http://www.serendipity.li/wot/plissken.htm.*

24. Dewdney, A. K. "Operation Pearl." *http://www.serendipity.li/wot/operation_pearl.htm*.

25. Anderson, Mark. "Concentration Camps in US: Are They Real?" *http://www.americanfreepress.net/htm/hilder_concamps_7239.html*.

26. *AboveTopSecret* Website. "Groom Lake Air Force Base - Area 51." http://www.bibliotecapleyades.net/offlimits/esp_offlimits_3.htm.

27. Thorn, Victor. "More to U.S. Detention Camps Than Feds Admit." American Free Press. August 31, 2009, 4.

# CHAPTER 4

## Damages to the World Trade Center in 2001

### *Shutdowns of the Twin Towers before September 11, 2001*

Larry Silverstein had leased the WTC from the New York Port Authority on July 24, 2001, and had insured it for $3.5 billion in a transaction that would have allowed Silverstein to simply default and walk away from the lease in the event of a catastrophic loss. He obviously had the authority to shut it down.

Three individuals named in Internet articles have described such shutdowns. Scott Forbes, who had worked since 1999 for Fiduciary Trust, supports them. In a personal letter that was subsequently published, Forbes said:

> In 2001 we occupied floors 90 and 94-97 of the South Tower and lost 87 employees plus many contractors.

> On the weekend of [September 8-9, 2001], there was a "power down" condition in WTC tower 2, the south

tower. This power down condition meant there was no electrical supply for approximately 36 hours from floor 50 up. I am aware of this situation since I . . . had to work with many others that weekend to ensure that all systems were cleanly shutdown beforehand . . . and then brought back up afterwards. The reason given by the WTC for the power down was that cabling in the tower was being upgraded. Of course without power there were no security cameras, no security locks on doors, [while] many, many "engineers" [were] coming in and out of the tower.

Forbes added the following comment to an e-mail letter to Dr. Griffin on June 2, 2004:

I've been amazed at the response to my original weblog posting . . . . All I can tell you is that what I said is entirely true and that I can refer to others who can validate it. What surprises me, and the original motive for my posting, is the fact that no authority will acknowledge that there was a 36-hour power down in the top half of tower 2 over the weekend period 9/8-9/9. I have no hidden agenda other than trying to get the truth acknowledged and investigated.

Supporting Mr. Forbes is a statement by Ben Fountain, a financial analyst with Fireman's Fund, who worked in the South Tower. Mr. Fountain stated that during the previous few weeks before 9/11, the towers had been evacuated a "number of times," which he considered to be "unusual."

The statements by Mr. Forbes and Mr. Fountain clearly support the authority of Mr. Silverstein to shut down WTC-1, 2, and 7 and the fact that he did so on more than one occasion before September 11, 2001.[1]

## Structural Details of the Twin Towers

The three stairways in each twin tower were bunched together and built for only a few hundred people at a time to walk three or four stories according to the 1968 code of New York City. This building code required the same number of exit stairways for a six-story building as for a 110-story building. That made it possible for the Port Authority to offer 75 percent of its floor space for rent, 21 percent higher than the best yield achieved in older skyscrapers, which had to commit much *more* space to exit routes. This additional space was partly provided by using gypsum board and spray-on fireproofing over steel, which gave only two hours of fire protection.[2]

## Escape Procedures

After the 1993 bombing, the Port Authority had spent $2.1 million on emergency lighting and exit signs, which were lit by light-emitting diodes and powered by batteries for ninety minutes.

At the time of the 1993 World Trade Center bombing, dozens of WTC workers fled from heavy smoke by climbing to the roof. Police helicopters rescued them from this place of refuge.

But in 2001, such an escape was not possible. "Indeed, the roof was off-limits," but the Port Authority did not explicitly inform the occupants of its towers that the roof would not be available in a fire. No signs in the stairwells said, "Go down, not up." Many people who were trapped on the upper floors did try to reach the roof, but they could not because the doors were locked. This is known from cell phone calls made by frantic victims. It is not hard to imagine their horror after fleeing toxic smoke, heat, and flames and then to discover that there would be no escape. At that point, hundreds of trapped individuals must have known they were doomed.

For a variety of reasons, the Port Authority had decided, with the agreement of the Fire Department, to discourage the use of helicopters in emergencies at the building. Ordinary building occupants were never briefed on the policy change after 1993, and there were no signs explaining that the doors were locked although the Port Authority's emergency drills directed people down the stairs, not up.[3]

[AC] This locked-door policy was obviously convenient for the murderous inside-job perpetrators of 9/11. The abandoned helicopter rescue system also eliminated any chance that survivors might have been able to describe bombs exploding inside the buildings. Because of the smoke and heat, helicopter rescues would have been difficult but not impossible, in the author's opinion, because he believes that one helicopter could have blown smoke sideways while a rescue helicopter could have removed people. [AC]

## *The North Tower, WTC-1*

The north side of the North Tower was struck at the ninety-sixth floor by the alleged Flight 11 at 8:46:30 a.m., traveling at 450 mph. The plane's forward motion came to a halt, and the plane itself was broken up. Hunks of it erupted from the south side of the tower, and a part of the landing gear landed five blocks to the south. The jet fuel ignited and roared rapidly across the sky.

[Author's Comment—AC] Referring to Col. Nelson's discussion in Chapter 3 of identifying numbers being on all important parts of military and civilian passenger planes, that landing gear should have displayed a number identifying it as having been on the specific American Airlines Boeing 767-223ER which was allegedly AA Flight 11. If the landing gear did not have the correct number, it could explain why Mayor Giuliani prohibited the taking of photographs at Ground Zero and even confiscated cameras. [AC]

Flight 11 had traveled the full length of Manhattan Island, 14 miles from north to south, in less than two minutes. By tipping its wings just before impact, Flight 11 cut a swath through seven floors and severely damaged all three escape staircases, which were clustered in the central core of the building. Steel, concrete, and fragments of offices and glass rained onto the plaza. A wall of fire spread across ten to fifteen floors. A fireball of exploding jet fuel shot down the elevator shafts, past the lobby, and as far as four levels below it. In the lobby, the fuel had exploded, blackening a stretch of wall near one of the elevator banks and blowing the doors off the cars. Within two minutes of impact, people were coming to the upper-floor windows, driven toward air by the smoke and fumes.

In the six floors of Cantor Fitzerald and in Windows on the World, just above it, nearly 900 people were trapped. Arguments continued briefly as to breaking windows to get air, but soon , "We smashed the computers into the windows to get some air," Rosenblum reported by cell phone to Barry Kornblum, a colleague who was not in the office.

The building had easily absorbed the impact of the airliner because its 240 pinstripe columns, 14 inches wide and 22 inches apart, actually held the building up. The surviving pinstripe columns on the north face of the North Tower formed an arch around the wound, creating new paths for the weight of the building to travel along the unscathed columns, like a punctured mosquito netting.

On the ninety-first floor of the North Tower, two floors below the bottom of the impact zone of Flight 11, a crew of six electricians hunted for a stairway in a warren of collapsed ceiling tiles and fallen walls. Most of floor 91 seemed to be empty because the employees of the American Bureau of Shipping, the only commercial tenant on the floor, had already started down the only stairway not smashed. However, one electrician called, "Anybody there?" A woman in a red hat appeared, saying, "I'm the last one." Then they heard two people from an area near the elevator. The "electricians hollered to them, leading them by voice toward a central corridor" and then into the dark, surviving staircase. Everyone had gotten off the ninety-first floor, but no one could come down from the higher floors because the stairs to the ninety-second floor were blocked tight.

The 170 people in the top-floor restaurant, Windows on the World, 1,300 feet in the air, were trapped. All stairwells were blocked. The building had barely stopped shuddering when smoke first appeared in the restaurant even though the tip of the right wing of Flight 11 had merely cut into the ninety-ninth floor, 85 feet below. The smoke billowed through channels and ducts.

People in the 106th floor also could not get out, and there was no available water for drinking, putting out fires, or dampening clothes because the plane had severed pipes. "Even the simplest advice, to wet towels and stuff them in the doorsills, became another avenue of frustration."[4]

So urgent was the need to breathe fresh air that people piled four and five high, their bodies hanging out, in one window after another. Sometimes people jumped, and sometimes they were nudged by desperate people behind them.

Among the one thousand people trapped in the upper floors, more and more fell or jumped to their deaths. Because of the heat and smoke, police helicopters were unable to land on the roof, and exits to the roof were also locked on the inside.

Many more people jumped or fell from the North Tower than from the South Tower because the North Tower had been hit seventeen floors higher than the South Tower, and people started to evacuate the South Tower before the airliner struck it. Consequently, about three times as many people (i.e., close to a thousand) were confined in the North Tower space that was about one-half of the South Tower space.[5]

The Fire Department radios, which were supposed to make it possible for the fire and police departments to communicate, did not operate because the agencies could not agree on which one was in charge of the frequencies. A fire commander consequently had to contact his own dispatchers who would forward his request to the police. Fire Chief Joseph Pfeifer attempted to contact the dispatcher by radio and by phone but was unable to do so. The police aviation team had been anticipating a call from the firefighters but instead continued to fly. However, the fire department chief decided that the smoke and heat were too much and at 9:08 spoke over the police radio, "I don't want to see anybody landing on either one of these towers."

The first police helicopter, a Bell 412, to arrive at the North Tower was capable of carrying 10 people in addition to the crew. It had a 250-foot hoist, which could be used to pluck people from a roof. However, the heavy smoke condition made it impossible to see any opportunity for rescues. At 8:58, one of the pilots spotted United Flight 175 roaring toward them through the sky. "Jesus Christ, there's a second plane crashing," he yelled as he and his copilot pulled up quickly while the plane shot beneath them, bursting through the South Tower and sending a giant ball of flame coughing out the other side. Within minutes, the roof of the South Tower had also vanished behind the smoke.

# The Stairwells in the South Tower

Impact 9:02 A.M. Collapse 9:59 A.M.

## 110
### Access to roof
Callers report trying to get to the roof but finding the doors locked.

## 93
### Aon
Gregory Milanowycz, an insurance broker, calls his father. He and about 30 others are trapped in the northeast corner of the floor. "The elevators aren't working. The stairwell collapsed. We can't go up. We can't go down. We are stuck here."

## 84
### Euro Brokers
About 50 of the company's 61 employees who die are on this trading floor when the plane hits.

## 78
### Sky Lobby
After the north tower is hit, many in the south tower evacuate to the sky lobby to catch an express elevator. An announcement that the building is safe leaves many unsure whether to return to their offices or leave. Many die instantly when the second plane hits.

## 76
### Stairway A
An elevator crashes into the stairwell in this area, evacuees say, spewing debris, including large sections of the wall, into the passage. Several men prop up debris so that at least 18 people are able to slide through and escape.

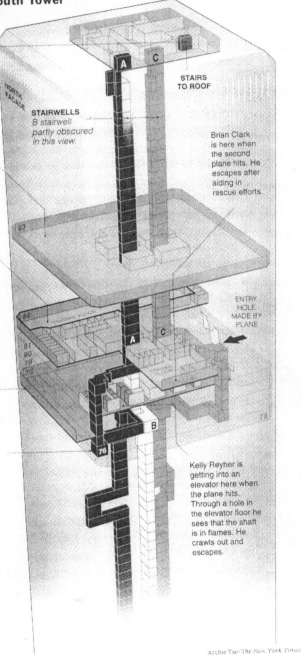

STAIRS TO ROOF

STAIRWELLS
B stairwell partly obscured in this view.

NORTH FACADE

Brian Clark is here when the second plane hits. He escapes after aiding in rescue efforts.

ENTRY HOLE MADE BY PLANE

Kelly Reyher is getting into an elevator here when the plane hits. Through a hole in the elevator floor he sees that the shaft is in flames. He crawls out and escapes.

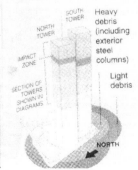

SOUTH TOWER
NORTH TOWER
IMPACT ZONE
SECTION OF TOWERS SHOWN IN DIAGRAMS
NORTH

Heavy debris (including exterior steel columns)

Light debris

Archie Tse/The New York Times

The need for intervention was horribly apparent to the helicopter pilots as they watched the fires advance through the upper floors while people on those floors hung out of the windows. One pilot, hovering off the North Tower, said on the radio at about 9:30, "About five floors up from the top [sic], you have about fifty people with their faces pressed against the window trying to breathe." They began to break windows with computers soon after.[6]

Fire companies had to walk up because none of the 99 elevators was in working order. It would be a matter of hours, not minutes, to reach top floors so that the fires high in the tower would have a galloping, destructive head start. Each fireman had to carry more than 56 pounds. In the ladder companies, some firefighters carried an extinguisher and hook, weighing 38 pounds. Others carried an ax and an all-purpose pry bar, weighing 25 pounds. One firefighter from each unit carried a lifesaving rope, 150 feet long and weighing 22 pounds. Each man also carried a radio, the Motorola Saber, but it did not work in the upper floors because no boosters had been installed in the buildings.

As the firefighters ascended single file past a stream of people descending, they knew that they could not put out fires in five floors but would have to let them burn out. It would be a rescue operation though they might put out a patch of flame to open up a stairway. More than 225 fire units went to the trade center—half of all the companies working that day. More than one thousand firefighters reported there.[7]

# The Stairwells in the North Tower

Impact 8:46 A.M. Collapse 10:28 A.M.

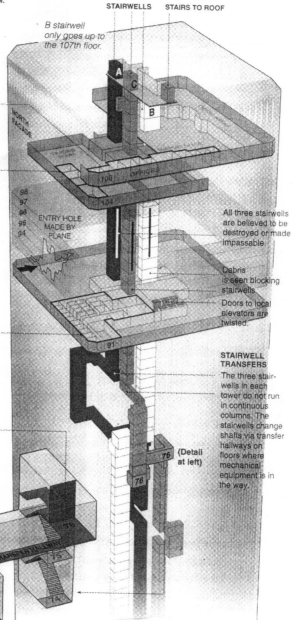

## 106-107
### Windows on the World
Heavy smoke fills the floors immediately. Stuart Lee, a vice president at Data Synapse, is trapped in an office in the northwest corner.

## 104
### Cantor Fitzgerald
Smoke infiltrates the floor. Eventually, fire blocks the stairwells. Employees seek refuge in these offices, including about 50 in a conference room.

## 92
### Carr Futures
"It's really bad here—the elevators are gone," Damian Meehan, a trader at Carr Futures, tells his brother in a telephone call.

## 91
### American Bureau of Shipping
The impact causes little damage to the office. All staff members evacuate. Only two of the three stairwells are accessible, and only one of those, stairwell C, appears passable. Above this floor, no one will survive.

## 76
### Stairway C
Evacuees encounter a door in the transfer hallway that cannot be opened. They go back up a floor and switch to another stairwell before continuing down and out of the building.

STAIRWELLS    STAIRS TO ROOF

B stairwell only goes up to the 107th floor.

NORTH FACADE

98
97
96
95
94

ENTRY HOLE MADE BY PLANE

All three stairwells are believed to be destroyed or made impassable.

Debris is seen blocking stairwells.

Doors to local elevators are twisted.

### STAIRWELL TRANSFERS
The three stairwells in each tower do not run in continuous columns. The stairwells change shafts via transfer hallways on floors where mechanical equipment is in the way.

76 (Detail at left)

Sources: Interviews with survivors and people who had contact with victims; Leslie E. Robertson Associates; FEMA; Port Authority; N.Y. Fire Department dispatch records

Archie Tse/The New York Times

The South Tower was struck at a corner at 9:02:59 a.m. by United Airlines Flight 175, flying at 545 mph, which had banked slightly at the last second so that its wingspan ran diagonally across nine floors, from floor 77 through floor 85, causing much of its fuel to be spewed out of the tower in two directions. Because stairwells were spread out there so that they could detour around elevator machinery that occupied much space, Stairway A was largely intact. Two people in an elevator were knocked from their feet as "the heat burst across them in a ferocious, roasting wave that kept coming, ten or fifteen seconds of staggering intensity. As they stumbled into the sky lobby, there were the remains of people who had been breathing and thinking and chatting a few seconds earlier. Now they were flat on their back or torn apart, dead, or horrifically injured and alive. Inside one elevator, eighteen people were alive but sealed in."

Moreover, the fires in both towers were mostly obscured by billowing clouds of black smoke, indicating insufficient oxygen to achieve complete combustion and a really hot fire. By 9:30 most of the six thousand people who had entered the South Tower on their way to work had left the building or were beginning to do so. Fewer than one thousand of the South Tower workers had not yet left the building, and six hundred would die there.

Floor 78 of the South Tower had many people who were badly hurt. Perhaps two hundred had been killed when the plane hit. Elevators would not go above the fortieth floor. Most people inside the South Tower did not know about the open Stairway A; it was little used. Of those who did find this stairway, many were bruised, burned, or had broken bones. Even on the seventy-eighth floor, survivors crept into the stairwells. It was dark. People, even with injuries, helped others. At the fiftieth floor, three badly injured survivors met firefighters coming up who advised them to find an elevator ten floors below.

Flight 175's wings had struck floors 77-85 and grazed the seventy-eighth floor lobby at the last second; its wingspan had run diagonally across nine floors, from 77 through 85, and grazed the seventy-eighth floor lobby. Stanley Praimnath's room was on the eighty-first floor, where part of a wing was lodged in a doorway. Of all the people in his office who had dutifully evacuated to the lobby and just as dutifully gone back upstairs [they had been told it was safe to do so, ed.]. He was apparently the only one alive, and he was trapped in the rubble beneath his desk. He heard no one in the darkness as he called for help.

As Brian Clark, a survivor from the eighty-fourth floor, descended on stairway A with four others from Euro Brokers, he heard Praimnath crying for help in the eighty-first-floor rubble. Clark and DiFrancesco found and freed Praimnath; then Clark and Prainmath walked together down the stairs.

Firefighters walked as fast as possible to get to the seventy-sixth floor to assess the fire problem. Battalion Chief Orlo J. Palmer and Fire Marshal Ronald P. Bucca reached the seventy-eighth floor of the South Tower, one floor below the fire. Using his radio, Palmer said, "We've got two isolated pockets of fire. We should be able to knock it down with two lines." Then he called for two engines to remove many dead civilians from the seventy-eighth floor. At 9:50, a stream of what appeared to be molten aluminum from the melting airliner was pouring from a window on the corner of the eightieth floor.[8]

The tape shows that the two firemen were not turned back by heat, smoke, or a wall of flames. They were able to function within the fire zone and were prepared to help the injured and combat the few isolated fires they found. Palmer even mentions that the stairway up to the next level, i.e., floor 79, was passable. Minutes later the building came down on their heads.[9]

A large, commercial-class aircraft (757/767 class) was flying close to the WTC towers during the attacks, between 8:46 a.m. and 9:03 AM, as seen visually and as photographed in still and video photography. This aircraft was not mentioned in the 9/11 Commission Report, does not appear in any version of the official story, and is largely unknown even in critical studies of 9/11. Nevertheless, this white aircraft, having dark engines and vertical stabilizer, actually orbited in close proximity to the towers for several minutes while the North Tower burned and the South Tower was struck.

[AC] This plane could have provided a flying platform nearby to manage part of the 9/11 attacks, and it was a platform which could move in and out quickly and relatively discreetly. It could also explain Bush's statement that he saw the first plane strike the WTC before the rest of the world could have seen it happen. [AC]

This fact is significant because the three major airports servicing the city of New York are La Guardia and JFK International to the east and Newark International across the Hudson to the west, all having holding patterns that did not intersect the borough of Manhattan at any point. Lower Manhattan was a no-fly zone for commercial jets, with air traffic near the WTC towers being additionally restricted to a minimum ceiling of 3,300 feet within a radius of one nautical mile. "These were the VFR (Visual Flight Rules) parameters in effect on the morning of 9/11."[10]

## *World Trade Center Buildings 5 and 6*

An emergency medical technician [EMT], Patricia Ondrovic, who was with the Fire Department of New York, had parked her ambulance with several other parked ambulances along Vesey Street and backed up to the curb so that the backdoors of the ambulances were facing WTC-6, near the 6's corner by the alleyway between WTC-5 and 6, just three to five minutes before the South Tower collapsed, when she was told that another plane was coming and to get in her ambulance to move fast when "there was a loud 'roar'—lots of crashing sounds." She was attempting to put her stretcher back into the vehicle, but she was knocked down to the ground by an explosion that she thought came from the lobby of WTC-5, and "a sea of people, mostly the various agencies on scene, fire, police, EMS, were all running" toward her.

She stood up and started running west toward the river on the sidewalk to be ahead of them when "parked cars were blowing up and some were on fire." She remembered parts flying off the cars and was hit by a door, which flew off one car as she was running past. Very shortly after she started running, everything became one big black cloud.

She tried to run into the lobby of WTC-6 for cover, but federal police standing in the open doorways waved her out and told her, "You can't come in here, keep running." As she turned, she "saw a series of flashes around the ceiling of the lobby, all going off one-by-one like the Xmas lights that 'chase' in pattern," and she heard "popping" sounds that were at the same time as the flashes. She thought they were "timed explosives."[11]

## *Mini-Atomic Explosion in WTC 6*

A mini-atomic explosion in the seventh subbasement of WTC-6 "caused a pool of molten steel to last there for weeks, and that caused elevated levels of uranium in the dust analysed." All its eight hundred or so employees had been evacuated after WTC-1 was struck. This massive, unexplained explosion devastated WTC-6, the eight-story U.S. Customs building. The blast in WTC-6 occurred between the burning North Tower and the forty-seven-story Salomon Brothers Building, known as WTC-7. It happened immediately after UA 175 smashed into WTC-2 at 9:03 a.m. While the upper portion of the South Tower was shrouded with smoke, this "mysterious explosion shot 550 feet into the air above the U.S. Custom House at WTC-6."

The mysterious explosion has been completely suppressed by a media blackout. No national newspaper other than *American Free Press* wrote about it. WTC-6 and WTC-5 burned for hours, but neither building collapsed.[12] CNN's public affairs department confirmed that the video footage of an apparent explosion at ground level was made at 9:04 a.m., just one minute after Flight 175 struck the South Tower and long before either tower collapsed. Photos show a very noticeable, huge circular hole having a deep crater that was blasted from this building. In addition to the timing delay after the Flight 175 impact, this noticeable hole is clear evidence that the massive explosion occurred in building 6. However, building 6 was not hit by an airplane and was still standing after the towers collapsed and indeed until it was purposely demolished.

Because building 6 was considered "very dangerous" by FEMA, there was "no data collection" from it. Nevertheless, the FEMA report stated, "Building Five was the only building accessible for observation [by the team of engineers] . . . the observations, findings and recommendations are assumed to be applicable to all three buildings."

The Customs Service, the Departments of Commerce, Labor, and Agriculture and the Bureau of Alcohol, Tobacco, and Firearms were occupants of building 6. All "declined to explain either the early blast or the massive crater at the center of the Customs House ruins."[13]

## *World Trade Center Building 7*

The "Final Report on the Collapse of World Trade Center Building 7" was issued by NIST, the National Institute of Standards and Technology, in November 2008. The Executive Summary on page xxxv begins with the following two paragraphs:

> WTC 7 was a 47-story office building located immediately to the north of the main WTC Complex. It had been built on top of an existing Consolidated Edison of New York electric power substation which was located on land owned by The Port Authority of New York and New Jersey. On September 11, 2001, WTC 7 endured fires for almost seven hours, from the time of the collapse of the north WTC tower (WTC 1) at 10:28:22 a.m. until 5:20:52 p.m., when it collapsed. This Executive Summary was the first known instance of the total collapse of a tall building primarily due to fires.

WTC 7 was unlike the WTC towers in many respects. It was a more typical tall building in the design of its structural system. It was not struck by an airplane. The fires in WTC 7 were quite different from those in the towers. Since WTC 7 was not doused with thousands of gallons of jet fuel, large areas of any floor were not ignited simultaneously. Instead, the fires in WTC 7 were similar to those that have occurred in several tall buildings where the automatic sprinklers did not function or were not present. These other buildings did not collapse, while WTC 7 succumbed to its fires.

[AC] After a brief review of this government report, it is clear that it is a politically driven job, not an engineering one. It uses civil engineering and architectural terms, but its reasoning and conclusions deviate from reality.

[AC] Under "Principal Findings of the Investigation" is this statement:

> The fires in WTC7 were ignited as a result of the impact of debris from the collapse of WTC 1 which was approximately 110 m (350 ft) to the south.[14]

[AC] There is no proof of debris impact causing ignition. WTC-7 was outside of the original World Trade Center. Except for smaller WTC buildings, other buildings neighboring the WTC and damaged by hurled debris did not ignite, the Deutche Bank building being an example. Moreover, considering the very great benefits to many powerful people from destruction of financial records and of Mayor Giuliani's emergency command center, there is reason to suspect that these fires were set on purpose. In other words, although firefighters observed fires under way, there was motivation for arson to have been committed in order to be sure that a seemingly plausible excuse for the building's collapse would be available.

[AC] In this book, no further attention will be paid to this governmental hoax. Detailed descriptions of what happened to WTC-7 are in chapter 6. [AC]

# Chapter 4 Notes

1. Griffin, David Ray. *The New Pearl Harbor: Disturbing Questions about the Bush Administration and 9/11*. Updated Edition. 2004. Northampton, Massachusetts 01060. Olive Branch Press, 46 Crosby Street, Olive Branch Press, 46 CrosbyStreet, 180, 181.

2. Dwyer, Jim and Kevin Flynn. *102 Minutes: the Untold Story of the Fight to Survive inside the Twin Towers*. 2005. New York, New York 10011. Henry Holt and Company, 115 West Eighteenth Street, 105, 110, 111.

3. Ibid., 128-131.

4. Ibid., 35-40, 46.

5. Ibid., 136-138.

6. Ibid., 130, 131, 135, 136.

7. Ibid., 196-198.

8. Ibid., 95, 204-206.

9. Gaffney, Mark H. *The 9/11 Mystery Plane and the Vanishing of America*. 2008. Walterville, OR 97489, Trine Day LLC, PO Box 577, 173.

10. Carlson, Jon. "NYC Photos, Flight 93 Witnesses Identify 9/11 White Jet." *http://www.rense.com/general64/white.htm*, 3, 4, 8, 10-13.

11. Killtown. February 10, 2006, 2, 4—6, 15. http://killtown. blogspot.com/2006/02/911-rescuer-saw-explosions-inside-

12. 100777.com. "Unexplained 9-11 Explosion at WTC Complex.

13. Marrs, Jim. *The Terror Conspiracy: Deception, 9/11 and the Loss of Liberty*. New York, NY 10003. The Disinformation Company, Ltd., 163 Third Avenue, Suite 108, 48, 49.

14. NIST NCSTAR 1A, WTC Investigation, "Final Report on the Collapse of World Trade Center Building 7," issued November 2008, begun in 2002, xxxv, xxxvi, 50-56.

# CHAPTER 5

## Collapses of the Twin Towers in the WTC

### *Typical Controlled Demolition Features*
### *Compared to WTC Collapses*

**Sudden onset of collapse**. In a controlled demolition, the beginning or onset of a building's collapse is indeed sudden and without warning. However, heating steel does not cause it suddenly to buckle or break; instead, it begins gradually to sag and bend. A steel-frame building, when sufficiently heated by a fire, also begins gradually to sag and bend, but unless the entire floor is heated equally, the building begins to topple over. To face reality, videos of the Twin Towers' collapses show that each building was perfectly motionless until it began to collapse, except for the top thirty floors of the South Tower, thereby demonstrating that each collapse was occurring as in a controlled demolition.

**Falling straight down**. A tall building about to be demolished must never fall sidewise on to nearby buildings. Instead, its demolition must be planned so that it falls into its own footprint.

Obtaining that result with fire and without explosives would indeed be a miracle.

**Nearly free-fall downward speed.** Buildings being demolished with explosives collapse at almost free-fall speed because the supports for the lower floors are progressively destroyed just before the upper floors reach that demolition level whereby the upper floors encounter no resistance. Exactly that happened at the WTC on September 11, 2001, as revealed by videos showing that "the rubble falling inside the building's profile falls at the same speed as the rubble outside." As explained by Dave Heller (2005):

> [T]he floors could not have been pancaking. The buildings fell too quickly. The floors must all have been falling simultaneously to reach the ground in such a short amount of time. But how? . . . In [the method known as controlled demolition], each floor of a building is destroyed at just the moment the floor above is about to strike it. Thus, the floors fall simultaneously, and in virtual freefall.

[Author's Comment—AC] It should be noted that the floors did not truly fall simultaneously but at the rate of eleven floors per second, thereby demonstrating how precisely the successive floor destructions had to have been timed, unless mini-atomic explosives had been used to destroy perhaps ten floors with each explosion, as discussed in Chapter 11.[AC]

**Sliced steel.** When steel-frame buildings have to be demolished, explosives are used to slice the steel columns and beams into pieces. A commonly used high explosive is RDX, which slices steel like a "razor blade through a tomato." The slicing is done to segment the steel columns and beams "into pieces matching the lifting capacity of the available equipment." After studying various photos of the WTC collapse sites, Jim Hoffman (2004) said that much of the steel seems to be "chopped up into sections that could be easily loaded onto the equipment that was cleaning up Ground Zero."

**Pulverized into fine powder.** Controlled demolitions are additionally known to produce much dust because "explosives powerful enough to slice steel will pulverize concrete and most other nonmetallic substances into tiny particles." Jim Hoffman (2003) reported: "Nearly all of the nonmetallic constituents of the towers were pulverized into fine powder." The fineness of the dust can indicate the demolition method because increased fineness indicates increased demolition energy. Col. John O'Dowd of the U.S. Army Corps of Engineers commented that "at the World Trade Center sites, it seemed like everything was pulverized" (History Channel, 2002).

**Dust clouds.** Controlled demolitions also produce dust clouds when explosions eject the dust from the building with great energy. By comparing videos on the Web, 9/11 truthers have noted that the collapses of the Twin Towers produced clouds that were very similar to clouds produced by earlier controlled demolitions. An example is Seattle's Kingdome. However, the collapses of the Twin Towers produced proportionally much bigger clouds, indicating much more energy was involved.

**Horizontal ejections.** Controlled demolition commonly includes horizontal ejections of other materials, besides dust, from the areas in the building where explosives are placed. Photos and videos made on September 11, 2001, show that "[h]eavy pieces of steel were ejected in all directions for distances up to 500 feet while aluminum cladding was blown up to 700 feet away from the towers."

**Demolition rings.** Controlled demolition additionally occurs as demolition rings when a series of small explosions runs rapidly around a building. Such rings of small explosions were heard by firefighters inside the towers.

**Instant ejections of pulverized concrete**. Moreover, thick clouds of pulverized concrete were ejected within the first two seconds when the relative motion of the top of the tower to the intact portion was only a few feet per second. One second later, these clouds extended about 200 feet above the roof and about 200-300 feet to each side. Moreover, these clouds were pyroclastic, too hot to mingle with ambient air, a characteristic shown by volcanic clouds. This feature particularly rules out any possibility of gravitational collapse.

**Sounds of explosions**. Using explosives to demolish a building produces typical sounds that can be heard by nearby people. Hundreds of firefighters and New York City police personnel testified under oath to sounds of explosions which they had heard, often while within the towers, on that terrible day of September 11, 2001.

**Molten steel**. Molten steel is found after controlled demolitions, and such pools of "literally molten steel" were indeed observed by Peter Tully, president of Tully Construction. Mark Loizeaux, president of Controlled Demolition, Incorporated, noted "hot spots of molten steel," which were found "at the bottoms of the elevator shafts of the main towers, down seven [basement] levels" when the rubble was being removed.

These facts decisively rule out the official theory, but the convincing feature of these collapses was that they were *total!* Specifically, each 110-story twin tower collapsed into piles of rubble only a few stories high even though the core of each tower consisted of forty-seven massive steel box columns.

Attempts to defend the official theory, such as the article in *Popular Mechanics* (2005), typically ignore most of the above features of controlled demolitions. This widely promoted article "completely ignores the suddenness, verticality, rapidity, and totality of the collapses and also fails to mention the testimonies about molten steel, demolition rings, and the sounds of explosions."[1]

## Ground Shakings and Loud Noises within the Twin Towers Before the Beginnings of the Collapses of the Buildings

When analyzing the strange collapses of the Twin Towers on September 11, 2001, the shaking of the ground that accompanied these collapses has been important. Patricia Ondrovic, for example, as told in the three paragraphs identified by endnote no. 11 of chapter 4, had this experience:

> Well, one second I was trying to put my stretcher into the ambulance, the next thing I know I am thrown to the ground as the ground was shaking. Debris was flying at me from where the building I was parked in front of. There was a continual loud rumbling, there was just debris flying from every direction and then everything being covered in the black and gray smoke.

The collapse of the North Tower produced a seismic disturbance of 2.3, and the collapse of the South Tower registered 2.1. These questions continue to be of significant importance: when did this shaking begin and what caused it? While it may seem intuitively plausible that the rapid disintegration of such enormous buildings would produce seismic signals, it is likely that understanding the nature and times of the signals will give us more insight into the destruction of these buildings.

In 2006 the National Institute of Standards and Technology (NIST), which had issued a lengthy report in 2005 on the destructions of the Twin Towers, tried to answer several questions about the collapses. Two of the questions and answers, as found in NIST's 2006 publication, follow:

5. Why were two distinct spikes—one for each tower—seen in seismic records before the towers collapsed? Isn't this indicative of an explosion occurring in each tower?

    The seismic spikes for the collapse of the WTC Towers are the result of debris from the collapsing towers impacting the ground. The spikes began approximately 10 seconds after the times for the start of each building's collapse and continued for approximately 15 seconds. There were  no seismic signals that occurred prior to the initiation of the collapse of either tower. The seismic record contains no evidence that would indicate explosion occurring prior to the collapse of the towers.

6. How could the WTC towers collapse in only 11 seconds (WTC 1) and 9 seconds (WTC 2)—speeds that approximate that of a ball dropped from similar height in a vacuum (with no air resistance)?

    NIST estimated the elapsed times for the first exterior panels to strike the ground after the collapse initiated in each of the towers to be approximately 11 seconds for WTC 1 and approximately 9 seconds for WTC 2. These elapsed times were based on: (1) precise timing of the

—
103

initiation of collapse from video evidence, and (2) ground motion (seismic) signals recorded at Palisades, N.Y., that also were precisely time-calibrated for wave transmission time from lower Manhattan (see NCSTAR 1-5A).[2]

Witnesses noticed the ground shaking before the North Tower's debris hit the ground and even before its collapse began. Such an experience (from the oral histories collected by the Fire Department of New York [FDNY]) and the written accounts of the Port Authority Police Department [PAPD] of John Amato (9110421, FDNY, pp. 3,4) is described:

As we approached Chambers Street, kept walking, still no one had told us about the total collapse [of the South Tower]. We get down to about Barclay and Vesey Street, which is a block away from the overpass, the bridge overpass that goes across the West Side Highway.

All you hear is a rumbling in the street. It sounded like an earthquake. When I was a younger kid, I was in an earthquake and it felt like the same exact feeling. I looked, and I could see the antenna on the top of the roof coming straight down.

We all turned and just threw our rollups down and started running as fast as we could.

[AC] Note that feeling and sound are closely connected in this quotation and that the time of the antenna becoming lost to sight is exactly known from videos of the North Tower's collapse. Also note the "rumbling in the street" and "sounded like an earthquake" that occurred before the North Tower even began to collapse (as indicated by the antenna on its roof falling straight down).

[AC] It is also important to note that the "rumbling in the street" and "sounded like an earthquake" occurred just before or at the *beginning* of the North Tower's collapse, *not* "approximately 10 seconds *after* the times for the start of each building's collapse," as NIST asserted.[AC]

Three PAPD accounts, which also refer to the North Tower, are useful because each corroborates the Amato account. For brevity, only the B. Pikaard account (Part 2, p. 17) account follows:

> I was standing there about 15-20 seconds when Inspector Fields ran up to me and said the building was going to come down. The ground started to shake, I looked up and saw the top of 1 WTC start to collapse. I started to run . . .

[AC] Like Amato's account, Pikaard's account suggests that the shaking of the earth preceded collapse initiation. [AC]

Using the same oral histories and written accounts, the experiences of people in or near the South Tower were similar. John Rothmund's account (9110112, FDNY, pp. 5,6) of the early shaking of the ground follows:

> At that time we were looking at the top of the towers and all the rubble and people coming off and all of a sudden you heard—it sounded like another airplane, or a missile. It was like a slow shake. The whole ground just vibrated and shook. We just told everybody to run, run into a building, let's go, run, run, run . . .

The next thing you know, you hear a loud thundering noise. It sounded like a jet, a big rumble. I start looking around and I'm like, what is that? The next thing I know, I see the cop just take off. I'm like, where's he going?

Then I see the things on the floor, like Liberty—you know, just like the movies, bouncing up and jumping and shaking. I mean, not like an earthquake, like a 6 point something or something like that. But you see stuff on the floor shaking from side to side. I'm like, oh, my God, I look up and I was saying, oh, no, the building's going to fall down.

The following account of Timothy Norris (PAPD, Part 1, p. 34) about "the second tower" refers to the South Tower, in which he felt and heard vibration and noise that were closely connected while the earth shake seemed to precede collapse initiation:

Just at this time, another firefighter began to yell at us from across the street. He was looking up at the towers and yelled for us to hurry since he thought the second tower was about to fall. The two firefighters and myself again picked up the injured man and managed to walk three or four steps when we felt extreme vibration and an incredible noise "like a thousand freight trains." I knew instantly that the tower was falling down.

Anthony Croce (PAPD, Part 1, pp. 64-67) discusses the South Tower below in which he links noise closely to "violent ground vibrations" and then mentions the North Tower in which he saw the "corners of the building collapsing straight down" after the noise had already begun, thereby indicating the noise started well before the debris struck the ground:

> As I walked to the window I heard this incredible noise. It's difficult to describe what it had sounded or felt like. It was like being in an earthquake and under a thousand "L" trains all at once. The vibration ran through me with violent ground vibrations. I heard Lt. Kassamatis yelling for me to get out of there . . . . [describes running, thinking] I thought it was another plane crashing into the Plaza. I remember thinking that this was it, I was not going to make it. I heard a loud wind and glass shattering around me. An incredible force of wind and debris crashed thru the mezzanine and knocked me down.

> We were walking north on West St. and just as we got there I heard that noise again. I remember looking up at the North Tower and saw the corners of the building collapsing straight down.

## *Conclusions and Discussions Relating to Ground Shakings and Building Collapses*

From these accounts, the following is clear:

1) The ground trembled and objects on the ground visibly shifted and shook well before the debris from a collapsing tower hit the ground.

2) "A considerable degree of shaking began not only before debris struck the ground but before the South Tower began to descend."

3) The earth shaking coincided with an extremely loud noise.

The Twin Towers were huge buildings so that it is not surprising that their rapid destruction generated a great deal of noise. Witness testimony and surviving audio records allow three broad and overlapping sorts of sounds accompanying the collapses to be distinguished:

1) Discrete impulsive sounds which were typically described as booms, bangs, crashes, and explosions. During the South Tower's collapse at least two video recordings of "booms" are available, one being the firefighter video and another being the Sauret video in which eight booms are audible, at least six of them preceding the debris strike.

2) A "rumble" that combines both sound and feeling and is noticed as both a deep, continuous noise and a felt vibration.

3) A "roar," usually described as resembling the roar of a jet plane, that combines both a deep sound and a higher pitched sound—a whine or a whistle.

The rumble and the roar were extremely loud, and they increased in volume in the early stages of the collapse. Most importantly, these sounds began *before* the descent of the South Tower.

The situation appears to have been the same with the North Tower in which the rumble also preceded downward movement.

Video evidence has confirmed the foregoing auditory and visual evidence, suggesting the following:

1. The shaking of the earth seems to have reached an early peak at approximately 9:59:04 a.m., thereby making sense of the original findings of the Lamont-Doherty Earth Observatory's (LDEO) seismic evidence.
2. A second and higher peak came much later, representing the moment when debris hit the ground.
3. "The seismic event actually began before both of these points in time and, indeed, before any visible sign of collapse."[3]

The last three sentences of MacQueen's Abstract at the beginning of his article are as follows:

Major shaking of the earth and corresponding seismic signals, started well before the debris hit the ground. In fact, it seems certain that the shaking of the earth started before visible signs of building collapse. This evidence is incompatible with the official NIST hypothesis of the cause of the collapse of the Towers.

[AC] Only very powerful explosions, occurring before the beginning of a building collapse, could have possibly created such ground shaking, discrete impulsive sounds, rumbles, and roars. The explosions must have been caused by unusually powerful explosives that had been placed inside the buildings and probably below ground level before September 11, 2001. These preliminary explosions are also sufficient by themselves to prove that the government stories are false and packed with deceptions.

[AC] An explosion in the center of the core columns and at about the third basement level of a micro-fusion bomb or a mini-fission bomb, as discussed in Chapters 10 and 11, could reasonably have produced such ground shaking while destroying a vertically measureable portion of the most massive core columns, thereby initiating downward movement of the North Tower's antenna. Such a powerful explosion would have supplemented the explosion experienced by William Rodriquez just before the North Tower was hit high above by the first plane.[AC]

## The South Tower, WTC-2

As recorded by the Columbia University's Lamont-Doherty Earth Observatory in Palisades, N.Y. at 9:59:04 EDT, the South Tower pulverized itself in a span of ten seconds and became a mammoth cloud of dust that blasted into the lobby of the North Tower, curling up the stairways of its twin. "The blast of air from the South Tower traveled 131 feet into the lobby of the North Tower and then burst through the passageways across the complex," where it instantly lifted a woman into the air and slammed her into the window of Borders Books. The power of the collapse was so great that the earth shuddered in waves that were captured on a seismograph in Lisbon, New Hampshire, 265 miles away.[4]

## Discussion of the South Tower Collapse

During a lecture by Dr. Steven E. Jones of Brigham Young University, the collapse of the South Tower was discussed with reference to a photograph of the upper portion of the South Tower as approximately its top thirty floors were clearly toppling over and rotating. A photograph of the toppling upper portion of the South Tower is shown on the following page.

Dr. Jones made the following comment:

We observe that approximately 30 upper floors of the South Tower begin to rotate as a block, to the south and east. They begin to topple over, not fall straight down. The torque due to gravity on this block is enormous, as is its angular momentum. But then—and this I'm still puzzling over—this block turned mostly to powder *in mid-air!* How can we understand this strange behavior, without explosives? Remarkable, amazing—and demanding scrutiny since the US-government-funded reports failed to analyze this phenomenon. But, of course, the Final NIST 9-11 report *"does not actually include the structural behavior of the tower after the conditions for collapse initiation were reached."* (NIST, 2005, p. 80, fn. 12, emphasis added)

Dr. Jones commented that people seeking the truth of the matter should *not* ignore the data that was observed in videos during the actual collapses of the towers. That's what the NIST team admits they did. But ignoring highly relevant data in this way is a blatant nonscientific procedure. Dr. Jones said that this was supposed to have been an "open and thorough" investigation, but ignoring highly relevant data indicates political constraints.[5]

This upward bursting mass of gases, dust, and debris described by Dr. Jones as "this block turned mostly to powder in midair" is moving upwardly and sideways with great energy and clearly extends at least about 200 feet above the top of the South Tower and also extends about the same distance away from the building on all sides. The following observation also indicates great force: "This eruption of dust and debris initiated within one to two seconds. Three seconds into the collapse, the towers were spewing debris more than 200 feet outwards."[5]

[AC] Professor Jones simply underestimated the audacity of the people who arranged the WTC tragedies. It apparently did not occur to him that some U.S. government officials at the highest levels could be such psychopaths as to have used one or more extremely powerful bombs to blow those topmost thirty floors at least 200 feet upward and sideways in all directions while pulverizing and/or vaporizing the building's contents as a brown cloud, including its concrete floors, toilets, urinals, washbasins, desks, chairs, printers, computers, safes, wallboards, doors, elevators, stairways, stored water, steel, and people. It would have required the energy of such a bomb or bombs to have blown these pulverized materials at least 200 feet above and sidewise of the building while killing the 600 human beings in the top floors by vaporizing or shredding them and, immediately thereafter, pulverizing or vaporizing most of the eighty floors except for the steel.

—

[AC] However, this question is relevant: how did those "thirty upper floors" become separated from the lower eighty floors of the South Tower so that they could "begin to rotate as a block to the south and east" and then "begin to topple over, not fall straight down"? A steel-framed building simply does *not* separate into two parts unless very strong forces are applied to the building. So where did these forces come from? [AC]

Firefighter Richard Banaciski's described his experience in the South Tower:

> [T]here was just an explosion. It seemed like on television [when] they *blow up these buildings. It seemed like it was going all the way around like a* belt, all these explosions. [6]

[AC] As noted in the same reference, such explosions are known in the demolition industry as a "demolition ring." Cutter charges placed all the way around approximately the eightieth floor and detonated successively, beginning at the southeast corner, might have neatly separated those approximately thirty upper floors from the lower eighty floors and possibly pushed the upper floors to cause the block to begin to rotate and tilt.

[AC] The South Tower collapsed at 9:59 a.m., twenty-nine minutes before the North Tower collapsed at 10:28 a.m. [AC]

### The North Tower, WTC-1

Hardly anyone in the North Tower realized that its twin had collapsed in spite of the shuddering that followed. It was beyond conception. Office workers continued to go down and firefighters continued to climb, but two men on the fifty-first floor were nearly knocked to the ground.

It was equal to 1 percent of a nuclear bomb. It was enough power to supply all the homes in Atlanta or Oakland or Miami for one hour. It was so strong, the earth shuddered in waves that were captured on a seismograph in Lisbon, New Hampshire, 265 miles distant. Yet it made no sense in the building next door.

Patricia Cullen, standing at a window on the twenty-seventh floor while taking a break on her descent from the eighty-eighth floor, watched a massive cloud explode into her line of sight, a galloping darkness coming straight toward her building. "The floor trembled, the rumble passing from her feet to head. She fled toward the elevator lobby in the core of the building."

While moving in the stairwells, office workers and rescuers had little reliable information from the outside. The office workers could initially smell the odor of splattered jet fuel, but that did not last. Their feet and calves ached. The heat from all those thousands of people while making the dizzying reversals of direction at each stair landing was the present-tense realities of the escaping people.

Fortunately, the inferno was out of sight. So were the sights and sounds of bodies dropping from the highest floors.[7]

Essentially, each of the Twin Towers was built as three buildings stacked atop one another. The first ran from the lobby to the forty-fourth floor sky lobby; the middle ran from forty-fourth to the seventy-eighth floor lobby; the highest stretched from seventy-eight to the top of the building. WTC-1 was quiet in its "middle building," but its "top building" contained most of the people trapped above the impact area, and its "bottom building" was packed with office workers moving out and rescuers climbing slowly.

Three court officers and three Port Authority officers, moving lighter than the firefighters, reached the fifty-first floor. They found no one in the offices or in the stairways. Just then, the Port Authority officers' radios crackled with orders to evacuate.

Sixteen floors below the court officers, on the thirty-fifth floor, a battalion chief was resting with parts of five fire companies: ladders 5, 9, and 20 and engines 33 and 24. Their upward progress had been slowed by the streams of descending people and the weight of the gear they were carrying. At that moment, just as they were talking to Joseph Picciotto, the building began to shake and a cry of "Mayday! Evacuate the building!" came from Picciotto's radio.

Then at 10:01, seventy-five minutes after Flight 11 had struck, a police dispatcher ordered everyone to leave, saying that the South Tower had fallen. This news astounded policemen inside the North Tower. However, the largest group of rescuers in the building had radios that could not hear those messages.

A dozen or so firefighters had climbed into the fortieth floor areas to find members of their companies who had become separated during the ascent. Others were still trying to help injured or asthmatic office workers to move down the stairways. The bright, modern lobby of tan marble and polished chrome was a ruin with debris and several inches of pulverized concrete dust everywhere.

At 10:28 AM, twenty-nine minutes after the collapse of the South Tower at 9:59 a.m. and 102 minutes after Flight 11 hit the North Tower at 8:46 a.m., the North Tower seemed to spill out of itself, the dust boiling up above the roof, then pouring down the four facades toward the ground. Both towers showered debris in a wide radius as their external frames essentially "peeled" outwardly and fell from the top to the bottom. An estimated total of about 2,749 people were killed at the World Trade Center.[8]

When a fire chaplain replied to a request to go to confession as the North Tower was crumbling, he asked, "This is an act of war, isn't it?" The policeman next to him answered, "Yeah, I believe so," and the chaplain then declared, "Then I'm giving general absolution," never slowing down. His absolution came as approximately 1,000 people died at the top of the North Tower. They had survived the crash of Flight 11 at 8:46 but had not been able to find an open staircase at the top of the North Tower. Their fate had actually been determined nearly four decades earlier when fire stairs were eliminated as a wasteful use of valuable space and stairways were clustered in the core of the building.

After the collapse of the North Tower, there were open areas within the debris below the North Tower within which more than a dozen firefighters were trapped. Led by FDNY Battalion Commander Richard Picciotto and aided by other firefighters above the debris, all escaped even though the rubble field was blocked off by the still raging office buildings, WTC-5 and WTC-6, which were burning so fiercely that the fire department had given up on them and was merely trying to keep their fires from spreading to adjacent buildings. However, WTC-5 and WTC-6 did not collapse.[9]

## Comments on the Nature of the Collapses

Structural steel is an extremely tough and forgiving material, causing it to be the preeminent building material used in high-rise construction. Globally speaking, no other steel-frame building, before September 11, 2001 or since, has collapsed because of fire. Otherwise, hundreds of New York City firemen would not have begun the long climb up the stairwells to aid the victims. Experienced witnesses were shocked by the totality and near-perfect symmetry of the unexpected collapses that were unknown in random fire events but standard features of controlled demolitions, using carefully placed explosives.

Bronx firefighter Joe O'Toole stated that some of the beams lifted from deep within the catacomb of Ground Zero by cranes were dripping from the molten steel. Ground Zero chaplain Herb Trimpe said, "I talked to many contractors, and they said they saw molten metal trapped, beams had just totally been melted because of the heat." Leslie Robertson (structural engineer responsible for the design of the World Trade Center) said, "As of 21 days after the attack, the fires were still burning and molten steel was still running."[10]

Morgan Reynolds noted that about "a dozen of the fragmented ends of exterior columns in the North Tower were bent but the bends faced the 'wrong way' because they pointed toward the outside of the Tower." A heavy airliner crashing through the perimeter columns should certainly have bent them *inward*, thereby casting doubt on the government story.

### *Horizontal Ejections and Pulverizations of All Materials Except Steel*

One of the testimonies stated about the Twin Towers when they exploded near their tops, "materials shot out horizontally." Some of these materials ejected horizontally from the Twin Towers were massive sections of perimeter columns, weighing hundreds of tons, and some of them traveled five hundred to six hundred feet and even implanted themselves in neighboring buildings as can be seen in videos and photographs.[13]

Another anomaly was the pulverization of material. Throughout history, concrete buildings have been known to collapse during powerful earthquakes, and when this occurs, they typically fold up like an accordion, leaving a succession of concrete slabs, one piled on top of another, each plainly discernible in the rubble. But nothing like this occurred on 9/11. Photos of the mountain of wreckage at Ground Zero taken by Joel Meyerowitz and others show very few, if any, large chunks of concrete. The rubble pile consisted almost exclusively of twisted steel. The conspicuous absence of concrete is remarkable since concrete was the main constituent of the 500,000-ton towers. As noted, each floor of the 110-story building, roughly an acre in size, consisted of a slab of poured concrete, most of which was pulverized during the collapse into small pieces and fine dust.

Some have attributed this to the force of gravity, but videos of the collapse clearly dispute this. The buildings were not pulverized as they hit the ground; they disintegrated in midair. As the South Tower started to collapse, for example, the entire upper section tipped as a unit, then inexplicably turned to dust before people's eyes. As noted, much of the dust settled a foot deep on the sixteen-acre WTC site. The rest was deposited across lower Manhattan. Nor was the pulverization limited to concrete. Other construction materials also disappeared without a trace, including glass, office furniture, and tens of thousands of computers, not to mention the many victims. It's a fact that fewer than 300 corpses were recovered. Most of the victims were identified solely from body parts. Strangely, when workmen began to dismantle the badly damaged Deutsch Bank on December 8, 2006, they found more than 700 slivers of bone on the roof and within the structure. This bizarre report has never been explained. (Incidentally, the E. J. Lee study determined that the building was beyond saving and recommended demolition.)

And there were other anomalies. The video record plainly shows that during the WTC collapse, perimeter columns, weighing many tons, were hurled as far as 500-600 feet from the towers. One remarkable photo of Ground Zero taken from above shows that entire sections of WTC-1's western perimeter wall were thrown over 500 feet toward the winter garden.[11]

# Chapter 5 Notes

1. Zarembka, Paul, editor. *The Hidden History of 9-11*. Second Edition. 2008. New York 10013. Seven Stories Press, 140 Watts Street, 80-85. v

2. MacQueen, Graeme. "Did the Earth Shake Before the South Tower Hit the Ground?" July 9, 2009, 2, 35.

3. Ibid., 26-35.

4. Dwyer, Jim and Kevin Flynn. *102 Minutes: The Untold Story of the Fight to Survive inside the Twin Towers*. New York 10011. Henry Holt and Company, 115 West Eighteenth Street, 211-213.

5. Jones, Steven E. "Why Indeed Did the WTC Buildings Collapse?" Physics Department Colloquium at Idaho State University, Sept. 1, 2006. *Journal of 911 Studies, 35, 36*. http://reopen911.org/BYU.htm, 35, 36.

6. Griffin, David Ray. *The New Pearl Harbor Revisited: 9/11, the Cover-up, and the Expose*. 2008. Northampton, Massachusetts 01060. Olive Branch Press, 46 Crosby Street, 27.

7. Dwyer and Flynn, 214-216.

8. Ibid., 214-221, 242, 243, 256, 257.

9. Picciotto, Richard. *Last Man Down: A Firefighter's Story of Survival and Escape from the World Trade Center*. 2005. New York 10011. Henry Holt and Company, LLC, 218-220.

10. 9-11 Research.wtc7.net. "Molten Metal. Workers Reported Molten Metal in Ground Zero Rubble." http://911research.wtc7.net/wtc/evidence/moltensteel.html.

11. Gaffney, Mark H. *The 9/11 Mystery Plane and the Vanishing of America*. 2008. Walterville, OR 97489. Trine Day LLC, PO Box 577, 164, 165.

# CHAPTER 6

## The Collapse of WTC-7 Seven Hours after the Twin Towers Collapsed

### *Larry Silverstein's Involvement in WTC-7 and Its Demolition*

Larry A. Silverstein was appointed a director of Westfield America in May 1997. Since 1979, Mr. Silverstein has been President of Silverstein Properties, Inc., a Manhattan-based real estate investment and development firm which owns interest in and operates over 10 milion square feet of office space. Mr. Silverstein is a member of the New York Bar, and a Governor of the Real Estate Board of New York, having served as its Chairman. He is a trustee of New York University and is the founder and Chairman Emeritus of the New York University Real Estate Institute. He is Chairman of the Realty Foundation, Vice Chairman of the South Street Seaport Museum, and a board member of the Museum of Jewish Heritage.

—

Zionist Larry Silverstein built the forty-seven-story steel-framed WTC no. 7 in 1987 as part of the WTC complex, owned by the New York Port Authority. This dark, flat-topped skyscraper was north of the WTC superblock across Vesey Street. It was three hundred feet from the plaza and was built over a Con Ed electrical substation, which filled the first five floors, because of land scarcity. It was not hit by an airliner. WTC-7 contained thousands of sensitive files relating to very large financial scandals, including Enron and WorldCom.

The IRS, the Department of Defense, and the CIA had offices on the twenty-fifth floor. The Secret Service was on the ninth and tenth floors. The Securities and Exchange Commission, which had vast records of bank transactions, was on floors 11 through 13. Rudy Giuliani's Office of Emergency Management, his crisis center, was on the twenty-third floor. Salomon Smith Barney occupied floors 28-45. The mortgage of WTC-7 was held by the Blackstone Group. Its head was Pete Peterson, chairman of the Council on Foreign Relations, both being potentially active in any NWO MIHOP.[1]

In the preface to the second edition of his book, *9/11 Synthetic Terror: Made in USA*, Dr. Tarpley wrote:

> But first, a note on methodology. This book argues the rogue network MIHOP ("made it happen on purpose") position. That is to say, it represents the analytical point of view which sees the events of September 11, 2001 as a deliberate provocation manufactured by an outlaw network of high officials infesting military and security apparatus of the United States and Great Britain, a network ultimately dominated by Wall Street and City

of London financiers. It is our contention that any other approach not only misrepresents what actually happened in the terror attacks, but also must tend to leave the public naïve and helpless when it comes to identifying the present and future threat of state-sponsored, false flag synthetic terrorism, and therefore preventing repeat performances of 9/11 including on a far larger scale.

LIHOP stands for Let It Happen on Purpose. Vice President Cheney has been characterized as a MIHOP (and indeed the chief MIHOP, in the opinions of some 9/11 truth seekers), and President Bush has been characterized as a LIHOP.

Dr. Tarpley commented that David Ray Griffin's *New Pearl Harbor* was an example of what might be termed Bush-Cheney MIHOP. Such emphasis on Bush-Cheney as the possible masterminds of 9/11 creates a problem, however, "since the rogue network has demonstrably been around since the blowing up of the USS *Maine* more than a century ago—long before Bush and Cheney." Furthermore, Dr. Tarpley wondered "if serious plotters would ever dream of assigning an important role to a moron or to a *Bush* man who has had multiple heart attacks, who has had a pacemaker *Cheney* installed and who is living on borrowed time." He also commented that "the 'invisible government' will not necessarily be defeated if its puppets of the moment - Bush, Cheney, and company—are ousted."

Dr. Tarpley further observed that "the presence of trained professionals who actually produce the results observed, which the patsies could never produce, suffices to validate a MIHOP analysis for the entire operation." He also commented that "the Mossad is also known to be a very nefarious organization," but although "it is a well-established fact that the Mossad meticulously observed every phase of the preparation and execution of 9/11, what is missing is convincing proof of a direct operative role for the Mossad in 9/11."[2]

[Author's Comment—AC] The chief MIHOP would have had the authority to make the quick changes in plans that were needed when Flight 93 was seriously delayed in take-off. Cheney seems to have been frozen into following an established plan, so he was definitely not the chief MIHOP.

NWO stands for New World Order, a current term for world government. The Council on Foreign Relations (CFR) was founded in 1921 in New York City "by a group of 'intellectuals' who felt that there was a need for world government and that the people of the United States were not ready for it." Its meetings are secret as required by Article II of its bylaws. Its *Study No. 7*, published on November 25, 1959, gave the exact purpose of the CFR as advocating the "building (of) a new international order (which) may be responsible to world aspirations for peace (and for social and economic change). The words 'a new international order' are the current catch words for a world government."

Rear Admiral Chester Ward (USN, Ret.), a former member of the CFR, made these comments about the CFR:

> The most powerful clique in these elitist groups have one objective in common—they want to bring about the surrender of the sovereignty and the national independence of the United States.
>
> A second clique of international members in the CFR . . . comprises the Wall Street international bankers and their key agents.

Primarily, they want the world banking monopoly from whatever power ends up in the control of global government.[3]

According to Jim Hoffman, a software engineer and physicist from Alameda, California, where he authors the site 911research.wtc7.net, he simply saw a "classic controlled demolition." That explains 'why 7 WTC dropped so rapidly (in about 6.6 seconds, or almost at the speed of a free-falling object) and so neatly, into its own footprint."

For 7 WTC to collapse unaided at that speed, Hoffman says, would mean "its 58 perimeter columns and 25 central columns of structural steel would have to have been shattered at almost the same instant, so unlikely as to be impossible."[4]

In a PBS documentary aired in September 2002, Larry Silverstein, the WTC leaseholder, quotes himself as saying about WTC-7:

I remember getting a call from the, er, fire department commander, telling me that they were not sure they were gonna be able to contain the fire, and I said, "We've had such terrible loss of life, maybe the smartest thing to do is pull it. And they made that decision to pull and we watched the building collapse.[5]

[AC] The expression "pull it" is industrial slang for controlled demolition. Using it means that Mr. Silverstein must have known

#7 as a matter of fact that the necessary explosives were indeed in place and electrically synchronized or radio controlled to bring the skyscraper down correctly as a demolition.

[AC] But many hours of work by skilled demolition experts are required to place explosives in critical places in order to accomplish such precise collapse of a steel-framed building as noted by several experts. Who gave permission for these demolition experts to enter the buildings? Mr. Silverstein was the ultimate authority for giving such permissions. Indeed, Mr. Lewis M. Eisenberg, the Port Authority Lessor, must also have been a conspirator in the matter, for the immense Twin Towers and even the substantial WTC-7 must have required more time than was available during the forty-nine days of Silverstein's ownership for installing the explosive materials therein, especially if such work had to be done on scheduled weekends.

[AC] Mr. Silverstein's foreknowledge of precisely placed explosives in WTC-7 is self-evident. How much did he know about explosives in WTC-1 and WTC-2? Why did the 9/11 Commission fail to ask these questions?

[AC] Another important question is this: when did the Israeli spies and demolition experts first arrive in the U.S.A.?[AC]

## Mayor Giuliani's Command Center and Its Abandonment

Mayor Giuliani's creation of his emergency command center on the twenty-third floor of building 7, which had 25 core columns and 58 perimeter columns, is of some interest. Giuliani spent $15 million to make this command center self-sufficient and insulated from danger. The features of this floor included an independent and secure supply of air and water, bullet-and-bomb-resistant windows, and the ability to withstand winds of 200 mph.[6]

[AC] Accordingly, if Giuliani and his associates had been in this command center when the South Tower fell, they would have been protected from the huge dust clouds that developed and roared down the streets and should not have been harmed even by the fall of the North Tower, which was about 300-350 feet away. So why did they leave unless they had received reliable warnings that the building would soon collapse—that is, be demolished? [AC]

### Jennings and Hess, Who Experienced the Ignored Lobby Explosion and Dead Bodies Inside WTC-7

[AC] Another important question is this: was WTC-7 supposed to collapse in the morning? [AC]

A massive explosion did occur at about 9:15 in the morning as reported by Michael Hess, the city's corporation counsel, and Barry Jennings, New York City's deputy director of the Emergency Services Department. Immediately after the North Tower had been struck at 8:46 a.m., they had gone to Mayor Rudy Giuliani's Office of Emergency Management Command Center on the twenty-third floor of WTC-7 and found that everybody had gone, leaving still-steaming coffee and half-eaten sandwiches on the desks. Jennings called several people, and "one individual told me to leave and to leave right away."

They found that the elevator would not work because all the power had gone out. Then they started down the stairs. But when they reached the sixth floor of building 7, there was a huge explosion at the base of the building, and the landing they were standing on gave way. They returned to the eighth floor, broke a window with a fire extinguisher, looked out "both ways," and saw "both buildings [the Twin Towers] were still standing." They signaled for help to firefighters on the ground. Jennings later added, "The explosion was beneath me."

They were trapped on the eighth floor for about an hour and a half. Firemen came to rescue them but then ran away because of the collapse of the South Tower, which occurred at 9:59. Returning a little later, the firemen again started to rescue them but then ran away again because of the collapse of the North Tower, which occurred at 10:28. "All this time I'm hearing explosions."

> When they finally got to us and they took us down to what they called the lobby—'cause I asked them "Where are we?" He said, "This *was* the lobby." And I said, "You got to be kidding me." It was total ruins, *total* ruins. Now keep in mind, when I came in there, the lobby had nice escalators, it was a huge lobby, and for me to see what I saw, it was unbelievable. And the firefighter that took us down kept saying, "Don't look down." I asked, "Why?" And he said, "Do not look down." We were stepping over people, and you know you can feel when you're stepping over people. They took us out through a hole in the wall . . . And this big giant police officer came to me, and he says, "You have to run," and I said, "I can't run, my knees are swollen." He said, "You'll have to get on your knees and crawl, then, because we have reports of more explosions."[7]

Their rescue "must have been sometime between 11:00 and 11:30, because at 11:57, Hess gave an on-the-street interview several blocks away. Jennings also gave an on-the-street interview. Both men reported that they had been trapped for some time - Hess specified "about an hour and a half."[7]

A NYC policeman said he was injured in WTC 7 and removed on a gurney with his eyes covered, but "he was able to see dead bodies lying all over the floor as he was being carried out - BEFORE building 7 collapsed."

[AC] This NYC cop's view of dead bodies on the lobby floor of WTC building 7 confirms what Jennings and Hess experienced. Bearing in mind that the government said that there were no deaths in WTC-7, why so many deceptions? [AC]

Hess was interviewed by Frank Ucciardo of UPN 9 News "on Broadway about a block from City Hall" beginning shortly before noon. Jennings said that the big explosion that occurred at 9:15 a.m. and trapped them was simply the first of many that he heard while waiting to be rescued. **NIST DISTORTED JENNINGS'S TESTIMONY AND COMPLETELY OMITTED HIS REPORT ABOUT THE DESTROYED LOBBY AND DEAD PEOPLE THEY HAD TO STEP OVER.**

On August 19, Barry Jennings died. On August 21, 2008, NIST intended to release the first version of its final report, its "Draft for Public Comment," on the collapse of WTC-7.

Jennings was fifty-three years old when he very mysteriously died. No one was willing to provide any information as to how or why he had died. Dylan Avery hired a private investigator, one of the best in the state of New York, to find out what she could. He paid her a considerable fee with his credit card.

A message came from her twenty-four hours later, saying, "Due to some of the information I have uncovered, I have determined that this is a job for the police. I have refunded your credit card. Please do not contact me again about this individual."

The dedication page of Avery's book said, "To the memory of Barry Jennings, whose truth-telling may have cost him his life." Avery is one of the makers of the 9/11 video, *Loose Change*. [8]

> Avery originally hoped to use the Jennings interview in one of his "*Loose Change*" series of documentaries, which contend that elements of the U.S. government played an active role in orchestrating the events of 9-11 as a pretext for the implementation of the so-called "war on terror" and a predatory foreign policy in the oil-rich Middle East. Jennings at first gave permission for the interview to be shown as part of the film, but later asked that it be withheld because he feared there would be reprisals if his testimony were made public. [9]

[AC] Why was the mysterious death of Barry Jennings, a black NYC official, not investigated by the city police? Hopefully, an independent federal grand jury will take up the case and put Michael Hess and people from The Office of Emergency Management (OEM) on the witness stand. [AC]

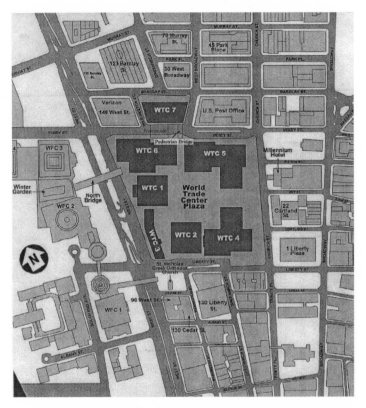

The World Trade Center in Lower Manhattan

## *Exterior Damage to WTC-7 from Ignored Explosions*

Two 9/11 researchers, Matthew Everett and Jeremy Baker, have independently suggested that WTC-7 was probably intended to collapse in the morning, shortly after the collapse of the North Tower, because its collapse would then have been less suspicious and could have plausibly been explained as resulting from the previous collapses of the Twin Towers, especially the North Tower, which was 300 feet away.

—

Everett, one of the editors of *The Complete 9/11 Timeline,* wondered whether the reason for a previous premature announcement at 11:07 that morning could have been "that WTC-7 had originally been scheduled to be brought down (with explosives) at 10:45 a.m.? . . . However, something—as yet unknown to us—happened that meant the demolition had to be delayed, and so building 7 was not ready to be brought down until late that afternoon."

Then Baker discovered a short video clip from ABC News showing "an enormous gash that extends down the center of WTC-7's facade from its roofline all the way to the ground." Explaining the importance of this discovery, Baker wrote:

> The force required to gouge the straight, clear, cavernous gash in WTC 7 represents a source of destructive power far greater than anything that was present that day and simply could not have been caused by falling debris.

Baker next asked:

> Could the straight, clean gouge in WTC 7's south face be an indication that a line of explosives running up the center of the building detonated but then stalled? Buildings typically have their centers blown out first when they are being demolished and this kind of failure is certainly not without precedent. Though this theory is surely speculative, is it unreasonable to ask the question: *What else could have caused such a bizarre wound in the south face of WTC 7?*

Larry Silverstein corroborated this finding by attempting to suggest an alternative cause for the gash, saying that the falling antenna from the roof of the North Tower had crashed down and "sliced through the facade in the front of 7. As it did so, it ruptured fuel lines in the building . . . [which] caught fire. That fire started to burn and burned intensively the rest of the day."

Baker was unimpressed, saying, "This ridiculous claim . . . is easily refuted by video evidence. Silverstein thereby showed that he was aware of this vertical gash down the front of WTC 7, which had not been previously acknowledged publicly." [10]

### *Expectation of WTC-7's Collapse at 10:45 a.m. as Announced at 11:07 a.m. on September 11, 2001*

There were reports that it was known in advance that building 7 was going to collapse so that a collapse zone of several blocks around WTC-7 was established several hours before the building collapsed. Firefighting was never started in WTC-7. When the chief officer in charge of WTC-7 got to Barclay Street and West Broadway, "numerous firefighters and officers were coming out of WTC-7 . . . because they thought that the building was going to collapse."

One reason for this expectation was a previous premature announcement at 11:07 that morning by CNN correspondent Alan Dodds Frank, who was in Lower Manhattan:

> [J]ust two or three minutes ago there was yet another collapse or explosion . . . . [A]t a quarter to 11, there

was another collapse or explosion following the 10:30 collapse of the second tower. And a firefighter who rushed by us estimated that 50 stories went down. The street filled with smoke.

Assuming that WTC-7 was intended to collapse at 10:45 a.m., it would have been about ninety minutes after the massive explosion experienced at 9:15 a.m. by Hess and Jennings while on the sixth floor landing of building 7. This interval would have been about the same as the interval between the collapse of the North Tower and the earlier explosion in its basement as experienced by William Rodriguez and others.

Why did they think this? According to Captain Michael Currid, who was the sergeant at arms for the Uniformed Fire Officers Association, "Someone from the city's Office of Emergency Management" had told him that WTC 7 was "basically a lost cause and we should not lose anyone else trying to save it." The Office of Emergency Management (OEM) was directly under Mayor Rudy Giuliani (it was the OEM Command Center in WTC 7 to which Hess and Jennings had gone to find Giuliani, only to discover that everyone had already left). It is especially significant that it was Giuliani's OEM that reportedly spread the word that WTC 7 was going to collapse, because this same office had been the source of the advance knowledge, reported earlier in terms of an exchange between Giuliani and Peter Jennings, that the Twin Towers were going to come down.[11]

[AC] On the other hand, if his emergency command center, having a perfect view of the Twin Towers, was used to direct the airliners into the towers, he was a definite MIHOP. It is indeed a reason to wonder why Rudy Giuliani left his twenty-third-floor bunker, which was bulletproof and even dustproof when he could have stayed there in perfect safety and comfort while both of the Twin Towers collapsed. However, suppose that Giuliani knew the plans of the murderous conspirators. More exactly, suppose that Giuliani knew that WTC-7 was intended to be demolished in the morning while Lower Manhattan was enveloped in enormous clouds of smoke and concrete dust. With bedlam surrounding the area—fire engines, police sirens, and screaming citizens fleeing in all directions—the conspirators could have brought down WTC-7 at 10:45 a.m., for example, so that they would have had the perfect cover story: falling debris from WTC-1 and WTC-2 had struck WTC-7 and caused it to crash to the ground. Best of all, from their perspective, there would have been no snooping cameras to record this obvious controlled demolition.

[AC] Giuliani would not have known that some malfunction would prevent WTC-7 from collapsing as planned. So he would have reasonably evacuated the building without delay, taking no chances. Unquestionable foreknowledge! [AC]

WTC-7 contained thousands of sensitive files relating to very large financial scandals. The Securities and Exchange Commission (SEC) apparently lost three thousand to four thousand active cases involving "the manner in which investment banks divided up hot shares of initial public offerings during the high-tech boom." Some of the biggest financial scams in history, including Enron and WorldCom, were among those cases. WTC-7 had office space for more than two hundred Secret Service employees. All the evidence stored in all SEC cases were destroyed. Citigroup said that backup tapes of corporate e-mails from September 1998 through December 2000 were additionally destroyed.[12]

## Sudden Destruction of WTC-7 at 5:20 p.m.

The building collapsed symmetrically into its footprint in 6.6 seconds, nearly at free-fall velocity and about seven hours after the destruction of the North Tower, beginning from t0he bottom up, as in standard controlled demolition with explosives while Silverstein watched. For 7 WTC to collapse unaided at that speed, Hoffman says "it's 58 perimeter columns and 25 central columns of structural steel would have to have been shattered at almost the same instant, so unlikely as to be impossible" (i.e., without explosives).[13]

[AC]The 9/11 Commission Report failed to state that WTC-7 (which had only two small, localized fires) had also collapsed. The National Institute of Standards and Technology (NIST) additionally had little to say about this collapse until its final report issued in November 2008. As briefly commented upon at the end of Chapter 4, it has been characterized by the author as a "governmental hoax."[AC]

Fires were initially observed by firemen on noncontiguous floors on the south side of WTC-7 at approximately floors 6, 7, 8, 10, 11, and 19. The exteriors of floors 8-18 were damaged to some degree, and there was additional damage to the south elevation, particularly to the southwest corner caused by the collapse of the North Tower. WTC-7 was 300 feet from the North Tower.

With regard to squib-timing during the collapse of WTC 7, Ian Woods commented:

> Horizontal puffs of smoke and debris are observed emerging from WTC 7 on upper floors, in regular sequence, just as the building starts to collapse . . . ."The upper floors have evidently not moved relative to one another yet, from what one can observe from the videos. In addition the timing between the puffs is less than 0.2 seconds so air-expulsion due to collapsing floors . . . is evidently excluded. Free-fall time for a floor to fall down to the next floor is significantly longer than 0.2 seconds: the equation for free fall, $y = \frac{1}{2} gt^2$, yields a little over 0.6 seconds, as this is near the initiation of the collapse.

> However, the presence of such "squibs" proceeding up the side of the building is common when pre-positioned explosives are used as can be observed at http://www.implosionworld.com/cinema.htm. Thus, squibs as observed during the collapse of WTC 7 going up the side of the building in rapid sequence provide additional significant evidence for the use of pre-placed explosives.[14]

## Significance of WTC-7's Collapse

David R. Kimball commented that few remember WTC Building 7's demise because after September 11th it had been treated, both in the media and in The 9/11 Commission Report, as if it never happened. Yet its significance and the significance of its nationwide obliteration from the media are great.

The 47-story tall WTC building 7 was one of the largest buildings in lower Manhattan. It occupied an entire city block and was 300 feet from the closest twin tower (the North Tower).

Building 7 suddenly and rapidly collapsed on September 11, 2001, at 5:20 PM, ECT. The collapse began as the penthouse subsided and continued as all of its 47 stories imploded into its own footprint in less than seven seconds. This collapse was in itself a major event, yet it "was reported as if it were an insignificant footnote." Incredibly, it is virtually impossible to find any mention of Building 7 in newspapers, magazines, or broadcast media reports after September 11th."

Five days later, NASA flew an airplane over the WT site. This airplane recorded infrared radiation coming from the ground and obtained thermal data which the U.S. Geological Survey analyzed to make a thermal map. "This map shows that five days after the collapse of Building 7, the surface temperature of a section of its rubble was 1,341°F .... This temperature is indicative of the use of explosives."

He concluded his article with the following three questions:

Who had the means and expertise to engineer such a demolition and acquire needed materiel, and who had access to WTC Building 7 PRIOR to September 11, 2001 in order to place the explosives?

An inquiry into the answer to this question might be a good place to begin a search for the real perpetrators of 9/11. Do we, the citizens of the United States, have the courage and honesty necessary to initiate an actual investigation, or will we continue living a Lie - and reap the consequences?[15]

[AC] How neat, complete, and fortuitous was this destruction of WTC-7, considering the amount of money involved, the danger of imprisonment for very powerful people if those cases had not been destroyed, and the fact that WTC-7 was not struck by an airliner! [AC]

## *Molten Steel in WTC-7's Rubble Pile*

Mark Loizeaux, president of Controlled Demolition Inc., who was hired for the building 7 cleanup, said that "molten steel was found at 7 WTC." Leslie Robertson, World Trade Center structural engineer, stated that on October 5, "21 days after the attacks, the fires were still burning and molten steel was still running." Fire department personnel, recorded on video, reported seeing "molten steel running down the channel rails . . . like you're in a foundry—like lava from a volcano."

The knowledge that this evidence even exists was denied by one of NIST'S top engineers, John Gross, during his appearance at the University of Texas in April 2006.

—

139

Richard Gage, AIA, commented in an email to NIST on January 4, 2007: "Steel melts at about 2,850 degrees Fahrenheit, about twice the temperature of the World Trade Center Tower 1 and 2 fires as estimated by NIST. So what melted the steel?" Gage wrote that analyzes of the slag at the ends of beams and in samples of previously molten metal found iron, aluminum, sulfur, manganese, and fluorine. These are the chemical evidence of thermate that the military use as an incendiary cutting charge. It cuts through steel like a hot knife through butter and produces molten iron as a byproduct.

Gage also pointed out that fire causes "large, gradual deformations and asymmetrical collapses. If the thermate is formed into ultra-fine particles, as has been accomplished at Los Alamos National Laboratory, it is called super-thermate, and is very explosive."[16]

[AC] A super explosive developed by the military could have been used on 9/11 only if the planners must have known with certainty that permission would be available from the US government and if the US government had actually given permission to the perpetrators to obtain and use it; thus MIHOP and an "inside job" are thereby proven.

[AC] Using super-thermate to cut the structural steel in the perimeter columns and core columns of the WTC buildings would have effectively melted steel close to each super-thermate charge and would surely have pulverized nearby concrete as well. However, the explosive radius of such a super-thermate charge is unknown. Unless they were placed close enough together as to be overlapping, this author believes that they would not have pulverized three-fourths of an acre on all floors of the Twin Towers. Nor is it likely that they would have had the power to hurl hundreds of tons of perimeter steel columns some 500 feet sidewise. For those reasons plus heat generation in the rubble pile for months after 9/11, the possibilities of fusion and fission nuclear explosives have been explored in subsequent chapters.AC]

## *Illegal Removal of Steel from WTC-7's Rubble Pile*

[AC] Evidence needed for determining what had caused the three skyscrapers to fall down was required by state and federal law to be preserved until they could be carefully studied and the cause of catastrophe determined. Yet the laws were ignored without punishment after 9/11! [AC]

Unintended structural failures are less common in steel-framed high-rises than in aircraft. Being the only such building in history in which fire is blamed for total collapse, Building 7's remains warranted the most painstaking examination, documentation, and analysis. Building 7's rubble pile was at least as important as any archeological dig. It contained all the clues to one of the largest structural failures in history. Without understanding the cause of the collapse, all skyscrapers become suspect, with profound implications for the safety of occupants and for the ethics of sending emergency personnel into burning buildings to save people and fight fires.

Yet, despite the paramount importance of the remains, they were hauled away and melted down as quickly as possible. The steel was sold to scrap metal vendors, and most of it was soon on ships bound for China and India. Some of the smaller pieces and a few token large pieces of steel marked "Save" were allowed to be inspected at Fresh Kills landfill by FEMA's BPAT volunteers.

This illegal evidence destruction operation was conducted over the objections of attack victims' family members and respected public safety officials.

Officials running the "cleanup operation" took pains to make sure the structural steel didn't end up anywhere but in blast furnaces. They installed GPS locator devices on each of the trucks hauling loads from Ground Zero at a cost of $1000 each. One driver who took an extended lunch break was dismissed. [17]

[AC] The rubble pile should have been dismantled carefully while documenting the position of each piece of steel and moving it to a warehouse for further study. None should have been sold or even moved without documentation; doing so was a felony.

[AC]According to the government story, no one had been caught in WTC-7's collapse, for it had been evacuated hours before it happened, and the pile was well confined to the building's footprint. This official story omits the information provided by Hess and Jennings about bombs within WTC-7 and about stepping over dead people as they walked through the demolished lobby of WTC-7. Did government officials and the media simply ignore those dead people? Who were they? Were they listed among the "approximately 2,780 deaths," in spite of WTC-7 being officially identified as having no casualties? What killed them? Was it the explosion experienced and heard by Hess and Jennings or was it something else, such as asphyxiation by freon? [AC]

## *Requirements for Organized Demolitions of Skyscrapers*

Dr. Frank Legge, Logical Systems Consulting, Perth, Western Australia had this comment on the collapses of WTC-1, 2, and 7:

> To organize the controlled demolition of these three large buildings would obviously require possession of very substantial resources and remarkable freedom of access. The following had to be achieved before the event: the secret and skilful installation of a network of explosives in three buildings; the establishment of a control centre from which the demolitions could be initiated and monitored; the provision of the ability to commence demolition prematurely if a building started to topple [this occurred with WTC 2, the south tower]; the incapacitation of the normal Air Force interception of wayward aircraft; and the hijacking of four aircraft without raising suspicions. All this had to be achieved in the face of numerous warnings by field workers in the FBI, and by intelligence agencies of other countries, that a major attack was imminent.

Dr. Legge also made this observation and deduction from the videos:

WTC 7 collapsed straight down. This requires that, at
the moment of collapse, if caused by fires weakening the
supports, not only did the north and south pair of walls
have to be of equal strength, but also the east and west
pair. Without such symmetry this tall building would
inevitably have toppled over. Even if the fires had been
intense and widespread this dual symmetry would have
only a very low probability of existence. Given the uneven
distribution of the small fires at the time of collapse the
probability of the required symmetry vanishes, hence
fires did not cause the collapse.[18]

## Significance of Obliterating WTC-7's Collapse from Nationwide Media

Barrie Zwicker, a Canadian journalist with fifty-five years of
experience, when his book, *Towers of Deception*, was published in
2006, commented upon the strange difference between 6-9 days
passing before an independent investigation was ordered after
the sinking of the Titanic, the JFK assassination, the *Challenger*
disaster, and the Pearl Harbor attack and 441 days passing before
an independent investigation was ordered after the events of
September 11.

He noted that the "evidence that elements of the US government
were complicit in 9/11 is, frankly, overwhelming," as is demonstrated
by "the growing number of well-referenced books by authors with
excellent bona fides." He thought that this is "a puzzle foremost in
the minds of this huge constituency of skeptics."

Zwicker also noticed that "when a coherent picture—surely what readers, viewers, and listeners want—is needed on a really controversial topic . . . . , the media buy quickly into the initial official version . . . . Contradictory facts and interpretations begin to be sidelined or dismissed altogether . . . ."

> Much overlooked to our peril is that there's an 800-pound gorilla in our synthetic perceptual environment: the increasing "invention of reality" by covert agents working for "invisible "governments." The ultimate is what Bakunin called "the propaganda of the act."

> This undeniable aspect of the reality of our world is dangerously underreported, even as clandestine operations, by definition undemocratic and deceitful in the extreme, receive ever more funding. In *9/11 Synthetic Terror*, Webster Tarpley claims reality today is "overdetermined" by fake events.

> The stakes could hardly be higher. The official story of 9/11 is the linchpin for the so-called "war on terror," being sold 24/7 as the imperative reality of our time. The "war on terror" has replaced the Cold War template as the justification for the escalation of already obscene squandering of Earth's precious resources on militarism, the gutting or endangerment of every worthy goal from social equity to social justice to civil liberties, peace and the very survival of the life support system of our planet.

At the same time the so-called "war on terror" is transparently self-serving for those who promote it. It reaps profits for the arms and security industries, bestows power on the "intelligence community," the "counterterrorism experts" and the military, and boosts poll numbers for politicians.

Zwicker commented that Pres. George Bush and those behind him trafficked in fear because "fighting the terrorists" was the only issue on which the majority of voters fell in line behind the US president. Then he made this critically important observation:

> The "war on terror" is really a war of terror against domestic populations. Everything harks back to "remember 9/11." What could be more important than to have mainstream media lead an extended critical public analysis of the official story?[19]
>
> [AC] What this author is striving for is exactly to present a coherent story of the events of 9/11, with paragraphs faithfully identified as to references and with author's comments clearly distinguished from referenced materials so that readers will understand what happened and have ideas as to what to do to overcome this cover-up and the many deceptions by government and media. Ideally, an independent federal grand jury can do such uncovering and also bring much delayed justice to this nation. [AC]

# Chapter 6 Notes

1. 911review.org Homepage. "7 World Trade Center." http:// elitewatch.911review.org/7WTC.html.

2. Tarpley, Webster Griffin. *9/11 Synthetic Terror Made in USA*. Fourth Edition. 2007. Joshua Tree, CA, 92252. Progressive Press, PO Box 126, vi-ix.

3. Epperson, Ralph A. *The Unseen Hand: An Introduction into the Conspiratorial View of History*. 1985. California 91359. Publius Press, Tucson, AZ, 196, 197.

4. Jacobson, Mark. "The Ground Zero Grassy Knoll: A new generation of conspiracy theorists are at work on the secret history of New York's most terrible day." New York. Nymag.com.

5. Zarembka, Paul, Ed. *The Hidden History of 9-11*. Second Edition. 2008. Elsevier Ltd. New York, NY 10013. Seven Stories Press, 140 Watts Street, 98, 99.

6. 9-11 Research.wtc7.net. "Building 7. The Secrecy-Shrouded Building Holding Giuliani's Command Center." http://911research. wtc7.net/wtc/background/wtc7.html.

7. Griffin, David Ray. *The New Pearl Harbor Revisited: 9/11, the Cover-up, and the Expose*. 2008. Northampton,Massachusetts 01060. Olive Branch Press, 46 Crosby Street, 45-52.

8. sacramento craigslist. "Testimonial Evidence for Explosives." http:// sacramento.craiglist.org/rnr/1377931868.html.

9. Duveen, Peter. "9-11 hero's testimony sparks controversy on the first anniversary of his death." Http://www.petersnewyork.com/Jennings. html.

10. Griffin 2008, 48-50.

11. Ibid., 50-52.

12. What Really Happened.com. "Larry Silverstein, WTC 7, and the 9/11 Demolition." *http://whatreallyhappened.com/WRHARTICLES/cutter.html?q=cutter.html.*

13. New York ny mag.com. "The Ground Zero Grassy Knoll: A new generation of conspiracy theorists is at work on a secret history of New York's most terrible day." *http://www.printthis.clickability.com/pt/cpt?action=cpt&* title=The+Ground+Grassy+Knoll+-+Knoll+-+A + New . . .

14. Woods, Ian. "9/11: The Greatest Crime of All Time. The Best of Global Outlook (Vol. II.) , 57.

15. Kimball, David R. "Government Refuses to Consider Cause of 47 Story World Trade Center skyscraper Building 7 Demolition." *http://www.libertyfor*life.com/eye-openers/911/wtc7demolition.htm.

16. Gage, Richard. "Undisputed Facts Point to the Controlled Demolition of WTC. Response to NIST'S Invitation for Written Comments.", 2-4.

17. WTC.net. "The Destruction of Building 7's Remains." http:wtc7.net/steeldisposal.html.

18. Legge, Frank. "9/11 - Evidence for Controlled Demolition: A Short List of Observations." Journal of 9/11 Studies. June 2006/Volume 1, 4, 5.

19. Zwicker, Barrie. "Towers of Deception: The Media Cover-up of 9/11."

# PART II
## Government Story for Twin Tower Collapses and Refuting Arguments

# CHAPTER 7

## Official Story Explaining the Collapses of the Twin Towers and Technical Argument against NIST Excuses

It didn't seem real . . . There are thousands of these steel beams that just fell like pickup sticks.

> John Albanese, volunteer firefighter and amateur photographer.

What struck us - guys like Warren Jennings and myself, who have spent basically all our lives in the scrap business - we'd never seen steel this heavy this huge, this massive. It was just unbelievable.

> Michael Henderson, general manager,
> Marine Terminals, Metal Management NE.[1]

## *Official Story Explaining the Sudden Collapses of the Twin Towers*

NIST gave a threefold explanation as to how the impacts of the planes plus the ensuing fires could have caused the collapses of the towers:

> (i) The impact of the planes severed many steel columns and knocked the fire-proofing off of many more, (ii) the fires were so big and hot that they weakened the remaining columns to the point where additional pressure would cause them to fail, and then (iii) the upper portion of the buildings, above the strike zones, exerted this additional pressure by falling on the lower portion.

Shortly after 9/11, President Bush advised people not to listen to "outrageous conspiracy theories about the attacks of 11 September." Then Philip Zelikow, who directed the work of the 9/11 Commission, also warned against "outrageous conspiracy theories." But what is the difference between a non-outrageous theory and an outrageous one? The government theory is a conspiracy theory in which members of al-Qaeda are the conspirators.

The official theory about the Twin Towers says that they collapsed because of the combined effect of the impact of the airplanes and the resulting fires. This theory clearly belongs in the category of outrageous theories for a number of scientific reasons.

## *Answers of the National Institute of Standards and Technology (NIST) to Frequently Asked Questions*

After the first edition of *The Hidden History of 9-11*, edited by Paul Zarembka, appeared, NIST (National Institute of Standards and Technology) published a document entitled "Answers to Frequently Asked Questions," henceforth, AFAQ.

[Author's Comment—AC] The NIST "Answers" document discusses several issues not explicitly addressed in the NIST Report, but it does *not* make NIST's explanation of the WTC destruction more plausible. Instead, it provides more evidence that this explanation is not sensible. Really, it's just a myth! [AC]

Dr. David Ray Griffin, one of the contributors to the Zarembka volume in "The Destruction of the World Trade Center: Why the Official Account Cannot be True" and "Update: The Destruction of the World Trade Center: Why the Official Account Cannot Be True," discussed the following answers to frequently asked questions (AFAQ):

Given the fact that "a document from the Port Authority of New York and New Jersey . . . indicated that the impact of a Boeing 707 aircraft would result in only local damage which could not cause collapse, why did the impact of individual 767s cause so much damage?" NIST's reply blamed "the large mass of the aircraft [and] their high speed and momentum," pointing out that "a Boeing 767 aircraft is about 20 percent bigger than a Boeing 707."

Dr. Griffin acknowledged that this statement was true but also deceptive because it ignored comparative speeds. The 767s hit the North and South Towers at 440 and 540 mph respectively, whereas the calculated 707 of the 1960s traveled at 600 mph, thereby more than compensating for the 707's smaller size.

[AC] It is also pertinent that the Boeing 707 aircraft had four engines, whereas both the 767 and the 757 aircraft had two engines. [AC]

Another AFAQ was "How could the WTC towers have collapsed without a controlled demolition since no steel-frame, high-rise buildings have ever before or since been brought down due to fires?" NIST replied, "The collapse of the WTC towers was not caused either by a conventional building fire or even solely by the concurrent multifloor fires that day. Instead, NIST concluded that [the impacts of the airplanes played major roles]."

Dr. Griffin discussed NIST's second part of its explanation, relating to the size and heat of the fires, by pointing out the deceptions used by NIST, such as alleging that the air temperature in the towers reached "about 1,000°C (1,800°F)" and then saying that "when bare steel reaches temperatures of 1,000°C, it softens and its strength reduces to roughly 10 percent of its room temperature value." NIST thereby implies that the steel columns in the towers actually got that hot, ignoring the conductivity of steel and the enormous amount of interconnected steel in each tower, forming a tremendous heat sink so that a long, long time would have been needed "for even a fairly big fire to heat up any of the steel columns to its own temperature."

[AC] Moreover, all the 247 perimeter columns on a heated floor would have had to reach that softening temperature at the same time in order to prevent the tower from toppling. In the case of the South Tower, where the airliner struck near a corner and the fuel fire was brief and only near that corner, this would have been clearly impossible. There must have been some other reason for the

toppling and rotating of the top thirty floors of the South Tower.
[AC]

Dr. Griffin further argued as follows:

NIST compounds its deceptiveness in this new document by
failing to point out that its own scientists had found no evidence
that any of the steel columns had reached temperatures above
250°C (482°F). Given that fact, NIST had no evidence that any of
the columns even reached 425°C (797°F), which, as Eagar points
out, is when "structural steel begins to soften." NIST's suggestion
that core columns had reached temperatures of 1,000°C (1,832°F)
is, therefore, "about as wildly unempirical as could be imagined."

Another AFAQ was "How could the WTC towers collapse
in only 11 seconds (WTC 1) and 9 seconds (WTC 2)—speeds
that approximate that of a ball dropped from similar height in a
vacuum?" NIST gave this answer:

> [T]he momentum (which equals mass times velocity) of
> the 12 to 28 stories (WTC 1 and WTC 2, respectively)
> falling on the supporting structure below (which was
> designed to support only the static weight of the floors
> above and not any dynamic effects due to the downward
> momentum) so greatly exceeded the strength capacity
> of the structure below that it (the structure below) was
> unable to stop or even to slow the falling mass.

Dr. Griffin pointed out that this idea "that the massive steel
frames of the [lower structure of the] towers provided no more
resistance to falling rubble than [would] air" is one of the reasons
that critics of the official account claim that explosives must have
been used to remove the 287 columns supporting each building.

Moreover, Dr. Griffin stated, NISTS's statement was clearly false in asserting that "the supporting structure below . . . was designed to support only the static weight of the floors above" because articles in *Engineering News-Record* in 1964 predicted that the Twin Towers would remain stable even if one-fourth of their columns were lost and if loads on the perimeter columns were increased by 2,000 percent."[2]

# Chapter 7 Notes

1. Reynolds, Morgan. "Why Did the Trade Center Skyscrapers Collapse?" *http://lewrockwell.print.this.clickability.com/pt/ cpt?action=cpt&title=0Why+Did+the+Trade=Center+ Skyscrapers+Collapse?*, 1.

2. Zarembka, Paul, Ed. *The Hidden History of 9-11*. Second Edition. 2006, 2008. New York 10013. Seven Stories Press, 140 Watts Street, 315-321.

# CHAPTER 8

# NIST Data
# And General Arguments
# Against the Official Stories that
# Prove them to be Myths

## *NIST Temperature Tests of WTC Structural Steel*

The National Institute of Standards and Technology (NIST) was authorized by the U.S. Congress in August 2002 to investigate the collapse of the World Trade Center on September 11, 2001. Their report was released in September 2005.

NIST made a series of fire tests to investigate the possible weakening of the WTC support columns. In the first test, an uninsulated steel column was placed in a furnace at 1,100°C (2,012°F). The surface temperature of the column reached 600°C (1,112°F) in merely thirteen minutes. At this temperature steel loses significant strength. ("Construction grade steel begins to lose strength at 425°C [762°F] and is only about half as strong

—
158

at 650°C [1,202°F."] When they repeated the test with a steel column treated with SFRM (spray-applied fire resistant material) insulation, the column's surface did not reach 600°C after ten hours.

In its report NIST argued that the crashed airliners "damaged or dislodged 100 percent of the protective insulation within the impact zone and spilled many thousands of gallons of jet fuel over multiple floors." NIST then made the crucially important claim that the resultant blaze created temperatures of 800-1,000°C (1,472-1,832°F), thereby seriously weakening the now-exposed steel and causing a "global structural failure."

NIST scientists developed a novel way to evaluate the effect of fire temperatures on the WTC steel. Their approach was "easy to implement and robust enough to examine the entire component in the field." Having found that the original primer paint used on steel was altered by high heat, they were able to determine the level of temperature exposure by analyzing this paint, which had been used on the WTC steel beams and columns.

The result surprised NIST scientists because they "found no evidence that any of the steel samples, including those from the impact areas and fire-damaged floors, had reached temperatures exceeding 1,110°F (649°C). Sixteen recovered perimeter columns showed evidence of having been exposed to fire, but even so, out of 170 areas examined on these columns, only three locations had reached temperatures in excess of 250°C (482°F). Moreover, NIST found no evidence that any of the recovered core columns had reached even this minimal temperature."

Two possible explanations have been suggested: (1) "the jet fuel . . . burned out in less than ten minutes" and (2) the fuel load was surprisingly low.

## *Fuel Load Calculations by NIST*

FEMA's 2002 report noted

> Fuel loads in office-type occupancies typically range from
> about 4-12 psf [pounds per square foot], with the mean
> slightly less than 8 psf . . . At the burning rate necessary
> to yield these fires, a fuel load of about 5 psf would be
> required to maintain the fire at full force for an hour.

When NIST calculated the fuel load for a typical WTC floor,
they obtained an average of only about 4 psf. That meant that the
WTC towers were too fuel poor to support "the frequent depictions
in the media of a ferocious inferno raging beyond anything in human
experience." The paint tests also demonstrated that the 9/11 fires
failed to heat the steel columns sufficiently to cause them to weaken
and buckle so that NIST's conclusion that damaged SFRM insulation
was responsible for collapsing the towers became ridiculous.

[AC] These figures seem reasonable in view of the "box within
a box" design used for the Twin Towers and the abundant amount
of space between the boxes, whereby office furniture would have
been less crowded than customary. [AC]

## *The Effects of Sustained and Elevated Temperatures Upon Steel Buildings*

The strength of each tower and its resistance to impact of an
airliner enabled each tower to absorb the impact easily "because
they were hugely overbuilt, redundant by design."[1]

—

[AC] The government's fire intensity theory ignores (a) the black smoke near each airliner impact area that indicates insufficient oxygen for creating a hot fire, (b) the thermal conductivity of steel that would have caused heat from a hot spot to travel in every possible direction to cooler places while warming the steel along which it had traveled and (c) the fact that the Twin Towers were fuel-poor (4 psf) compared with other office buildings, as previously described. At some welded joints, the heat would have been able to move in several directions, creating a very large heat sink. A fuel fire burning for fifty-six minutes (in the South Tower) simply lacked the intensity and longevity for compromising a steel structure, which requires a psf of at least 5, a much longer burning time, and much more oxygen. [AC]

For example, a fifty-six-story steel building in Venezuela remained standing after a recent seventeen-hour fire. As another example, the 1991 Meridian Plaza fire in Philadelphia burned for eighteen hours, and the fire was so extraordinary that flames came from dozens of windows on many floors, and "the fire was so energetic that [b]eams and girders sagged and twisted," but "[d]espite this extraordinary exposure, the columns continued to support their loads without obvious damage." The building did not collapse.

Finally, before 9/11, no steel-framed building had ever collapsed because of fire even if engulfed in flames for hours, and none has ever collapsed because of fire anywhere else in the world since then.[2]

## *Living People Walking in the Hole of the North Tower*

Among a wide variety of facts undermining the fire collapse theory, photographs show people walking around the hole in the

—

North Tower "where 10,000 gallons of jet fuel were supposedly burning." A video and photographs show a blond woman with light-colored slacks looking over the edge of the 94th floor and waving her arm. She has been identified as Edna Cintron but was not "mentioned in the Popular Mechanics myth debunking book." Moreover, most of the North Tower's flames had already vanished after burning for only 16 minutes by the time that the South Tower was hit."[3]

## No Inward-bent Columns Observed in the North Tower

About a dozen of the fragmented ends of exterior columns in the North Tower hole were bent, but the bends faced the "wrong way" because they pointed toward the outside of the Tower. The laws of physics imply that a high-speed airplane with fuel-filled wings breaking through thin perimeter columns would deflect the shattered ends of the columns inward.

It is more reasonable that "the outward bends in the perimeter columns were caused by explosions from the inside the tower rather than bends caused by airliner impact from outside."

## Perimeter Columns Cut With Linear-shaped Charges

The "uniformly neat ends of the blown perimeter columns are consistent with the linear shaped charges that demolition experts use to slice steel as thick as 10 inches." Such linear-shaped charges also explain "the perfectly formed crosses found in the rubble" as well as the rather neatly shorn steel found everywhere.

## No Engine Was Recovered in the Rubble
## from the North Tower

In Boeing airliners, "each engines is enormous and dense, consisting mainly of tempered steel and weighing 5-6 tons, depending upon model." Yet no engine was recovered in the North Tower rubble, and no hydrocarbon fire could possibly vaporize such steel. It is also important to bear in mind that these airliners are huge. They weigh eighty-two tons empty and have a maximum takeoff weight of up to 193 tons.[4]

[AC] It is true that among the "Oral histories of Plane Impacts and Bounced Back Evidence from North Tower Impact" that are recited in chapter 3, an engine was seen "near a little plaza close to West Broadway and west Vessey." However, FEMA took charge of Ground Zero the next day and forbade even photographing of such evidence. Recovery of the engine was surely impossible.

[AC] To assert that the fire in one corner of the South Tower would have become hot enough over the entire floor to cause all of the 247 perimeter columns to soften or melt simultaneously in fifty-six minutes is simply absurd. (If such softening or melting did not occur simultaneously, the very tall building would have toppled over if a collapse had been caused by heat from a fire.) This theory also ignores the heat conduction of steel, whereby the entire tower could act as an enormous heat sink, and further ignores the forty-seven steel columns in each central core. For example, most of the North Tower's flames had already vanished after burning for only 16 minutes by the time that the South Tower was hit. In other words, a pancake type of floor collapse would have left the forty-seven core columns standing for hundreds of feet in the air. [AC]

—

## Steel Wreckage at Ground Zero

One of the most important eyewitnesses was Abolhassan Astaneh-Asl, a professor of civil engineering at the University of California at Berkeley. Immediately after 9/11, he received a National Science Foundation grant to spend two weeks at Ground Zero, studying steel from the buildings. In speaking about what he learned in October 2001, he reported that steel flanges "had been reduced from an inch thick to paper thin." He also reported seeing 10-ton steel beams that "looked like giant sticks of twisted licorice" and also steel that was smoothly warped at connection points, which could happen, he said, only if the steel had become yellow or white hot—"perhaps around 2,000 degrees."[5]

[AC] Moreover, a pancake-style collapse, floor after floor, requiring steel trusses to be torn from all steel columns at the perimeter and from all steel columns at the core, floor after floor, could never have occurred at nearly free-fall speed. Such speedy collapses could have occurred, however, if the perimeter and core columns and the connections to the floor trusses had been severed by cutter charges slightly less than a tenth of a second before each floor began to collapse. These precise cuttings would have required thousands of cutter charges to have been expertly placed in each twin tower.[AC]

Instead, the towers had collapsed into a bizarre, giant, unprecedented "rubble field, acres and acres of mass and terrifying destruction." Compacted debris was made up of beams, girders, some chunks of concrete, and very, very fine dust. There were "mountain after mountain of packed debris, interrupted by crater after crater." Some mountains were 200 feet high at some points, with 100-foot drops at other points. There was nothing human or personal in this rubble field. Nothing *real*. Every specific thing, every identifiable thing, was just disintegrated, pulverized, gone. Also, beneath these piles, there were another six or seven stories of wreckage compacted below ground level and extending to bedrock.[6]

Karin Deshore , captain *EMS) provided this description:

> Somewhere around the middle of the World Trade Center, there was this orange and red flash coming out. Initially it was just one flash. Then this flash just kept popping all the way around the building and that building had started to explode. The popping sound, and with each popping sound it was initially an orange and then a red flash came out of the building and then it would just go all around the building on both sides as far as I could see. These popping sounds and the explosions were getting bigger, going both up and down and then all around the building.[7]

## *Pulverization of All Contents of Twin Towers Except for Bent Steel*

Demolition experts say that high-velocity explosives are actually more powerful as they build up a powerful shockwave than low-velocity explosives such as untamped black powder and ANFO that make a whoosh and roar while belching forth fire and smoke as shown in movies.

From a WMV video download (907KB) came this statement:

> You don't find a telephone, a computer. The biggest
> piece of a telephone I found was half of the keypad You
> have two hundred and ten story office buildings. You
> don't find a desk. You don't find a chair . . . The building
> collapsed to dust.

Peter Tully, president of Tully Construction, which specializes
in concrete, made this comment to *American Free Press*:

> Think of the thousands of file cabinets, computers, and
> telephones in those towers—I never saw one—everything
> was pulverized. Everything that was above grade—above
> the 6th and 7th floor—disintegrated—it was like an
> explosion.

When AFP asked if he had ever seen concrete pulverized as it
was at the WTC, he answered, "No—never."[8]

> Dr. Frank Legge commented,
> To organize the controlled demolition of these three
> large buildings would obviously require possession of
> very substantial resources and remarkable freedom of
> access. The following had to be achieved before the
> event; the secret and skilful installation of a network
> of explosives in three buildings; the establishment of
> a control centre from which the demolitions could be
> initiated and monitored; the provision of the ability to
> commence demolition prematurely if a building started

to topple (this occurred with WTC 2, the south tower),
the incapacitation of the normal Air Force interception
of wayward aircraft, and the hijacking of four aircraft
without raising suspicions. All this had to be achieved
in the face of numerous warnings by field workers in the
FBI, and by intelligence agencies of other countries, that
a major attack was imminent.

The demolition of the Twin Towers had to be done from the
top down in order to create the illusion—and the deception—that
the damage from airliner impacts and fires in the top sections
had caused the collapses. However, achieving this effect required
much more explosive than conventional controlled demolitions in
which the buildings are demolished from the bottom up so that the
weight of the entire building presses down and assists collapse. The
explosives also had to be set off in a precise descending sequence.
The vast amount of dense dust which was flung out violently,
together with pieces of steel, from the collapsing region provides
the most immediately obvious evidence of such explosives. Videos
and photographs show that the collapses were preceded by a series
of horizontal dust puffs or squibs which progressed downwardly at
intervals of several floors.[9]

[AC]Significantly, the collapses were little longer than in free
fall in a vacuum. A likely reason for the South Tower falling first is
that the WTC organizers had to time demolition with the dying
of the fires in the two towers in order to sustain the official theory
that an intense fire caused each collapse after the airliner impacts
had dislodged insulation, thereby causing buckling failures, which, in
turn, would allow the upper floors to pancake onto the floors below.
So they set off thermate and other charges at about the eightieth floor

of the South Tower and inadvertently caused the top 30-34 floors to separate from the seventy-ninth floor, begin to rotate, and then to topple about twenty-two degrees. Panic-stricken, they detonated one or more bombs, which eliminated those top 30-34 floors within three seconds. Then they immediately detonated more bombs to bring down the remaining 76-79 floors in about six more seconds.[AC]

## *Illegal Destruction of Evidence After Fatal Fires*

As noted by Morgan Reynolds:

> The criminal code requires that crime scene evidence be saved for forensic analysis, but FEMA had it destroyed before anyone could seriously investigate it. FEMA was in position to take command because it had arrived the day before the attacks at New York's Pier 29 to conduct a war game exercise, "Tripod II," quite a coincidence. The authorities apparently considered the rubble quite valuable: New York City officials had every debris truck tracked on GPS and had one truck driver who took an unauthorized 1 ½ hour lunch fired." [10]

[AC] In view of this painstaking tracking of the trucks by New York City officials, it is likely that Mayor Rudy "Scoop and Dump" Giuliani must have had much to do with illegally removing WTC evidence. Breaking the law about preserving such evidence is a felony. No one is above the law. So why hasn't Giuliani been tried, found guilty, and put in prison? A federal grand jury in Manhattan should be able to learn much about such illegal destruction of evidence, especially if it can issue presentments, as authorized by the Fifth Amendment to the U.S. Constitution, and is thereby free of such obvious corruption as occurred after 9/11. [AC]

## *Observations by Scientists*

Among fifteen reasons for doubting the official government account for collapses of the Twin Towers, James H. Fetzer noted that the "melting point of steel at 2,800°F is about 1,000°F higher than the maximum burning temperature of jet fuel-based fires, which do not exceed 1,800°F under optimal conditions," whereby the fires in the Twin Towers cannot have caused the steel to melt, which means that melting steel did not bring the buildings down. He also pointed out that heavy steel construction buildings like the Twin Towers are simply not capable of "pancake collapse." Such collapses can only occur with concrete structures of "lift slab" construction. Welded-steel buildings of "redundant" construction are unable to collapse in that way unless every supporting column has been removed at the same time. Each twin tower was built with more than one hundred thousand tons of steel.

Mr. Fetzer further observed that for as long as five weeks after 9/11, pools of molten metal were found at the subbasement levels. The amount of heat required to melt such large quantities of steel and keep the pools in molten condition for such a long time could not have been produced by the plane impact or jet fuel-fire or pancake collapse scenario, thereby implying that it is not the correct scenario.

An additional observation by Mr. Fetzer was that there was insufficient kinetic energy for the collapse of one floor onto another to cause the pulverization of the impacted floor, "even if the impact of the planes and the ensuing fires had been enough to cause the steel to weaken and one floor to collapse upon another, which required a massive source of energy beyond any that the government has considered."[11]

## *Explosions Before and After Aircraft Impacts*

William Rodriguez heard explosions both before and after the aircraft impacts in the North Tower. The first explosion (fourteen seconds before impact) caused the floor beneath his B1 subfloor office, having fourteen occupants at that time, to shake and the cement walls to crack. The very loud, massive explosion seemed to come from between B2 and B3 floors. In response to a question about the possibility of aircraft fuel having traveled down the elevator shafts to cause the explosion, William Rodriguez testified:

> Very strange indeed since there were only one elevator shaft (the 50A car) that went all the way to B6, the operator was inside, Mr. Griffith and he survived with a broken ankles. He should have died burnt since on this theory the ball of fire went down. He is alive and well and I will interview him in the future to clear the disinformation.[12]

[AC] Rodriquez and the fourteen people with him were in an excellent position to know that the "very loud, massive explosion" occurred below ground level and before the plane impact upon

170

the North Tower and that more explosions occurred after the plane impact. These unchallengeable facts prove beyond doubt that significant explosions did happen independently of the plane impact and that the government fraudulently omitted them from its elaborate report. [AC]

## *Revisions of Impact Times by NIST*

The very loud and massive explosion heard and felt by William Rodriquez and fourteen others in the maintenance office on the first sublevel of the North Tower and by twenty-two people on the B2 sub-basement level on September 11, 2001 cracked the cement walls in the office, vibrated the floor, and shook everything in the office. This explosion also caused a seismic spike at the Lamont-Doherty Earth Observatory at Columbia University (LDEO) at 8:46:26 a.m. This spike was nine seconds earlier than the FAA radar time of 8:46:35 and fourteen seconds earlier than the radar-based time of 8:46:40 when the alleged AA Flight 11 died at about the 90th floor of the North Tower.

As to the South Tower, there was an original seismic spike recorded by the LDEO at 9:02:54 a.m., and the alleged UA Flight 175 crashed at the radar-based time of 9:03:11 a.m., a difference of 17 seconds.

NIST (National Institute of Standards and Technology) added five seconds to the impact times and collapses in an apparent time-manipulative effort to make the seismic spikes "supposed" times of "impacts," instead of powerful sub-basement explosions

The following conclusions in 2006 by Craig T. Furlong and Gordon Ross, members of Scholars for 9/11 Truth, are important:

> Several seismic stations recorded seismic signals originating from two events which occurred at the WTC site, immediately prior to both aircraft impacts. Because these signals preceded the impacts there can be no doubt that the seismic signals recorded were not those associated with the aircraft impacts on the Towers. These signals were in fact the seismic spikes associated with the huge basement explosions reported by witnesses. Only by a revision of the previously well-regarded seismic times has NIST been able to attempt to say the times of the aircraft impacts coincide with the seismic signals, and even then, their 8:46:30 first impact time is a fake. Meanwhile, the evidence of basement explosions prior to the impact of AA Flt 11 has not been explored or examined at all, even with so great a cloud of witnesses.

> The inescapable conclusions drawn from this analysis and the facts contained herein, cast extreme doubt on the government's claim that these attacks were carried out solely by Middle Eastern terrorists, who would not have had the ability or opportunity to plant explosive devices, nor to detonate them so as to be masked and partially hidden by the aircraft impacts. The real perpetrators, those who actually did plant these devices, clearly had free access to the Towers. The total number of people who had this opportunity was small and a list of these people should be easily available.[13]

[AC] That list has clearly not been available during the years since 2006, but it should be obtainable from Mr. Silverstein who had the authority to close the Twin Towers over weekends. It seems to be another mystery and web of deceptions that an independent grand jury can solve. [AC]

Morgan Reynolds observed that the opening in the North Tower was not big enough for a Boeing 767 (allegedly the plane, officially tail number N334AA, used for Flight 77). In particular, a Boeing 767 has a wingspan of 155 feet, but the maximum distance across the hole in the North Tower was about 115 feet, a hole undersized by some 40 feet. Furthermore, there were no reports of plane parts, especially wings, that could have been shorn off in the collision and bounced to the ground on the northeast side of the tower. Moreover, the two engines for this plane are enormous and dense, consisting mainly of tempered steel and weighing 5-6 tons, depending upon model. Most importantly, no engine has been recovered in the rubble, and vaporizing them by a hydrocarbon fire would have been impossible.[14]

Dr. Steven E. Jones, after experimenting with molten metals, concluded that the yellow white color of the molten metal pouring from an eightieth-floor window of the South Tower implied a temperature of about 1,000°C (1,832°F), which was too high for the dark-smoke hydrocarbon fires burning in the building and also because molten aluminum appears silvery gray in daylight, whereas molten iron appears yellow white at that temperature. After falling about 150 yards, the molten metal still retained a reddish orange color, not the behavior of falling, molten aluminum but of molten iron, which he believed to be "consistent with thermite or one of its variants."[15]

Eight scientists studied two WTC dust samples collected soon after 9/11 by applying scanning electron microscope (SEM) and X-ray energy dispersive spectrometry (XEDS) methods, with an emphasis on observed microspheres in this dust. The microspheres were tiny solidified droplets, which were roughly spherical in shape (spherules). The scientists commented that

> the formation of spherules in the dust implies the generation of materials somehow sprayed into the air so that surface tension draws the molten droplets into near-spherical shapes. That shape is retained as the droplet solidifies in the air. Spherules observed in the WTC dust include iron-rich, molybdenum-rich and silicate varieties. The temperatures required to melt iron, silicates, and molybdenum, and to vaporize lead and aluminosilicates . . . are summarized in Table 1.

## Table 1

Temperatures Required to Melt or Vaporize Certain Metals and Metal Compounds

| Process and material | °C | °F |
| --- | --- | --- |
| To form Fe-O-S eutectic (with mol% sulfur) in steel | 1,000 | 1,832 |
| To melt aluminosilicates (spherule formation) | 1,450 | 2,652 |
| To melt iron (spherule formation) | 1,538 | 2,800 |
| To melt iron (III) oxide (spherule formation) | 1,565 | 2,849 |
| To vaporize lead | 1,740 | 3,164 |
| To melt molybdenum (spherule formation) | 2,623 | 4,753 |
| To vaporize aluminosilicates | 2,760 | 5,000 |

The scientists stated that not only is it necessary for materials in the dust to have undergone extremely high temperatures in order to melt and then form small spheres, it is also necessary that some violent physical disturbance occur in order to shatter the molten materials into the observed sizes, which were 1.5 mm down to about one micron in diameter. Then surface tension in the liquid droplets would cause spherule formation.

The scientists observed that the temperatures necessary to melt iron and molybdenum, and to vaporize lead and aluminosilicates, were "completely out of reach of the fires in the WTC buildings (maximum 1,100°C)." They wished "to call attention to this discrepancy" between the data and "the official view implicating fires as the main cause for the ultimate collapses of the WTC towers and WTC 7."

They further stated that the "data provide strong evidence that chemical reactions which were both violent and highly exothermic contributed to the destruction of the WTC buildings," whereas NIST neglected this high temperature and fragmentation evidence.

These scientists noted that

> In combustion science, there are three basic types of flames, namely, a jet burner, a pre-mixed flame, and a diffuse flame . . . . In a diffuse flame, the fuel and the oxidant are not mixed before ignition, but flow together in an uncontrolled manner and combust when the fuel/oxidant ratios reach values within the flammable range. A fireplace is a diffuse flame burning in air, as was the WTC fire. Diffuse flames generate lowest heat intensities of the three flame types . . . the maximum

—

flame temperature increase for burning hydrocarbons (jet fuel) in air is, thus, about 1000 °C - hardly sufficient to melt steel at 1500° C.[16]

[AC] Such neglect by NIST of "this high temperature and fragmentation evidence" is prima facie evidence that the federal government committed fraud upon the American people. It would only have been done by the highly educated NIST personnel because emphatic orders had come from on high, namely, the White House. Obviously, an independent grand jury is badly needed. [AC]

## Light Bluish Smoke From WTC Rubble Contained Much Extremely Toxic, Ultrafine Particles

When Thomas A. Cahill, an expert on airborne aerosols and director of the DELTA Group at the University of California at Davis, saw the light bluish smoke rising from the rubble of the World Trade Center, he knew that the plumes contained large amounts of the very smallest particles, which are extremely toxic and ultrafine, that is, less than one-millionth of a meter in size, and smaller. "Unlike the much larger dust particles from the destruction of the twin towers, these ultra-fine and nano-particles are particularly hazardous because of their extremely small size, which allows them to pass throughout the body and penetrate into the nucleus of the human cell."

On October 2, 2001, a Davis air-monitoring unit was installed on the roof of the twelve-story building at 201 Varick Street, at the edge of the "exclusion zone," which was about one mile north of

WTC's smoking rubble. It began to sample the air on that day and continued until late December after the last fires in the rubble were finally extinguished.

Cahill was asked why it took so long to begin a scientific evaluation of the air contamination coming from the destroyed WTC. He answered that he had assumed that many agencies and scientists were monitoring the air quality in Manhattan after 9/11, but he found out that EPA did nothing.

Cahill also said that the debris pile at the WTC acted like a chemical factory, which cooked together the components of the buildings and their contents, including enormous numbers of computers. Not surprisingly, this factory "gave off gases of toxic metals, acids and organics for at least 6 weeks."

Cahill also commented that the DELTA Group's work revealed most of the particles in the plumes were in the category of the smallest ultrafine and nanoparticles, from 0.26 to 0.09 microns. He further stated that such ultrafine particles require extremely high temperatures, "namely the boiling point of the metal." His data proved that incredibly intense hot spots, capable of boiling and vaporizing metals and other components from the debris, persisted beneath the rubble for weeks.[17]

# Chapter 8 Notes

1.  Gaffney, Mark H. *The 9/11 Mystery Plane and the Vanishing of America.* Walterville, OR 97489. Trine Day LLC, PO Box 577, 159-161, 168, 169.

2.  9-11 Research.com. "Other Skyscraper Fires. Fires Have Never Caused Skyscrapers to Collapse." http.//911research.wtc7.net/wtc/analysis/compare/fires.html.

3.  Straight Dope Message Board. "'Edna Cintron' standing in World Trade Center on 9-11." http://boards.straightdope.com/sdmb/archive/index.php/t-534880.html.

4.  Reynolds, Morgan. "Why Did the Trade Center Skyscrapers Collapse?" *http://lewrockwell.printthis.clickability.com/pt/cpt?action=cpt&title=Why+Did+the+Trade+Center+.,1,* 5.

5.  Griffin, David Ray. *The New Pearl Harbor Revisited: 9/11, the Cover-up, and the Expose.* 2008. Northampton, Massachusetts. Olive Branch Press, 33.

6.  Picciotto, Richard. *Last Man Down: A Firefighter's Story of Survival and Escape from the World Trade Center.* 2002. New York. Berkley Books, 218-220.

7.  Marrs, Jim. *The Terror Conspiracy: Deception, 9/11 and the Loss of Liberty.* 2006. New York, NY 10003. Disinformation Company Ltd. , 163 Third Avenue, Suite 108, 39-51.

8.  What Really Happened. "Evidence of Demolition Charges in WTC 2." *http://www.whatreallyhappened.com/wtc2_cutter.html.*

9.  Legge, Frank. "Evidence for Controlled Demolition: a Short List of Observations." *Journal of 9/11 Studie*s. June 2006/Volume 1, 5.

10. Reynolds, 2.

—

11. Fetzer, James H. "Why Doubt 9/11?" Scholars for 9/11 Truth. http://www.scholarsfor 911truth.org/WhyQuestion911.html, . ,

12. Furlong, Craig T. and Gordon Ross. "Seismic Proof - 9/11 Was An Inside Job." (Updated Version II). 2006, 5.

13. Ibid, 10, 11.

14. Reynolds, 5.

15. Jones, Steven E. "Why Indeed Did the WTC Buildings Collapse? http://reopen911.org/BYU.htm, 7-12.

16. Jones, Steven E., Jeffrey Farrer, Gregory S. Jenkins, Frank Legge, James Gourley, Kevin Ryan, Daniel Farnsworth, and Crockett Grabbe. "Extremely high temperatures during the World Trade Center destruction," 1, 4-10.

17. Bollyn, Christopher. "Why Did Iron Boil in the Rubble of the World Trade Center?" *http://www.erichufschmid.net/TFC/Bollyn-ProfCahill.html*, 1-3.

―

# CHAPTER 9

## Experiences and Testimonies about WTC Explosions and Governmental and Media Cover-Up

### *Individual Testimonies*

Dr. Ward provided descriptions by Fireman Lou Cacchioli of his experiences while he tried to save as many people as he could with little regard for personal safety: "There were bombs . . . Elevator doors completely blown out . . . We heard this huge explosion that sounded like a bomb . . . another huge explosion like the first one hits . . . Oh my god , these bastards put bombs in here like they did in 1993! Then as soon as we get in the stairwell, I hear another huge explosion like the other two. Then I heard *bang, bang, bang*—huge bangs."

Dr. Ward quoted from a book by Dr. David Ray Griffin, entitled *Explosive Testimony*:

> *Firefighter Richard Banaciski* said: "There was just an explosion [in the south tower]. It seemed like on

television [when] they blow up these buildings. It seemed like it was going all the way around like a belt, all these explosions."

*Engineer Mike Pecoraro* was working in the sixth subbasement of the North Tower and said that after an explosion he and a coworker went up to the C level, where there was a small machine shop. "There was nothing there but rubble. We're talking about a 50 ton hydraulic press—gone!" On the B level, they found a steel-and-concrete fire door which weighed about 300 pounds and was wrinkled up "like a piece of aluminum foil."

*Officer NJFD Sue Keane*: It sounded like bombs going off. That's when the explosions happened . . . . I knew something was going to happen . . . It started to get dark, then all of a sudden there was this massive explosion.

*Auxiliary Lieutenant Fireman Paul Isaac:* "There were definitely bombs in those buildings." Isaac added: "Many other firemen know there were bombs in the buildings, but they're afraid for their jobs to admit it because the 'higher-ups' forbid discussion of this fact." *Isaac further broke the gag order by acknowledging its existence,* "It's amazing how many people are afraid to talk for fear of retaliation or losing their jobs," regarding the FBI gag order, placed on law enforcement and fire department officials, preventing them from openly talking about any inside knowledge of 9-11.[1]

[Author's Comment—AC] Such an FBI gag order means that the head of the US Justice Department must have issued that gag order. That logically means that the FBI was involved in planning and/or perpetrating 9/11 or was at least ordered by the president of the United States to protect and conceal the planners and perpetrators thereof. Conclusion? *9/11 must have been an inside job*; those nineteen Arabs who suddenly disappeared were just paid patsies, not martyrs.[AC]

On August 12, 2005, the New York Times announced the release of more than 12,000 pages of oral histories in the form of transcripts of interviews with 503 firefighters and emergency medical responders. The interviews were conducted between October of 2001 and January of 2002 under the order of New York City's fire commissioner at the time of the attack, Thomas Von Essen, who wanted to preserve first-hand accounts of the attack.[2]

## *Top Portion of South Tower*

Governmental deception and cover-up is also involved in the matter of fire temperature and intensity within the towers that, according to NIST, caused the core and perimeter columns near the fire to soften simultaneously and drop on to lower floors, causing them to collapse as if made of wet paper. However, two NYC firemen actually reached the impact/fire zone of the South Tower about fourteen minutes before it collapsed.

Battalion 7 Chief Orlo J. Palmer and Fire Marshall Ronald P. Bucca had reached the seventy-eighth floor sky lobby in the South Tower, where they had found many dead bodies and seriously injured people. Palmer's radio exchange said, "Ladder 15, we've got two isolated pockets of fire. We should be able to knock it down with two lines . . . . I'm going to need two of your firefighters Adam stairway to knock down two fires. We have a house line stretched we could use some water on it, knock it down, okay . . . . We have access stairs going up to 79, 'kay."

"Battalion Nine: Alright, I'm on my way up, Orlo."

[AC] NIST knew about this evidence but ignored it. That was plainly deception. NIST maintained that the seventy-eighth floor of WTC-2 had fewer combustibles than other floors because it was a sky lobby while much more intense fires were raging on the floors above the two brave firemen. It was those fires that did cause fatal weakening of the columns, according to NIST.

[AC] What reveals NIST's blatant deception and cover up, partly by failure to investigate, is that survivors from these higher floors did manage to escape by using stairwell A (called "stairway Adam" by Palmer). They tell a story that is very different from NIST's story. Indeed they make a liar of NIST.[AC]

One of these survivors was Brian Clark, an executive vice-president of Euro Brokers on the eighty-fourth floor. As Clark came down the stairs, he heard someone crying out for help. It was Stanley Praimnath, an employee of Fuji Bank who was on the eighty-first floor when the alleged Flight 175 crashed into the South Tower. In fact, a wing of the plane reportedly passed within twenty feet of him. Nevertheless, Praimnath escaped without serious burns although he was still trapped in the rubble beneath his desk on the eighty-first floor. Clark and another man found and freed him. Then Clark and Praimnath escaped together down the stairs.

It should be noted that both men were in the fire zone during and immediately after the impact when the fires were most intense because of the spilled jet fuel. If NIST were correct that the temperatures in the core were 1,000°C (1832°F) or higher, both men would have died within seconds. Clark describes the fire in these words:

> You could see through the wall and the cracks and see flames just, just licking up, *not a roaring inferno,* just quiet flames licking up and smoke sort of eking through the wall.[3]

The U.S. Congress authorized the National Institute for Standards and Technology (NIST) to investigate the collapse of the World Trade Center on September 11. Its report was released in September 2005.

The agency insisted that its "200 technical experts" had conducted "an extremely thorough investigation." NIST boasted that its staff "reviewed tens of thousands of documents, interviewed more than 1,000 people, reviewed 7,000 segments of video footage and 7,000 photographs, analyzed 236 pieces of steel from the wreckage, performed laboratory tests and sophisticated computer simulation," yet found "no corroborating evidence for a controlled demoltion."[4]

Examination by NIST of two samples from column 801 on floors 80 and 81, several floors above the firemen and very near the path of Flight 175, showed physical damage but no evidence of the kinds of distortion, that is, buckling, bowing, slumping, or sagging, that would have occurred if the steel had been weakened by an inferno. The novel NIST method for evaluating the impact of the fire on the WTC steel was "easy to implement and robust enough to examine the entire component in the field." It depended upon analyzing the original primer paint on the steel samples.

> But the results were surprising. FIST found no evidence that any of the steel samples, including those from the impact areas and fire-damaged floors, had reached temperatures exceeding 1,100°F (600°C). Sixteen recovered perimeter columns showed evidence of having been exposed to fire, but even so, out of 170 areas examined on these columns only three locations had reached even this minimal temperature . . . .

The NIST report provides "no physical evidence whatsoever that the fires in the core of WTC-2 were raging infernos."[5]

[AC]The reports by NIST on the collapses of the Twin Towers and Building 7 are clearly sufficient evidence of serious government corruption that an investigation by an unshackled grand jury should promptly begin.

[AC] The Internet contains many conflicting stories about 9/11. The airliner crash into the North Tower seems less certain because of the lack of videos showing the impact and at least one comment about the impact hole being too small for a Boeing 767. In other words, a military drone, having a smaller size than a Boeing 767 and painted to resemble an airliner, is reasonably likely to have hit the North Tower. However, videos of Flight 175 just before it struck the South Tower show characteristics of a military plane because attachments on each side and near the plane's bottom are visible, as discussed earlier with respect to a photo that was analyzed by a Spanish university.]

## Nationwide Media Conspiracy of Silence about 9/11

Barrie Zwicker wrote that there was *abundant evidence* "that 9/11 was an inside job, a false flag operation" that was "executed by a network of covert agents under orders from the neocons, those whom Bill Moyers of PBS calls 'the shadow government.'" To him it appeared "clearly to be the most brazen of dozens of similar iconic events through history calculated to stampede public opinion into support of the rulers' agenda—in this case resource theft and global domination. In this scenario, such Arabs as were involved were patsies, dupes."

Mr. Zwicker commented that the questions he was repeatedly asked at public meetings included the following:

> Why are the mainstream media closing their eyes to all the evidence? Why are they refusing to review the books? Why aren't they covering this meeting? Why are they censoring all the hard questions?

> Why don't we see our views reflected in the mainstream media? Why aren't the media telling the people the truth?

Zwicker repeated this denial of reality overheard by a U.S. social critic, Steve Bhaerman, "Well, that may be true, but I don't believe it." Zwicker commented that this demonstrated a belief system involving "the struggle for our survival, or not."

[AC]Perhaps the most important investigation that can be done by an unshackled grand jury is to find out who controls the nation's media. If it is the people having the same intense interest as the neocons with reference to the expansion of Israel, they involve America's security and seriously endanger the people in the United States.[AC]

# Chapter 9 Notes

1.  Ward, Ed. "Bombs in the WTC Buildings Proves Nothing to Racist-Fascist Bigots." *The Price of Liberty*, 1-3. *Http://www. thepriceof*liberty.org/06/08/21/ward.htm.

2.  Dwyer, Jim. "City to Release Thousands of Oral Histories of 9/11 Today." http://www.nytimes.com/2005/08/12/nyregion/12records. html.

3.  Gaffney, Mark H. *The 9/11 Mystery Plane and the Vanishing of America.* Trine Day LLC, PO Bos 577, Walterville, OR 97489, 172-174.

4.  Ibid., 159.

5.  Ibid., 168, 174.

6.  Zwicker, Barrie. *Towers of Deception: The Media Cover-up of 9/11.* 2006. New Society Publishers, P.O. Box 189, Gabriola Island, BC VOR 1Xo, Canada, 22,27, 32.

# PART III
## Suitable Cutter Charges and Explosives for Demolishing WTC Buildings

# CHAPTER 10

## Powerful Explosives Suitable for Demolishing the WTC Buildings

### *Continuity of WTC Explosions on September 11, 2001*

An article in *911 Review* provides a succinct description of the 9/11 events at the WTC in these words:

> The "towers" destruction cannot be accurately described without the word "explosion" because huge clouds billowed out from the towers, starting around the crash zones and grew rapidly as they consumed each tower, converting them to fine powder and fragments of steel, and depositing the bulk of the remains outside of each tower's footprint in a radial pattern.

> Incredibly, this stark reality has and continues to be so consistently and widely denied in government, media, industry, and academia, that few Americans have even

entertained the idea that the towers were intentionally demolished. One of the key underpinnings of that denial is the fact that the explosions were continuous, extending for the entire 15-second duration of each tower's collapse. Although witnesses describe loud pops at their onsets, thee (sic) extended duration and loud roar of the explosions apparently prevented most people from thinking of them as explosions. Also, the repeated description of the events as collapses by the broadcast networks must have had a powerful effect in shaping people's understanding of them, particularly given the heightened state of suggestability (sic) induced by the profound state of shock and disbelief most of [them] were in.[1]

FEMA helped to destroy the physical evidence after 9/11 but did provide some information on the fallout pattern from the collapses of the Twin Towers plus a description of the *pressure waves* accompanying the collapses in its report as in these two sentences from Chapter 1 of *The WTC Report*:

The sudden collapse of each tower sent out pressure waves that spread dust clouds of building materials in all directions for many blocks. The density and pressure of the dust clouds were strong enough to carry light debris and lift or move small vehicles and break windows in adjacent buildings for several blocks around the WTC site.[2]

In his classic article, *"How Strong Is the Evidence for a Controlled Demolition?"* which appeared in *Plaguepuppy's Cafe*, Jeff King asked these questions:

> How is it possible that this uniquely horrific event has been subjected to so little rigorous investigation or forensic engineering analysis?

> And what possible innocent motivation could there be for the great haste with which so much irreplaceable physical evidence was destroyed?

> Could there be something going on here that is so awful and yet so obvious that any serious investigation would threaten its exposure?

King expressed his belief that "even in the almost complete absence of physical evidence, there is enough photographic and video evidence and corroborating eyewitness reports" to indicate strongly that 9/11 was a "controlled demolition."

King concluded that a controlled demolition on this scale would imply the "existence of a powerful and well-connected group of insiders with access to the buildings over a long period of time." Then, in answer to his first question, "they would have to be in enough positions of power and authority to ensure that there could be no real forensic analysis of the collapses, a task that was well and truly accomplished."[3]

[Author' Comment—AC] This individual, Jeff King, has concluded that 9/11 was necessarily an inside job.[AC]

—

# Thermite and Thermate Cutter Charges for Cutting Steel Columns

Dr. Steven E. Jones, Department of Physics and Astronomy, Brigham Young University, Provo, UT84602, presented evidence for the controlled-demolition hypothesis. He suggested that the available scientific data indicated that through the use of pre-positioned cutter charges, "the collapse of the Twin Towers could be explained." Such cutter charges would have been high-temperature ones, such as thermite, HMX or RDX, or some combination thereof, routinely used to melt/cut/demolish steel. He noted that molten, red-hot pools of metal remained for weeks at the bottoms of the Twin Towers and WTC-7. Also significant were four-inch thick steel plates sheared and bent in the disaster.

He suggested that thermite reactions could have resulted in substantial quantities of molten iron at very high temperatures—initially above 2,000°C (3,632°F) and "even evaporate steel which it contacts while reacting.". He further suggested that sulfur could have been combined with the thermite, producing thermate, which accelerates the destructive effect on steel. Because both thermite and thermate contain their own supplies of oxygen (in ferric oxide, which is combined with powdered aluminum to produce thermite), the combustion cannot be extinguished by water or by smothering the fire. Sulfidation of structural steel was observed in some of the few recovered steel members from the WTC rubble, as reported in Appendix C of the FEMA report.[4]

The following table (see *http://www.processassoci'ates.com/process/heat/metcolor.htm*) provides data regarding the melting temperatures of lead, aluminum, structural steel, and iron, along with approximate metal temperatures by color. Note that the approximate temperature of a hot metal is given by its color, quite independent of the composition of the metal. (A notable exception is falling liquid aluminum, which due to low emissivity and reflectivity appears silvery gray in daylight conditions after falling through air for 1-2 meters, regardless of the temperature at which the poured-out aluminum left the vessel.)

## Table 2
### Melting Temperatures of Certain Metals and Metal Temperatures as Indicated by Color

|  | °F | °C |
| --- | --- | --- |
| Lead (Pb) Melts | 621 | 327 |
| Faint Red | 930 | 500 |
| Blood Red | 1075 | 580 |
| *Aluminum Melts | 1221 | 660 |
| Medium Cherry | 1275 | 690 |
| Cherry | 1375 | 745 |
| Bright Cherry | 1450 | 790 |
| Salmon | 1550 | 845 |
| Dark Orange | 1650 | 890 |
| Orange | 1725 | 940 |
| Lemon | 1830 | 1000 |
| Light Yellow | 1975 | 1080 |
| White | 2200 | 1205 |
| Structural Steel Melts | 2750 | 1510 |
| *Iron Melts | 2800 | 1538 |
| *Thermite (typical) | >4500 | >2500[5] |

—

195

Niels H. Harrit, Department of Chemistry at the University of Copenhagen, and Jeffrey Farrer, professor of physics at Brigham Young University (BYU), Provo, Utah, were the primary authors of an article titled "Active Thermitic Material Discovered in Dust from the 9/11 World Trade Center Catastrophe," published in *The Open Chemical Physics Journal*, 2009, 2, 7-31. The article displays electron micrographs of a bilayer chip having a gray layer and a red layer. The properties of the chips were analyzed by using optical microscopy, scanning electron microscopy (SEM), X-ray energy dispersive spectroscopy (XEDS), and differential scanning calorimetry (DSC).

Dr. Harrit and Dr. Farrer were among nine scientists who worked for eighteen months to know "what really happened that fateful day" of September 11, 2001. These scientists concluded that the red component of the bilayer chips is a high-tech explosive known as super thermite. It is a nanomaterial composed of ultrafine grains of iron oxide ($Fe_2O_3$) mixed with nanosized aluminum metal (Al) embedded in a matrix of silicon oxide and organic compounds. The technology to make these highly exothermic nanocomposites existed as early as April 2000. The reactant particles may be suspended in a solgel matrix applied to a substrate, such as steel. Such solgels are very stable and safe to handle in liquid form and can be applied to surfaces as a spray or even with a paintbrush.

They discovered distinctive red/gray chips in all the samples of the dust created during the destruction of the World Trade Center, collected from separate sites. These chips showed marked similarities in all four samples. "The red material contains grains approximately 100 nm across which are largely iron oxide while aluminum is contained in tiny plate-like structures. Separation of components using methyl ethyl ketone demonstrated that elemental aluminum is present. The iron oxide and aluminum are intimately mixed in the red material. When ignited in a DSC device the chips exhibit large but narrow exotherms occurring at approximately 430°C, far below the normal ignition temperature for conventional thermite."

The scientists suggested that this red material was not used as a cutter charge itself but rather as a means to ignite high explosives, such as in superthermite matches. They concluded "that the red layer of the red/gray chips we have discovered in the WTC dust is active, unreacted thermitic material, incorporating nanotechnology, and is a highly energetic pyrotechnic or explosive material."

The 221st National Meeting of the American Chemical Society held in San Diego during April 2001 included a symposium on Defense Applications of Nanomaterials, and one of the four sessions was titled nanoenergetics. "At this point in time all of the military services and some DOE and academic laboratories have active R&D programs aimed at exploiting the unique properties of nano-materials t.hat have potential to be used in energetic formulations for advanced explosives."[6]

In a Danish TV2 interview, when asked about" 9-11 conspiracy theories," Dr. Harrit said, "Viewers should ask themselves what evidence they have seen to support the official conspiracy theory. If anyone has seen evidence, I would like to hear about it. No one has been formally charged. No one is wanted. Our work should lead to demands for a proper criminal investigation of the 9/11 terrorist attack. Because it never happened. We are still waiting for it. We hope our results will be used as technical evidence when that day comes."

—

As to "who" did 9-11, at the "business end" of the operation, they were clearly people who had unimpeded access to introduce 10-100 tonnes of nano-thermite (super-thermite) into the North Tower, the South Tower and the WTC7 building of the World Trade Center (WTC) complex i.e. US officials or US surrogates (e.g. Israelis) with official government or corporate security clearance.

The evidence for nano-thermite explosives in the WTC dust directly implies US involvement in the atrocity because only American government or corporate officials (or their officially-sanctioned foreign surrogates) could have had the requisite security clearances to introduce 10-100 tonnes of nano-thermite into the WTC.[7]

[AC]Dr. Harrit's statement that 10-100 tonnes of super-thermite would have had to have been introduced into the three WTC skyscrapers that were demolished is one of the reasons that this author has subsequently provided information about possible use of micro-fusion, mini-fission, and HAARP/ beam weapons. In other words, simply making 10-100 tonnes of a recently developed (see April 2001 conference, page 26) explosive indicates that a large development and manufacturing operation must have immediately been started. The mere quantity of this exotic explosive that had to have been transported and selectively distributed throughout the three demolished skyscrapers indicates a challenging operation by itself, simply to provide "superthermite matches" for a more conventional explosive, such as thermite, that presumably had to have been provided in much larger quantities if micro-fusion, mini-fission, and/or HAARP/beam weapons had not been used. Hopefully, enough information about these varied explosives will be available to enable readers of this book to judge for themselves as to what happened on September 11, 2001.[AC]

## Bombs (Micro-fusion) to Provide Intense Upward Heat Waves: A Medical Opinion

Ed Ward, MD concluded on September 25, 2006 that the U.S. government used third—or possibly fourth-generation hydrogen bombs for the destruction of the World Trade Center (WTC) buildings. Such bombs would have been relatively pure hydrogen bombs, such as the W54, "a micro-nuke weighing 51 pounds and capable of being fired from a slightly modified ordinary bazooka. Different versions of this micro-nuke ranged from 0.01 to 1 kiloton in yield. Between the mid-1950's and the mid-70's, both large-yield dirty and small-yield clean versions of 2nd generation H-bombs were refined." Such atomic munitions suitable for demolition work were declassified in January 1967.

Some of Dr. Ward's reasons for concluding that a micro-nuke had been used to collapse each of the three WTC skyscrapers are as follows:

> widespread cancer in the responders, molten steel, melted cars, steel beams hurled hundreds of feet, aerosolized metals, vaporized steel witnessed and video, aerosolized and pulverized concrete, elevated tritium levels, vanishing (vaporized) victims, only sliver fragments of victims on roof tops, EMP—Electro Magnetic Pulse effects on

—

199

communications, hundreds of eyewitness testimony of ancillary explosions by heroic rescuers and victims, massive dispersal of debris, demolition expert states hydrogen bomb needed for this type of demolition, audio of a massive explosion prior to collapse, video of ancillary explosions, audio of ancillary explosions, significant reduction in debris pile, ancillary thermate found in wreckage, shock wave of a mini-yield nuclear blast knocked people off their feet, vaporization of 200,000 gallons of water, removal of wreckage without investigation.

Dr. Ward also noted that the spectrum and percentages of cancer were massive, including at least four classifications of blood-cell cancer: leukemia, lymphoma, Hodgkin's, and myeloma. There were also many more classifications of soft tissue cancers, including brain cancer and breast cancer. He stressed that "one thing and only one thing . . . can cause all these cancers and problems—RADIATION."

In less than an hour, WTC-2 (South Tower) collapsed and covered Manhattan in at least 1/3 of a million tons of particulate debris. After WTC-7 fell, Manhattan was covered with two billion pounds of pulverized and aerosolized buildings, whose total weight had been estimated at 3 billion pounds. Debris removal has been given as 1.2 billion pounds. Based on these rough numbers, 2/3 of the buildings by weight were turned to dust or vaporized.[7]

Additional comments regarding post 9/11 cancers include:

"By the end of 2006, there had been 400 diagnosed cancers in the WTC," of which 75 were blood cell cancers. "A short list of the varied cancers includes thyroid (30), tongue and throat, (25), testicular (16), brain (10), breast, prostate, and other soft tissue tumors in other areas of the body."

Other comments by Dr. Ward in support of the use of micro H-bombs are as follows:

> After the outer structure of WTC 2 falls, a portion of the central core remains standing for almost 25 seconds then it appears to melt and vaporize . . . . The cores at the base of the WTCs are 16" thick steel rectangles—each side is 4" thick. (BTW, there is no conventional explosive or thermate combination that can produce this effect. Nor can any nanothermate, superthermate, super-duper thermate and explosives combination produce this effect.)

> The "well below levels of concern to human exposure" and "7 times less than the EPA limit" of Tritium in the environment are in actuality 27 to 35 times higher than should have been found in one sample, and 21 to 28 times higher than should have been found in the other sample. In spite of this fact it was deemed that no other testing was needed. In spite of the fact that no *amount of radiation is considered "safe," i*t is merely "acceptable." This shows proof that even in the same general area there were varying degrees of dilution of the 10 ml samples prior their being collected and tested. Note that there is no notation about the size of the pools the samples were taken from.

Further evidence of tremendous heat can be seen in this 8 ton 6" thick I beam that is bent like a horseshoe without warping, kinking or splitting. (Again, there is no way for thermate to create this horseshoe, unless it is "miraculous" thermate. Nor, is there any unspecified vague "scalar" weapon that can do this even if the beam was isolated and not covered by some degree of 110 floors of concrete and steel.) Clearly, this is residual steel that has been exposed to massive and intense heat that is entirely consistent with a thermonuclear explosion and virtually nothing else can produce this single effect, let alone this and ALL the other irregularities. [8]

[AC] These beams were necessarily heated to at least a yellow-white color within less than ten seconds and probably within less than one or two seconds. Only an incredibly hot heat wave could have radiated such vast amounts of heat into these steel beams and then caused heat transfer through the beams almost instantaneously.[AC]

## *Cutting Charges for Perimeter Columns plus Microfusion Bombs for Core Columns (Finnish Military Expert)*

A Finnish military expert believed that the preparations for demolishing the WTC towers and WTC-7 were done so as to make them collapse completely, with extra napalm for dramatizing the effects of airliner hits. In fact, the Twin Towers buildings could have been exploded down to earth in the same way even without using the airplanes.

The Finnish expert believed that some targets were attacked because there were unique opportunities to attack "where the human bodies and all evidence of the crimes automatically disappeared when a hydrogen bomb exploded." Explosions which were heard in the towers before each "collapse" began may have been related to choosing these attacks. There is also a reason for the huge explosion in the customs building (WTC 6).

The Finnish military expert wrote that demolishing the WTC perimeter steel columns would have required 40 x 240 charges for each tower, an estimate that could be rounded off to 10,000 cutting charges, each weighing 50 pounds (a total of 250 tons). For WTC-7, at least four thousand charges would have been needed. These charges would have had to be ordered, prepared, and transported. In addition, at least one small thermonuclear bomb for the core columns of each of these three buildings would have had to be procured.

After ascertaining the right sizes and dimensions of suitable cutting charges, twenty-four thousand pieces and essential fitting detonators would have had to be ordered, time of delivery being several months. "All detonators must be equipped with some kind of safety mechanism, which will be removed by a radio signal at the final moment." Installing the charges would probably have required thirty men for four months, after spending two months on fitting detonators .

Delivery of the thermonuclear devices (micro-H-bombs) took place at the last moment, using elevators which were then locked down, guarded, and monitored. That is why on the weekend of September 8, 2001, and September 9, 2001, it was announced that floors up from the fortieth floor were being equipped with cables so that no normal employee would have had access to those working areas. A thermonuclear device having a lower yield was selected for WTC-7.

Demolition of the Twin Towers required at least half a year to prepare, including installation of ten thousand cutting charges in each twin tower and delivery to a cellar floor of a thermonuclear device at the last moment. Demolition of those ultra strong steel pillars in the central core using cutting charges only was not possible without arousing unwanted attention because these charges had to be in contact with the steel pillars and there was not enough enclosed space in the central core to hide such charges.

The explosions were timed so that 99.9 percent of people around looked at the tops of the towers, and perhaps two seconds later, the small thermonuclear bomb was exploded in the cellar of the South Tower, and again two seconds later, another very powerful charge was exploded in the WTC-6 customs building while nobody was looking that way. There were also continuous explosions of the thousands of cutting charges tearing the South Tower down at the speed-of-gravity-driven free fall.[10]

This Finnish expert commented that the demolition men met more challenging problems in the central cores of the Twin Towers because the forty-seven steel core columns were designed to hold many times the weight of each building. These central core columns were more robust than the perimeter columns and were thicker than the side armor of a battle tank so that cutting them, even with explosives, would have been extremely difficult. Charges would have been needed to surround the entire column with a powerful cutting charge on every floor intended to be blasted, and these charges would have needed to be placed in such a way that the users of the towers would not notice these preparations.

So instead of installing thousands of powerful cutting charges for the core columns, a modern thermonuclear explosive, that is, a small hydrogen bomb, was placed in the second level of each cellar, in the center of the core and the elevator shafts, and directed to explode upward as a narrow cone toward the roof of the tower and the upper parts of the outer walls. On its upward way, the waves of fire pressure partially penetrated about one hundred floors of concrete and steel with over ten million degrees of heat from the hydrogen bomb that boiled the water within the concrete in a moment. Concrete contains about 20 percent water. This water exploded extremely quickly into one thousand fold volume and totally pulverized the concrete. People and computers disappeared, turning into heat and light so that almost nothing of them was found in the ruins.[11]

The demolition operation for the World Trade Center was finished by destroying WTC-7, using a nuke and completely destroying the op center with its equipment. Concrete evidence,

—
205

such as the military flight beacon, the remote control devices for cutting charges, and the eavesdropping devices to detect events within the towers, all vanished without a trace.

Most of the media was controlled by people related to the attackers so that they told only misleading stories as if the crashing of the airliners and a weak fire could have caused the collapse of the towers. "The true attackers are the ones with strong and vigorous broadcasting around their false version of the events which is very different to what really happened."[12]

This unnamed Finnish military expert pointed out that the conditions in the WTC towers were not ideal for fire-induced collapse because there were far too many steel columns, which would lead heat away from the burning areas by conduction. Provided there were more substance to burn, a fire burning much longer, such as from ten to twenty hours, could slowly increase the steel temperature to perhaps 1,100°C (approximately 2,010°F), but if such a fire had caused columns to collapse on one or two floors, the collapse would have been limited and then would have stopped.

Pictures taken from video tapes of the "collapses" of the WTC showed that more explosions of the cutting charges could be seen as the explosions advanced quickly with a gap of a couple of floors as they cut the strong steel perimeter columns in the outer walls. "The explosions are timed so that it appears the tower collapses occur in the same timing as in a gravitational collapse."

"Burning radiation is absorbed in steel so quickly that steel heats up immediately over its melting point 1585°C (approx. 2890°F.) and above its boiling point around 3000 C (approx. 5430°F.)"

—

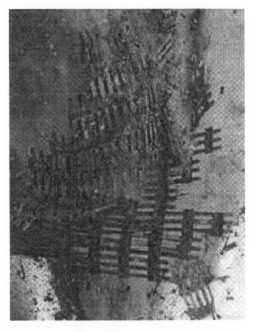

Steel segments falling and evaporating

Mini-atomic explosion at top
of a Twin Tower of the WTC

—

"The upward burst that is visible in this photograph is typical for atomic bomb explosions but is "not possible for a gravitational collapse or for cutting charges which are used horizontally.""

Extremely hot radiation is absorbed in steel so quickly that steel heats up immediately over its melting point of 1,585°C (approximately 2,890°F) and even above its boiling point of around 3,000°C (approximately 5,430°F). For that reason, as shown in videos, superhot portions of steel columns, torn from a wall by the pressure wave, are sublimated into a vaporized form and burst upward above the top of the tower. Such upward bursting, having a brown color, is not possible for a gravitational collapse or for the cutting charges which were used.[13]

The New York Fire Department did not announce until December 19 that the fires under the WTC rubble had been extinguished. That was three months after the 9/11 tragedy even though the fire department had poured millions of gallons of water onto the rubble to cool it. Elevated values of tritium were found by the University of California on September 13, 2001, and on September 21, 2001, within the boundaries of the WTC but not elsewhere in New York. In pure hydrogen bombs, isotopes of hydrogen are fused (D + T > n + a + 17.6 MeV). The military expert observed that simply pulverizing the concrete into fine dust could take more energy than the total gravitational energy available.

In the cellar, out of all the 47 ultra strong steel pillars, the steel was melted completely at the length of more than 20 meters (approx. 65 ft.). Even cars were melted and burned in the cellar. The pillars were far too thick for thermite, which some have suggested. An explosion of a thermonuclear bomb explains the phenomenon well.

Steel columns and pillars were ejected outwardly for distances of 60 to 175 meters (approximately from 170 to 574 feet) from the building facades. Cutting charges could not have done that. The expert believed that in the beginnings of the so-called collapses, the blast waves from nuclear bombs could have supplied the needed energy.[14]

A pure hydrogen bomb was an obvious way to obtain a bomb with a small size and a strong effect for the conspirators planning the 9/11 attacks because "[w]hen no atomic device is needed for igniting, the size of the hydrogen bomb gets even smaller and the yield (effect) can be set within a wide range, for example, between from 1 to 100."

"Nowadays, both the yield and the direction of the destructive force of a *small tactical hydrogen bomb* can be somewhat controlled."[15]

The next page is a schematic drawing supplied by the Finnish expert. The cited source is U.S. Department of Defense and U.S. Department of Energy, Glasstone—Dolan: "The Effects of Nuclear Weapons" (1980).

Compared to the drawing, "[t]he actual towers were much taller and the observed arch of destruction of the energy-directed thermonuclear device was correspondingly more narrow. The thermonuclear bomb used was a 'pure' hydrogen bomb, so no uranium or plutonium was emitted. The basic nuclear reaction is

Deuterium + Tritium > Alpha + n. The ignition of this was the fine part, either with a powerful beam array or antimatter (a very certain way to get the necessary effect of directed energy in order not to level the adjacent blocks of high-rise buildings, as well)."

The bomb was adjusted to send an extremely hot heat wave upwardly in a very narrow cone. This heat wave represented 70 percent of the energy in the bomb, the remainder being a blast wave that moved horizontally.

Ground Zero was a nuclear blast site. "The thermal energy may absorb heat at a rate of 10 E 23 ergs/cm$^2$ sec and near the bomb all surfaces may heat to 4000°C or 7200°F, igniting or vapourizing violently."

As shown in the following photograph, the heat cone impacting the perimeter columns has ripped away some fifty plus wall sections, most of them boiling and each of them weighing 22 tons apiece, and then threw them outside of the tower footage while superheating them internally to some 5,000°C.

At the WTC the clouds were unreal, far too energetic to be normal clouds resulting from explosions. They rapidly expanded into fivefold volume, which shows a lot of excess heat energy (pointing to thermonuclear device or hundreds of tons of military explosives like HDX). Those clouds also showed pyroclastic behavior, and those observations of this nature were correct. Even very large conventional explosive stacks blowing up cannot build pyroclastics because this needs really hot stuff, millions and not thousands of degrees Celsius present (in the case of volcanoes, large areas of molten magma will suffice too).[16]

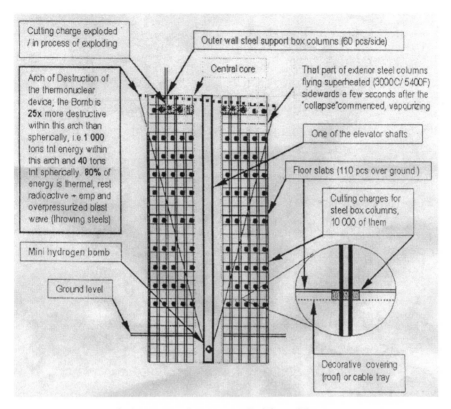

Schematic drawing of a Twin Tower
containing a Mini hydrogen bomb

[AC] Briefly stated and as understood, the Finnish expert's theory is that one micro-H-bomb was placed at the center of the core of each tower and at the second basement level to send an intensely hot heat wave upwardly as a narrow cone that would reach the perimeter columns at the sixth or seventh floor level and then continue to the top of the tower. This central cone was augmented by ten thousand cutter charges in each tower.

[AC] This theory has been criticized because the bomb would destroy all cutter charges above these floors and make it impossible for the squibs to appear as seen in several videos. The critic proposed using several micro-H-bombs within each tower which would be successively detonated downwardly, beginning near the impact area. Because each of the Twin Towers was built as three superimposed buildings, three micro-H-bombs could have been installed in each twin tower, the bottom H-bomb being the strongest and the upper ones successively weaker.

[AC] It also seems reasonable that the extremely hot cone of radiation and heat from a single micro-H-bomb at the center of the second basement level, having sufficient power to hurl a section of perimeter columns weighing many tons for nearly six hundred feet, would also have melted or broken all windows in the tower facades above the seventh floor during the cone's advance to the roof. Such window breakage would have been noticeable in videos in the ten seconds prior to complete collapse, and the window breakage would have been immediately followed by outward movements of heated air and probably also of pulverized and vaporized materials from all windows, instead of a few sidewise bursts identified as squibs. Three micro-H-bombs, of increasing power as the collapse proceeded, should have also affected the windows. Nothing of the sort has apparently been observed in videos, however, so that the author, who has no expertise in nuclear matters, believes that a micro-H-bomb, or even three such bombs, in each twin tower could not have been used, except in the basement explosions for destroying the massive core columns. [AC].

### *Destruction of WTC-1, WTC-2, WTC-7, and Other WTC Buildings with Several Small Nuclear Fission (Atomic) Bombs in Each Building*

The Anonymous Physicist (henceforth AP) has asserted that the WTC was likely demolished by using small nuclear (fission) bombs and that such demolitions were probably assisted by subsidiary conventional explosives. In response to claims that such small nukes did not even exist, he and Spooked wrote that "the .01 kiloton (kt) TNT is equivalent to about 1/1000th of the Hiroshima (20KT) blast." Then he quoted from a testimony of a government scientist, Peter Leitner, PhD, before a congressional committee in 1998 in order to provide proof of the existence of millinukes (mininukes) and micronukes:

> These experiments involve the ACTUAL TESTING of extremely low-yield fission devices (as low as the equivalent of several pounds of TNT) within a confined environment.

AP commented that "[s]everal pounds of TNT" is equivalent to about 1/10,000,000 (one ten millionth) of the Hiroshima blast. Thus the U.S. Govt admitted having micro-nukes, and beyond In 1998."[17]

AP also commented that the government explanation of 9/11 is "an impossible, ludicrous, and cruel set of hoaxes" because massive explosions were involved. He observed that "the Intel agencies have a massive set of Intel-controlled scientists, engineers, and architects to lie or omit many facts about the destruction of the three towers and other WTC buildings and the crucial aftermath." He briefly noted that "Directed Energy Weapons" (DEW) were hypothesized by some people because of the anomalies in the rubble pile. They had, however, "correctly pointed out that the videos of the 'plane crashes' are only CGI (Computer Generated Imagery) of impossible crash physics." He criticized the thermite hypothesizer because of his lies and his claim for "unextingushable fires" from any form of thermite, including "super nanocomposite thermite," which is a bogus, limited "hangout." Http://bogus911science. wordpress.com/

AP commented upon the Finnish military expert's theory that a single pure fusion fourth-generation nuclear fusion device brought down each tower but noted that fusion cannot account for the great heat underneath the towers and in the rubble pile for up to six months after 9/11.

AP also noted one scientist's claim that there were massive, hidden, nuclear reactors underneath the towers, which produced ternary fission and tritium production as well as great heat generating radioactive elements that were remnants of the alleged reactor cores. He pointed out that nuclear reactors cannot explode like a nuclear bomb and cause the observed vaporization, rapid expansion of clouds, and other nuclear effects.[18]

AP then set forth his own theory:

> Numerous small nuclear fission bombs caused the destruction of the towers, WTC7, and several other WTC buildings. http://www.wtcdemolition.blogspot.com/

> The 94% remainder of fission elements, supposedly U-235 with a half-life of some 700 million years, accounts for the heat generation via The China Syndrome Aftermath effect. http://wtc-chinasyndrome.blogspot.com/

> Tritium was produced in just the right amounts via ternary fission during nuclear criticality implosion. Numerous hypothesized effects, detailed by the

Anonymous Physicist, including fratriciding, and fizzling, explain the early failed destruction of WTC7, and the locations of the heat generating sources in many locations in the general rubble pile, and the even greater heat sources underneath the towers and WTC7. http://74.220.219.64/-myhealu9/AP/911.htm

Indeed while the towers are exploding outward and upward (vaporized contents rising), what initiated the destruction and caused the vaporization—and dust particle sizes much smaller than the regime's stooge alleges—could only have been small nuclear bombs. And these fission bombs were initiated by the *implosion* of subcritical, fissioning components into supercritical mass.

As evidence, AP cited victims with melted hanging skin, smallest dust particle size analysis, vaporized steel, and flowing steel underneath the demolished towers, which existed for up to six months. He pointed out that only nuclear bombs could account for such small particle size and that no conventional explosive, whether nanothermite, thermobarics, or other, can account for vaporized steel and flowing molten steel existing for six months underneath the towers—not during tower destruction nor during the aftermath. He asserted that no phenomena during WTC destruction, nor in the six-month aftermath, is left unexplained in this scenario.[19]

[AC] As understood, the term, China Syndrome Aftermath, is based upon the 1986 meltdown at Chernobyl in north central Ukraine when it was said that the hot mass as its aftermath, in which nuclear reactions were furiously generating heat, would melt itself all the way to China on the other side of the earth. [AC]

215

This physicist also wrote that his "many nukes" hypothesis for destruction of the WTC includes the use of redundant nukes, fratricidal nukes, and fizzled nukes.

AP explained that "a fission nuke uses up only some 1-6% of its fissile material in its chain reactions before the remainder is blown apart from the heat and pressure resulting from the chain reactions." The fission chain reaction includes eighty generations that are completed in a total of merely one microsecond; then the bomb's contents are blown apart.

The mininukes at the WTC, according to AP's theory, were emplaced in the centers of the towers and were selectively small enough that they did not vaporize the outer structure and thereby reveal the op plan. This arrangement enabled the outer structure to remain mostly undamaged while the mininukes were exploding at each level and in the subbasement area, and cutter charges were destroying the perimeter columns.

After the collapse of each tower, the heavy uranium atoms and fragments in the dust came down first onto Ground Zero. The many lighter chemical elements came down on top of them a little later and may have provided some radiation shielding. The resulting rubble pile was indeed hot and melted firemen's and dog's boots, requiring the rubble pile to be hosed down for many months and producing conspicuous amounts of steam as shown in countless photos. Fratricided or fizzled nukes within the more totally enclosed subbasement of each tower surely left more concentrated fission fragments in some areas and in the former basements. These fragments later caused very hot temperatures and molten steel weeks and months later.

AP asserted that the floors that were chosen for the initial explosions in each twin tower were those providing enough height and building material so that the first top-level exploding nukes would not vaporize through to the top, thereby creating a visible rising fireball which had to be avoided. So the floors for the "plane hit" explosions were carefully selected so that they would coincide with the location of the first nukes to explode.

Many people close to the Hiroshima hypocenter were vaporized, and exactly that happened to over 1,100 human beings in the WTC towers, whereby no intact strands of DNA were available for identification.[21]

> Even people who realize that nuclear explosions demolished the WTC often incorrectly believe that these explosions, because of their high temperature, caused the "lingering" heat. However, the Physics and the known effects of nuclear explosions prove that the million-degree temperature of, for example, a fission nuke, cools down to 10,000 degrees in one millisecond (a thousandth of a second), unless conventional fires result which might cause temperatures in the hundreds of degrees for hours or a few days at the most. A nuke's surroundings are likely to cool down to ambient temperature within minutes or hours, EXCEPT where any remaining radioactive fragments are releasing great heat from ongoing fission. Note that Hiroshima and Nagasaki did not have any China Syndromes because each had ONLY ONE NUKE that obviously DID NOT FIZZLE.[22]

A complete theory of 9/11 must include the demolitions that occurred on September 11, 2001, itself and crucially its aftermath of great hotspots and molten steel for up to five months afterward. This aftermath is supported by irrefutable, numerous eyewitnesses and photographs and at least one AVIRIS overflight temperature data set.

> I have stated that only nuclear criticality sites could be the source of heat GENERATION weeks, and months after 9/11. You can find, say on YouTube, numerous videos of thermite being used to melt things, yes, including metal—but no vaporization. Note that the thermite is not being used as an explosive when it is seen melting through a car, e.g. But some of those videos clearly show that after just a few minutes, the molten thermite residue cools off and no longer glows. It is highly likely that any thermite at the WTC on 9/11 would have cooled off within hours. Indeed, I have stated that even the momentary maximum temperature of a nuke's hypocenter (up to 100 million degrees) is known to cool off relatively quickly.[23]

One reporting source has stated that the very high temperatures at the surfaces of the WTC rubble piles existed for not five but six months after 9/11. For example, an article in GCN (*Government Computer News*)—a trade newsletter on the government IT field—says that the firefighters/responders' computer cataloging of 7,000 human remains found at the WTC from September 25, 2001 to May 30, 2002, stated that "for six months after Sept. 11, the ground temperature varied between 600 degrees Fahrenheit and 1,500 degrees, sometimes higher." Furthermore, it notes that "in the first few weeks, sometimes when a worker would pull a steel beam from the wreckage, the end of the beam would be dripping molten steel." Note that the "1,500 degrees, sometimes higher" is said to be the "ground temperature." This again indicates that the underground heat source must have been at a significantly higher temperature than at the surface to cause this surface temperature as there was nothing visible at the surface to cause this heat effect.

The high temperature hot spots of "1,500 degrees, sometimes higher" that were present until at least March 2002 could only have been caused by heat being generated by underground nuclear reactions—the China Syndrome.

The witnesses who reported molten steel included firemen, city officials, contractors, workers, and trained professionals who toured the ruin. One of the latter, Dr. Keith Eaton, chief executive of the London-based Institution of Structural Engineers, later wrote in *The Structural Engineer* about what he saw, namely, "molten metal, which was still red-hot weeks after the event," as well as "four-inch thick steel plates sheared and bent in the disaster." A similar account came from Leslie E. Robertson, the engineer of record, who helped to design the World Trade Center. Robertson's consulting firm Leslie E. Robertson Associates (LERA) worked in the WTC complex for forty years and, at the time of the tragedy, was still under contract to the Port Authority that administered the WTC. In a keynote address before the Structural Engineers Association of Utah, Robertson said, "As of 21 days after the attack, the fires were still burning and molten steel still running."

> As rubble is removed from piles, random pockets of steel, glowing brilliant red, are uncovered. Sometimes the steel just glows because there is nothing left nearby to burn. A curious phenomenon, no fuel to burn, but something,

heat migrating through the pile, continues to keep the steel at over 1,000°F. When that happens, work stops, equipment pulls back, and the firefighters put thousands of gallons of water on the piles to cool them down. Huge billowing clouds of steam are created, and we wait.[24]

A nuke or nukes being exploded near Patricia Ondrovic can explain why she saw and heard popping lights at the WTC-6 lobby ceiling and simultaneously saw cars near her—for no apparent reason—bursting into flames and why one car's door exploded off the car and hit her, knocking her down. At that very time WTC-1 was being destroyed, a little farther away from her, the nuke or nukes were being exploded under WTC-6 and WTC-5.

The nuke(s)' concomitant EMP(s) (Electromagnetic Pulse), passing through her immediate vicinity, intercepted the cars near her. Because this EMP wave induces a great current in metal but not in people or paper, it created great heat in the metal of the cars and resultant rapid expansion of that metal so that a given car door, being unable to expand beyond its confined space, exploded off the car and hit her.

It is a known phenomenon of nuclear explosions that ultrafine particles are created, and that is what became of the contents of the towers, except for the thick steel members. Nuclear radiation is another phenomenon, and a standard nuclear industry method used to lower it, particularly at hot spots, is to truck in large amounts of dirt. Judy Wood noted this and the covering of the WTC grounds with the dirt, as well as the continual hosing of the grounds with water—even the responders as well, according to some observers—plus the "frequent street scrubbing to get rid of the fuzzballs and nanodust." However, it was radioactive dust, not "fuzzballs."

Judy Wood's new evidence led AP to realize just how strangely the PTB had acted to hide the nuking of the WTC! Wood had cited Mayor Giuliani's strange acts of apparently trucking dirt in and out of the WTC, beginning that night! AP's interpretation of this activity was that Giuliani, in cahoots with the Feds/perps, knew that the UCal Berkeley scientists and others would soon arrive and would measure radioactivity at the WTC caused by the nukes they had used. They realized that they must lower this radioactivity and so they began to truck dirt in and out immediately, followed by washing down the area.

AP explained that numerous micronukes were placed in each tower, employing much redundancy, in order to be sure that sufficient numbers of these low-yield nukes would successfully explode as planned. Because some of the redundant micronukes were impacted by the exploding micronukes, the fissile material in the redundant nukes gave rise to the China Syndrome.

The reason for using so many redundant micronukes was partly because some micronukes fizzled for various reasons. AP explained that military and "policy makers" use the term "fratricide" to indicate the occurrence of one nuclear warhead impacting/adversely affecting a second one and preventing the second one from going nuclear. Long-term storage of nuclear bombs or warheads is another form of fratricide. During storage, nuclear warheads have "vulnerability to fratricide neutrons" and are also susceptible to many other problems that can cause them to fizzle.

The American perps who were planning the 9-11 atrocity took the following steps:

1. Emplaced many redundant nukes, in each WTC building, and at each level to be nuked. The levels

where the nukes were emplaced took fratricidal effects into account, as much as possible.

2. Used (somewhat hardened) sensors that would trigger (sequentially, as needed) redundant nukes at each level that they were to be set off at.

3. Used sensors that themselves were to be vaporized, if the first, planned nuke went off properly, so that the redundant ones would not go nuclear.

In WTC-7, the early explosions in the lobby and basement fizzled because of fratricidal or other effects, but they exploded while either failing to attain any criticality or by producing a nuclear explosion that was too small for demolition of WTC-7 to occur. The sensors were themselves damaged by partial explosions and then did not trigger redundant nukes to go off. Jennings describes several WTC-7 explosions, but they must have been non-nuclear.

AP stated that "the efficiency of a nuclear bomb is the percentage of its total available fissile material (such as uranium-235 or plutonium- 239) that actually undergoes fission during the criticality stage of implosion/explosion—roughly one microsecond. The remainder is still highly radioactive and can create a China Syndrome under certain conditions."

AP wrote that even a properly functioning fission bomb releases 94-99 percent of its highly radioactive fissile material into the environment where it will more slowly continue to fission and decay while releasing great heat.

But the micronukes used inside the WTC buildings, even the properly fissioning ones, were at least partially contained during the destruction of the buildings. As the buildings were being destroyed, even vaporized, the remaining fissile material was deposited all around the

WTC area, and some likely reached significantly beyond as well. Some fissile material from the subbasement nukes was likely trapped there in the largest concentrations to be found in the aftermath. Such radioactive fragments were also inaccessible to the usual radiation-lowering mechanisms that were extensively employed, beginning the very next day—water hosing and "coating" with sand/earth.[25]

Photographs of small underground nuclear blasts characteristically show an upward blast of material, plus debris off to the side like octopus arms. Photographs of the collapses of WTC-1 and WTC-2 show the exact same characteristic trademarks. It is also pertinent that radioactivity in air creates shades of brown. These WTC photographs clearly show the brown coloring of a nuclear blast in the updraft portion. "If the blast had been of hydrocarbon origin the color would have been between blackish and grayish depending on the amount of oxygen available. Whereas a nuclear blast does not need oxygen."[26]

## *Probable Use of HAARP/Beam Weaponry*

The following comments relate to the demolitions of WTC-1 and WTC-2, HAARP/beam weaponry, and Ground Zero activities.

> Seismic Record: The energy budget recorded in the seismic record on the day of 9/11 and the collapse of the buildings did not reflect the mass of building materials involved in the collapse, nor the nearly freefall of the collapsing buildings. The seismic record demonstrates an event on the scale of a quarry blast. WHERE WAS THE THUD??

Kinetic Energy: Two robust buildings with very robust steel beam reinforcement would release a sizeable amount of kinetic energy from the buildings falling—that would be all of the energy that went into the construction of the buildings. The release of that amount of kinetic energy is not reflected in the physical evidence on the seismic record. Into what physical process did that kinetic energy go?

Molecular Dissociation: The collapse of the buildings produced the highest mass per volume of very fine particles (nanoparticles) ever measured in an air sample in the United States. It takes a tremendous amount of energy to dissociate or break the molecular bonds of steel, concrete and other building materials that were "powdered" into very fine particles during the collapse of the buildings. The largest mass per volume of METALS ever measured in an air sample in the US were reported by Dr. Thomas Cahill who did air monitoring for 5 months. Metal is used in buildings because it is very strong - and would require large amounts of energy to reduce it to nanoparticles. Chemical explosives do not release enough energy to produce that volume of very fine particles. A much more energetic process was involved such as laser or beam energy which releases focused and concentrated energy as complex waveforms necessary to cause molecular dissociation.

Physical Evidence of Buildings Collapsing: In videos of the collapses on 9/11, the WTC buildings erupted into emulsion like a drinking fountain, and the rubble did not hit the ground. Even on tape huge pieces of aluminum building siding vaporized as they were freefalling, and never hit the ground.

Controlled Demolition: this was not a controlled demolition

Detritus pile: should be 1/3 the height of the building. The 100+ story buildings were about one-story high when the collapse of the buildings ended. A fireman on one of the news videos said the antenna that had been on the (sic) of B. 1 was on the top of a pile of rubble about one story high. The rubble pile should have been thirty-five stories if it was a conventional controlled demolition.

Rubble Never Hit the Ground - this defies gravity, where did the rubble go?

Footprints—Geometrically Round Holes: Contiguous round holes 24' in diameter were in the footprints of the WTC buildings 1 and 2, and a 60' deep geometrically round hole was in the middle of Liberty Street near the WTC. This is evidence of beam weapons. There was NO debris inside the footprints of the two WTC buildings . . . only bare dirt with circles in the dirt.

Livermore Nuclear Weapons Lab Beam Weapon Demo: in 1955 the microwave oven was invented and was a concept for a beam weapon. Lasers are used to molecularly dissociate materials by releasing tremendous amounts of energy as very advanced and complex waveforms. Livermore had long been involved in development of HAARP since 1978 in secret collaboration with the Soviet Union AND advanced beam weapons.

Dust: In videos of the collapse, larger particles fell and cascaded down from the buildings under the forces of gravity, but before they hit the ground, they vaporized and suddenly went into the atmosphere like an antigravity demonstration. Nanoparticles are so tiny that they are not subject to the forces of gravity so molecular dissociation occurred on the larger particles as they were free-falling, reducing them into nanoparticles (0.1 microns in diameter and smaller), which suddenly obeyed other physical laws—quantum mechanics. More evidence of HAARP/beam weapon technology applied during collapse.

Satellite photos showed dust going into the upper atmosphere—which had to be nanoparticles and may have been enhanced by other technology because most very fine particles/dust would stay in the Troposphere and be rained out in two months as we know from depleted uranium particulate releases from battlefield already.

1,400 Toasted Cars: located blocks from the WTC buildings, with door handles missing, engine blocks missing, blistering on some parts of the car finish, strange rust patterns on the bodies of the cars.

Paper Around Cars Not Burned: Whatever "vaporized" the engine blocks and the door handles on 1,400 cars did not ignite fragile and flammable paper lying all around the cars. If engine blocks and door handles selectively vaporized, why didn't the body of the car vaporize?

Pile of Cars Spontaneously Combusted: In a news video, the entire pile of cars started burning spontaneously at the same time with no visible cause; it was not a fire that started in one car and spread to others.

Rust occurred immediately on cars and trucks, and in FEMA photos, there was heavy rust on STEEL beams—steel does not rust, and it is a slow oxidation process that results in the rusting of iron. This rusting happened immediately.

Basements of WTC Buildings Undamaged: Stuffed mannequins in the basement with clothing on were carried out of the basement undamaged. If a hundred-plus-story building collapsed into its basement and left a thirty-five-story rubble pile, there would be nothing left in the basement. Even streetcars underground at the WTC were pulled out after the collapse and had no damage.

Prof. Cahill Air Monitoring Samples: The hardest and most durable materials vaporized (steel, concrete etc), and the most fragile materials (paper) cascading out of windows and all over the ground for blocks were undamaged.

Truckloads of Potting Soil: Right after the WTC disaster, the ground was "fuming," and sequential FEMA aerial photos show 130 dump trucks FULL of soil (filled almost to the top of the dump truck space) covered with tarps so that the dirt in the trucks was not visible to onlookers on the street, coming INTO the WTC area, dumping the soil and going out for more. This happened even before the rescues or cleanup started and it continued for some time. The piles of soil were left for a week and got higher each day in sequential photos. The soil "fuming" lasted until March 2002 (eight months).

Where Were All the WTC Bodies? Emergency room MDs Dr. Tony Daher and Dr. Lincoln Cleaver were interviewed on TV on 9/11 about the casualties. They said there weren't any after about noon on 9/11, no more casualties came to the ER. Firemen saw NO BODIES but talked about the antenna on top of building 1 that was at ground level on top of about one story of rubble.

Boots disintegrated on emergency responders after two hours. They had to get new boots every two hours—molecular dissociation. It was not from burning; their skin would have been damaged.

NO FIRES IN BUILDINGS: William Rodriguez, Senior Janitor at WTC said there were no fires in the buildings. He conducted rescue efforts, saved injured workers and had keys to every lock in both buildings.

USGS: Iron versus Steel: the USGS analyzed the mineral form of the rust on steel beams and iron objects at the WTC. They did not address the "steel does not rust" issue, but dodged it by referring to the rusted steel beams in the rubble pile as "iron beams" and gave mineral analyses of IRON minerals produced by oxidation.

Beam weapon evidence: was present at the top of the WTC buildings as 'lathering up' started before buildings started coming down. 'Lathering up' in videos preceded the collapse of all buildings, even Building 7 which supposedly Larry Silverstein when he said "Pull it" to firefighters meant controlled demolition. Color alteration and modification in news videos compared to other photos/videos at tops of buildings indicates "doctoring" of images.

"Lathering Up" Incriminating: Building 7 "lathered up" even before B. 2 went down. B 7 not damaged at all by B. 2 going down -right next to each other.

Freon tanks very odd, large tanks removed from WTC building and OSHA made bogus statement about what and why they were removed. Was freon used in takedown? A NYC cop I met with Cindy Sheehan said he was injured in B. 7 and removed on a gurney, but his eyes were covered so he could not see anything as they left the building. He reported he was able to see dead bodies lying all over the floor as he was being carried out - BEFORE building 7 had collapsed. Was this due to Freon asphyxiation put through the ventilation system like in recent Russian submarine disaster?

91001 Blog Forum Comment: We stand at the beginning of a new age. Our government has in its hands a method of disrupting the molecular basis for matter [HAARP/beam weapons], and its first impulse was to weaponize it. Is this so hard to understand? Like splitting atoms to create destruction was it hard to understand in 1945? [HAARP—the new and improved model]

Of course this new "invention" came when the United States ruled supreme. A weapon system of vast new power comes in time and we don't have an enemy worthy of it, so naturally we use it on ourselves, 'Wag the Dog'.[27]

[AC]This evidence indicates that HAARP/beam weapons were used on at least the Twin Towers particularly because this reference cites as evidence the use of nukes in combination with EMF devices.[AC]

# Chapter 10 Notes

1. 9-11 Review. "Continuous Explosions Leveled the Towers." http://www.911review.com/attack/wtc/explosions.html.

2. McAlister, Therese, Jonathan Barnett, John Gross, Ronald Hamburger, Jon Magnusson, *The WTC Report*, Chapter 1, 911research.wtc7.net/mirrors/guardian2/wtc/WTC_ch1.htm.

3. King, Jeff. "How Strong Is the Evidence for Controlled Demolition?" Plaguepuppy's Café. Http://www.911review.com/attack/wtc/explosions.ht,l.

4. Jones, Steven E. "Why Indeed Did the WTC Buildings Collapse?" Physics Department Colloquium at Idaho State University, Sept. 1, 2006. *http://reopen911.org/BYU.htm*.

5. Jones, Seven E. "Why Indeed Did the WTC Buildings Completely Collapse?" Journal of 9/11 Studies. September 2006/Volume 3.

6. Harrit, Niels H., Jeffrey Farrer, Steven E. Jones, Kevin R. Ryan, Frank M. Legge, Daniel Farnsworth, Gregg Roberts. James R. Gourley, and Bradley R. Arsen. "Active Thermitic Material Discovered in Dust from the 9/11 World Trade Center Catastrophe." *The Open Chemical Physics Journal*. 2009, 2, 7-31. http://www.globalresearch.ca/index.php?context=va&aid=13049.

7. Harrit, Niels. "Now Evident: WTC Collapse Was A Controlled Demolition. http://globalfire.tv/nj//09en/jews/wtc_blownup.htm.

8. Ward, Ed. "The US Government's Usage of Atomic Bombs—Domestic—WTC. http://www.thepriceofliberty.org/06/09/25/ward.htm.

9. Ward, Ed. "Update: The US Government's Usage of Atomic Bombs—Domestic—WTC," 4. http://www.thepriceofliberty.org/07/03/05/ward.htm.

—

10. Finnish military expert. "The 9/11 Operation: A Summary." http://www.saunalahti.fi/wtc2001/soldier1.htm, 1-4.

11. Military expert. "View of a Military Expert: Why the Towers of the World Trade Center Collapsed." http://www.saunalahti.fi/wtc2001/soldier5.htm, 1-3.

12. Finnish military expert. "The 9/11 Operation: A Summary." http://www.saunalahti.fi/wtc2001/soldier1.htm, 4.

13. Finnish Military expert. "View of a Military Expert: Why the Towers of the World Trade Center Collapsed." http://www.saunalahti.fi/wtc2001/soldier5.htm, 2, 3.

14. Finnish Military Expert. "Observations Suggesting the Use of Small Hydrogen Bombs." http://www.saunalahti.fi/wtc2001/soldier4.htm, 2.

15. Finnish Military Expert. "The Development of Bomb Technology Related to the 9/11 Operation." http://www.serendipity.li/wot/finn/3/soldier3.htm, 1.

16. Finnish military expert. "Crash Course on Hard-to-Know Military Explosives Details." http://www.saunalahti.fi/wtc2001/explosives.htm, 9.

17. The Anonymous Physicist. "Proof of the Existence of Mini-Nukes and Micro-Nukes." http://wtcdemolitionblogspot.com/2007/08/proof-of-existence-of-mini-nu . . . , 1.

18. The Anonymous Physicist. *Humint Events Online*. "9/11 Truth Flow Chart: Leaving the Bogus Hangouts, and Arriving At The Ultimate Truth of 9/11," http://covertoperations.blogspot.com/, 17-19.

19. Ibid., 20, 21.

20. The Anonymous Physicist. China Syndrome at the WTC. "Further Analogies between the WTC and Chernobyl China Syndromes of Molten Metal and Radiation Release," http://wtc-chinasyndrome.blogspot.com/,3.

21. The Anonymous Physicist. "If the WTC Nuclear Destruction Had the China Syndrome Aftermath, Why Didn't Hiroshima ?" *http://wtc-chinasyndrome.blogspot.com/*, 4-6.

22. The Anonymous Physicist. April 29, 2008. "Chernobyl's China Syndrome Gets New 'Coffin' and a Review of the China Syndrome at the WTC." 8

23. Ibid., 10.

24. Gaffney, Mark H. "The 9/11 Mystery Plane and the Vanishing of America." Walterville, OR 97489. Trine Day LLC. PO Box 577, 132, 133.

25. The Anonymous Physicist. World Trade Center Demolition. September 09, 2008. "Micro-Nukes in the WTC—Creating the China Syndrome: Important Matters of Completeness & Plausibility," 1-3. http://wtcdemolition.blogspot.com.

26. WAFT IT. "WTC 9/11 EVID ENCE." Cliff Livingstone. February 9, 2009. http://www.waftit.com/Nukeused1.htm.

27. HAARP & its role in the False Flag Operation of September 11, 2001 WTC demolition -How it's done (scientific video demonstrations included.)" *http://www.fourwinds10.com/siterun_data/government/fraud/911_attack/news.php?q=122* . . .

—

# CHAPTER 11

## The Use of Minifission and/ or Microfusion Explosives and/or HAARP/Beam Weapons for Destroying the Three WTC Towers

### *Evidence in WTC Rubble Proves Use of Fission and/or Fusion Explosives to Pulverize at Least the Twin Towers*

[AC] There are three additional criteria for the use of either numerous atom bombs or an underground mini-H-bomb or both for demolishing the Twin Towers and WTC-7. These are the absence of (1) remnants of all restroom facilities, (2) all corrugated and galvanized steel floor supports for floors, and (3) all lightweight concrete floors in the rubble after collapses of each of the three towers.

[AC] Elaborating upon these three criteria:

1. The presence of numerous men's restrooms and numerous women's restrooms on each of the 110 floors of each of

the Twin Towers can be taken for granted, with 20,000 individuals working in each tower. When each tower collapsed according to the government story, there should have been an enormous pile of toilets, urinals, and washbasins. Many would have been broken, but the fragments would have been recognizable, and in each pile there would have been at least two thousand feet of copper tubing, plus hundreds of steel or chrome-plated faucets and other accessories. No observer has commented on seeing such equipment.

2. Each tower had four million square feet of office space, supported by four-inch thick lightweight concrete floors on fluted or corrugated, galvanized steel sheets. The Twin Towers consequently should have produced eight million square feet of galvanized steel sheets among the rubble after their collapses. No observer or rescue worker among the rubble has made any comment about seeing even a small piece of such sheets, to the author's knowledge.

3. Lightweight concrete is made by mixing a detergent with the water added to sand and cement powder for making concrete. As the concrete sets, it contains numerous air bubbles which become small holes in the concrete. Such lightweight concrete is not as strong as conventional concrete containing gravel, but it is strong enough for supporting a floor when it is four inches thick and resting on a galvanized, corrugated steel sheet which is in turn supported by a highly redundant truss system. Instead of many blocks of broken concrete and some powder, as would normally be found after demolishing a building, there was a dusty powder (ultrafine) which covered many Manhattan city blocks. [AC]

—

## *Abundance of Zinc within the WTC Skyscrapers*

It is significant that many samples of WTC dust have an additional chemical signature—an enrichment of zinc in the iron spherules formed during the destruction of the Twin Towers. More specifically, airborne zinc concentrations were ten times higher than normal.

The galvanized twenty-two-gage corrugated steel sheets used for the decking to support the concrete floors had a coating of zinc on a sheet of metal comprising about 98 percent iron. Accordingly, the deckings contained 10 percent zinc by weight and were a major source of zinc. Estimating that 16 tons of steel decking were used per floor, the amount of zinc was about 1.6 tons beneath every floor of WTC-1 and WTC-2. Omitting the first floors of each tower and multiplying 2 by 109 by 1.6 equals 350 tons of zinc within the Twin Towers.[1]

## *Critical Importance of the Extremely Great Temperature Driving Force Needed to Explain Softening of Thick Steel Beams within One-tenth Second*

[AC] Anyone who has used an electric stove has experienced the difference between putting a small pot containing a cup of water on a burner heated to "medium" and putting the same pot on a burner heated to "hot" and already a bright cherry red. The result is that the hot burner produces boiling of the water much faster. The temperature difference between the pot at room temperature (say at 75°F) and the cherry red burner (1,375°F) is the driving force that quickly transfers heat from the hot burner into the metal of the pot

—

bottom and then into the water. This process generally requires a few minutes. To obtain the same result in one-tenth second would obviously require a far higher burner temperature, for those floors were collapsing at the rate of eleven floors per second. To bring a piece of structural steel (as thick as six inches) from 75°F to about 2,000°F in one-tenth second would just as obviously require a very great temperature difference, such as a million degrees or more. Those steel beams must have changed from being very rigid to being as limp as cooked spaghetti in that short a time.

[AC] Returning to the collapses of the Twin Towers, voluminous dust clouds appear in the numerous videos as the upper floors collapsed toward the bottom. Explosions of cutting charges, as they cut horizontally and vertically aligned beams in the perimeter columns and in the core columns of the top one-third sections of the Twin Towers into thirty-foot lengths and melted a band of steel at each cut, can explain the initial crumbling of each tower, beginning high in the tower near the zone of airliner impact. However, they do not adequately explain the disappearance of concrete floors and their supporting steel sheets, the disappearance of each enormous building's contents, the hurling of hundreds of tons of steel sidewise for up to five hundred feet, the partial disappearance of the massive core columns in the middle and bottom sections, and the creation of the voluminous dust clouds that expanded into a diameter several times the original tower diameter, beginning near the top rather than at the bottom of each tower.

[AC] Lightweight concrete simply lacks the thermal conductivity needed to transmit heat horizontally and rapidly from the location of each cut by the cutting charges beneath a floor. Heat from the cutting charges would not have been sufficient to make desks, computers, file cabinets, safes, and the like simply disappear

—

on each floor within a few seconds. Some other source of great heat must be found.

[AC] Detonation of a thermonuclear bomb (small H-bomb) at the second basement level and in the center of the core of each tower, with its intense heat wave at about 10,000,000°C, supplies the extremely great driving force needed to melt and vaporize successive trusses, vaporize successive galvanized steel sheets, and then to explode the four-inch thick lightweight concrete floors, one almost instantaneously after the other.

[AC] Since approximately the top thirty floors of WTC-2, the South Tower, were toppling 22° from the vertical and rotating, it was necessary for this heat wave to reach those toppling floors within about two seconds and then to vaporize the cap and finally to thrust the resultant dust cloud violently upwardly about two hundred feet above the tower within three seconds. If that had not happened, those top thirty floors would have crashed onto the street and left the lower eighty floors with no fire and no reason for further collapse. Then if the cutter charges had continued to cut beams without the weight of the top thirty floors while millions of people were watching on television screens, the government's story would have looked ridiculous to everyone. Moreover, if the lower eighty floors had not been demolished, the cutter charges beneath those eighty layers of concrete would have been discovered. [AC]

### Demolishing the Three WTC Towers with a Plurality of Fission (Atomic) Bombs

The issue of *Humint Events Online* for Thursday, July 17, 2008, acknowledges that several explosive devices may have been used in combination with conventional explosives (e.g. C-4) and that each may also have been used in some combination together. The article prefers to characterize the complete massive destruction of the WTC towers as having several key features:

1) incredible pulverization/"dustification" of all building contents in a matter of seconds

2) pulverized debris violently bursting outward during the destruction

3) a consecutive series of "explosive" waves traveling down the towers during the demolition

4) disappearance/vaporization of large numbers of interior core columns

5) various odd phenomena—likely EMP effects on vehicles and some electronic devices, odd holes in the ground and in surrounding buildings, early basement explosions, "hanging skin" in some surviving victims

6) extreme high heat in the ground zero rubble (widely reported/well substantiated)

7) large number of sicknesses/cancers in ground zero responders

8) suspicious treatment of remaining WTC steel—washing, extreme security on trucks taking it away, rapid sale to China

Both pros and cons are given for each explosive type. The pros for millinukes/micronukes are as follows:

1) can easily explain all the features of the destruction of the towers;

2)  powerful, well-known, well-established destructive technology;

3)  small but extremely powerful and so do not require massive emplacement of devices in the towers.

The single CON is "cover-up required for radiation at ground zero."[2]

[AC] The micro- or mini-H-bomb theory, including numerous cutting charges, explains the finding of tritium after the three collapses, the melting and even vaporizing of large amounts of steel, the formation of very hot pools of molten steel on the granite foundation beneath the street level, the large quantities of bent steel, the hurling of multiton perimeter assemblies hundreds of feet, and the conversion into dust of galvanized deckings, lightweight concrete, wallboard, doors, elevators, stairwells, office furniture, safes, computers, printers, copiers, restroom facilities, and human bodies, all within less than ten seconds. However, it does not explain the post-collapse generations of large quantities of heat within the basement levels of the Twin Towers and generally within the rubble pile, as observed subsequent to September 11, 2001, that persisted for up to six months in spite of heavy rains and large volumes of cooling water being poured onto the rubble pile.

[AC] Moreover, all of the above-listed capabilities of a single H-bomb or even triple H-bombs per tower can readily be attributed to a plurality of atomic bombs per tower. And such a plurality would have had the advantage of greater flexibility because of possible chosen variations as to power, spacing, and reinforcement. The relatively large numbers of small atomic (fission) bombs would also have created numerous fratriciding possibilities with resultant heat generation in the rubble after collapse. [AC]

Thomas A. Cahill, a retired professor of physics and atmospheric science at the University of California, Davis, noted that the color of the plume from Ground Zero after the rainfall of Sept. 14 was a light blue. That color meant that the pile was giving off very fine particles, which were characteristic of a very high temperature process. Yet "[t]he pile at ground zero wasn't hot enough to generate such fine particles."

The fires in the debris pile began at over 1,000°C and gradually cooled, at least on the surface, during September and October 2001. On September 16, temperature measurements of the debris pile found more than three dozen hot spots of varying sizes and temperatures between 500 and 700°C (900 and 1300°F), but they were surface temperatures. Cahill observed that "when they would pull out a steel beam, the lower part would be a glowing dull red, which indicated a temperature of 500 to 600°C (900 and 1,100°F). And we know that people were turning over pieces of concrete in December that would flash into fire—which requires about 300°C (600°F). So the surface of the pile cooled rather rapidly, but the bulk of the pile stayed hot all the way to December."[3]

The following testimonies seem to be pertinent for supporting the numerous fission bomb theory:

Ross Milanytch watched the horror at the WTC from his office window on the twenty-second floor of a building a couple of blocks away. "I [saw] small explosions on each floor. And after it all cleared, all that was left of the buildings, you could just see the steel girders in like a triangular sail shape. The structure was just completely gone," he said.

John Bussey, a reporter for the *Wall Street Journal*, watched the collapse of the South Tower from the ninth floor of the newspaper's office building. "I . . . looked up out of the office window to see what seemed like perfectly synchronized explosions coming from each floor. One after the other. From top to bottom, with a fraction of a second between, the floors flew to pieces."[4]

[AC] The numerous fission bomb theory seems to adequately explain the generation of large quantities of heat for up to six months in the basement levels of the towers and within the rubble pile, in addition to having the capacity of pulverizing or vaporizing of concrete floors, galvanized sheets supporting the floors, stairwells, doors, office furniture, safes, people, and glass. Such fission bombs could have provided the power needed to hurl hundreds of tons of steel for nearly six hundred feet. The theory also explains the formation of the pools of very hot molten steel in the basements of all three towers and quite reasonably says that atomic reactions within the debris pile and in the basement were producing this heat. It also provides an explanation for the radiation that necessitated washing the steel being shipped to China and bringing in dirt immediately after the collapses in the evening of September 11.

[AC] If ten mininukes (small atom bombs) had been used in each of the Twin Towers, their locations within the core would have been about every fifth and alternately every sixth floor. Assuming the topmost mininuke, having a selected quantity of explosive power, had been placed in the center of the 105th floor and another one had been placed in the center of the eightieth floor, they would, if detonated simultaneously, have caused the top thirty floors and the roof of the South Tower, tilting 22° at that moment, to dissolve simultaneously into the giant cloud seen in videos being projected into resulting debris flung upwardly and outwardly in every direction for two hundred feet. Next the eight remaining mininukes would have been detonated successively downward within the next eight seconds. That procedure would have enabled the eighty upright floors, beneath the tilting floors and the six hundred-feet wide cloud into which they had been dissolved, to appear untouched and then to be dissolved into downward falling dust as the tower crumbled.

Cutting charges could have been disposed every thirty feet of the perimeter columns and at the junctions of each transverse beam with a core column and a perimeter column, thereby providing the "perfectly synchronized explosions coming from each floor" that John Bussey had observed.

[AC] It seems more likely that mini-atom bombs were the main explosive devices for destroying the three WTC towers than micro-H-bombs (except for the basement core columns), although thermite and/or thermate cutting charges would have also been needed and must have been used extensively on the perimeter columns and on the trusses.[AC]

## *HAARP/beam Weapons for Vaporizing Steel*

Because large quantities of structural steel and aluminum siding apparently disappeared during the destruction of the three WTC towers, it is likely that these weapons, capable of molecularly dissociating chemical compounds as strong as structural steel, were used to obtain more rapid and complete destruction of the three buildings.[5]

## *A Feasible Means of Delivering WMD to New York City before September 11, 2001*

An El Al military cargo plane, a Boeing 747-200F, left Amsterdam's Schiphol airport at 6:21 p.m. on October 4, 1992, en route to Tel Aviv and crashed seven minutes later into a high-rise apartment complex. Its cargo of 114 tons of weapons of mass destruction (WMDs) included "dimethyl methylphosphonate and two other substances needed to make the deadly nerve gas Sarin," plus 882 pounds of depleted uranium.

A senior editor with a Dutch newspaper testified that he had been in Biafra and Vietnam "but I never saw anything like that crash. It was like looking into a steel smelter . . . The concrete of the flats was glowing red."

It was one of the worst air disasters in Dutch history, but officials of the Schiphol Air Traffic Control (SATC) "conspired with Israeli officials to lie to the public claiming the plane was 'only transporting flowers and perfume.'" The purpose of this cover-up was "to conceal Israel's unlawful chemical weapons arsenal and the international network that supports it."

The crash was caused by relentless scheduling of overloaded flights. The resultant stress in the metals holding the plane together caused one of the 747 engines to fall off and the violent shaking caused the second engine to fall off.

"A TV Amsterdam (TVA) report identified Schiphol as one of several European airports that allows El Al to transfer cargo without supervision."

Six long years after this disaster, courageous investigative journalists with the Dutch newspaper *NRC Handelsblad* exposed the true contents of the crashed plane and the destination for the nerve gas components, the Israeli Institute for Biological Research.

According to the Dutch press, "Security officials had been waving Israeli air cargo through Schiphol, El Al's European hub, since the 1950's." Because Dutch authorities had no jurisdiction over Israeli activities in Schiphol, where the El Al security detachment was a branch of Mossad, "Schiphol has become a hub for secret weapons transfers." And it continues because "[t]here are rules but there is an exception—El Al is allowed to ignore the rules."

"Mysterious planes loaded with tons of illegal chemicals, biowarfare agents, and nuclear materials were flown from New York to Schiphol to Israel on a regular schedule on Sunday nights—in violation of American laws and international laws that the U.S. has vowed to uphold."[6]

[AC] Since such violations happened en route to Israel from New York, why not also the reverse? Israel is known to possess at least two hundred nukes and very likely has had micro-H-bombs, mini-A-bombs, and HAARP/beam weapons for years. It is speculative, but why not ship some of them from Israel via Schiphol airport to a New York City airport shortly before September 11, 2001, and thereby avoid troubling paperwork in the United States while enabling the CIA and the U.S. neocons to claim total hands off? [AC]

[AC] As described in Chapter 21, the specific El Al flight that left JFK Airport at 4:41 p.m., September 11, 2001, with the assistance of US military officials, could easily have carried away the nineteen Arabs identified as the "hijackers." [AC]

# Chapter 11 Notes

1. Greening, F. R. "The Collapse of WTC 1 and 2: A New Theory."Muslim-Jewish-Christian Alliance for 9/11 Truth, 9, 10. http://mujca.com/procrustes.htm.

2. "WTC Destruction Theories: 'DEW' versus Thermite/Thermate/ Super Thermate versus Milli-Nukes/Micro-Nukes." Humint Events Online: Dedicated to Unmasking 9/11, the "War on Terror" and Other Major Frauds Perpetuated by the Global Elites/"Powers That Be." http://covertoperations.blogspot.com/2008/07/wtc-destruction-theories-dew-versus.html.

3. Dalton, Louisa. "Chemical Analysis of a Disaster." *Chemical & Engineering News, October 20, 2003*, Vol. 81, No. 42. http://pubs.acs. org/cen/NCW/8142aerosols.html, 6, 7.

4. Marrs, Jim. *The Terror Conspiracy: Deception, 9/11 and the Loss of Liberty*. 2008. New York, NY. The Disinformation Company, Ltd., 163 Third Avenue, Suite 108, 41.

5. Livingstone, Cliff. WAFT IT. WTC 9/11 Evidence, 2.

6. Forbes, Ralph. "Mossad Role in Airport Security Troubling." *American Free Press.* January 18, 2010, Issue 3.

# PART IV
## Slight-of-Hand Attack upon the Pentagon

# CHAPTER 12

## Deaths and Damages in the Pentagon from Preinstalled Explosives and a Missile Involving the Alleged American Airlines Flight 77

### *Official Time, Cause, and Extent of Human Deaths and Injuries in Pentagon on September 11, 2001*

The official time of attack upon the Pentagon, the official cause of the Pentagon damage, and the official extent of the human deaths and injuries are as follows from The 9/11 Commission Report:

> At 9:37, the west wall of the Pentagon was hit by hijacked American Airlines Flight 77, a Boeing 757. The crash caused immediate and catastrophic damage. All 64 people aboard the airliner were killed, as were 125 people inside the Pentagon (70 civilians and 55 military

service members). One hundred six people were seriously injured and transported to area hospitals.[1]

## Actual Time of Attack and Removal of Evidence

The official story about what happened at the Pentagon seems reasonable at first, but the closer one looks at this story of a third hijacked airliner, American Airlines Flight 77, having flown into America's military command center, the more mysterious and dubious it becomes. According to the story, the airliner created a fire that killed more than 185 persons and caused a section of the west wall to collapse.

The time of the attack has been changed several times by Pentagon spokespersons. It was initially 9:48 a.m. but has been lowered to 9:37 a.m., as stated in *The 9/11 Commission Report*. The correct time, as determined by witnesses at the scene and by multiple battery-operated wall clocks in the west corridors of the Pentagon that had been stopped by the attacks, is 9:32 a.m. "This timing is critical because it appears that some events connected to the Pentagon strike occurred both before and after the now-official time of 9:37 a.m."

[Author's Comment—AC] There must have been plenty of evidence at the actual crime scene, but most of this evidence was removed by a variety of suspicious official actions in the wake of the attack. These include the seizing of security videos that have never been made public, the immediate and rapid mop-up of the crime scene, and the destruction of, or suppression of, nearly all the physical evidence inside the building in the days and weeks following the attack. A small number of eyewitness accounts and

post-crash photographs taken by witnesses by happenstance are all
that is now available, but they change the official story into simply
a myth—or a hoax.[2] [AC]


## Vice President Dick Cheney


On May 8, 2001 President Bush had placed Vice President
Cheney in charge of

> [A]ll federal programs dealing with weapons of mass
> destruction consequence management within the
> Departments of Defense, Health and Human Services,
> Justice, and Energy, the Environmental Protection
> Agency, and other federal agencies.

This mandate included all "training and planning" which needed
to be "seamlessly integrated, harmonious and comprehensive" in
order to maximize effectiveness. This mandate also created the
Office of National Preparedness in FEMA, overseen by Dick
Cheney."[3]


## American Airlines Flight 77


AA Flight 77 left Dulles Airport near Washington, D.C.,
at 8:20 a.m., ten minutes late. It soon went off course. After its
transponder went off at 8:56, it disappeared from the air traffic
controller radar screen in Indianapolis. The controller looked for
primary radar signals along its projected flight path but could not

find the plane. At 9:05, it reappeared on Indianapolis flight control's primary radar scope and continued to travel west and seemed to get as far as Kansas, where it turned around.

The last normal communication with AA Flight 77 was at 8:52. In the next four minutes, the hijackers allegedly commandeered the big airliner away from the two pilots, tugged them out of their seats, strapped themselves in, became acquainted with the very complicated cockpit dials, and smoothly turned the 757 around toward Washington, D.C., with Hani Hanjour at the controls. (Hanjour had had problems with flying small planes.)

The 300-mile flight to Washington was done in thirty minutes. The speed must have been 600 mph, about 100 mph faster than Dulles radar controllers saw it traveling and faster than its maximum speed! Then at 9:25, air traffic controllers at Dulles Airport reported a fast-moving plane heading toward the White House.

The *proof* that Flight 77 had hit the Pentagon is so shaky that many major media sources only show where the plane reportedly *crashed* and do not show any of the alleged flight path.[4]

Transportation Secretary Norman Mineta testified that Vice President Dick Cheney was in command of the White House's emergency operations center. Mineta testified under oath to the 9/11 Commission in relation to the following conversation he heard about Flight 77 and gave the time as 9:25 or 9:26:

> During the time that the airplane was coming in to the Pentagon, there was a young man who would come in and out and say to the vice president, "The plane is 50 miles out." "The plane is 40 miles out." And when it got down to "The plane is 10 miles out," the young man said

to the vice president, "Do the orders still stand?" And the vice president turned and whipped his neck around and said, "Of course the orders still stand! Have you heard anything to the contrary?"

Peter Tiradera commented that Vice President Cheney was getting somewhat peeved and gave a response that obviously carried a tinge of sarcasm. He was apparently upholding previous orders that no event would change. It was as if he were following a preconceived plan that had been set into operation, with orders arranged in advance. Secret Service agents repeatedly attempted to tell Cheney of this potential threat and had "Stinger" SAMS available that could have brought down the approaching plane. The young Secret Service agent was referring to Vice President Cheney's stand down order (DoD directive J-3 CJCSI 3610.01A).[5]

Having arrived in the PEOC (Presidential Emergency Operation Center) at 9:20 a.m., Transportation Secretary Norman Mineta issued an order from the PEOC at 9:45 a.m., as soon as he became aware of the nature and scale of the attacks, that was unique in American history, with Cheney nearby and nodding approvingly:

> Mineta shouted into the phone to Monte Belger at the FAA, "Monte, bring all the planes down." It was an unprecedented order—there were 4,546 airplanes in the air at the time. Belger, the FAA's acting deputy administrator, amended Mineta's directive to take into account the authority vested on airline pilots. "We're bringing them down per pilot discretion," Belger told the secretary.

"[Expletive] pilot discretion," Mineta yelled back. "Get those goddamn planes down."

Sitting at the other end of the table, Cheney snapped his head up, looked squarely at Mineta and nodded in agreement.

Belger's attempted amendment of Mineta's order, allowing "per pilot's discretion," meant that pilots would decide which airport was the quickest to reach and the safest for landing.[6]

At 9:25, controllers at Dulles Airport saw a fast-moving plane apparently headed toward the White House.

Beginning at 9:33, radar data reportedly showed the aircraft crossing the Capital Beltway and heading toward the Pentagon, which it flew over at 9:35. Then, starting from about 7,000 feet above the ground, the aircraft made a difficult "downward spiral, turning almost a complete circle and dropping the last 7,000 feet in two and a half minutes.[7]

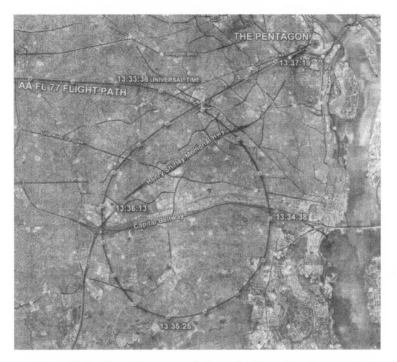

Spiralling descent of aircraft alleged to be
AA Flight 77 as it approaches the Pentagon

Strangely, "Danielle O'Brien, one of the air traffic controllers at Dulles who reported seeing the aircraft at 9:25, said, 'The speed, the maneuverability, the way that he turned, we all thought in the radar room, all of us experienced air traffic controllers, that that was a military plane.'" Another witness, seeing the plane from a fourteenth-floor apartment in Pentagon City, said that it "seemed to be able to hold eight or twelve persons" and "made a shrill noise like a fighter plane." Lon Rains, editor at *Space News*, said, "I was convinced it was a missile. It came in so fast it sounded nothing like an airplane." Still another witness, who saw it from his automobile, was reported as saying that it "was like a cruise missile with wings."

—

However, the official story eventually became that it was actually a really big airplane, a Boeing 757 . . . in fact, Flight 77 itself.[8]

## Ted Olson's Identification of Flight 77 as the Aircraft That Struck the Pentagon

However, identification of the aircraft which struck the Pentagon was not immediately obvious. A Pentagon Web site statement that it had been hit by a "commercial airliner, possibly hijacked," spread quickly through the media. The source was military officials speaking on condition of anonymity.

One other statement used for connecting Flight 77 with the Pentagon strike came from Theodore "Ted" Olson, the U.S. Justice Department's solicitor general. He said that he had received two telephone calls from his wife, Barbara Olson, the well-known author and television commentator. The calls were at 9:25 and 9:30. The reported conversations said that Flight 77 had been hijacked.

However, Ted Olson's report about these conversations with his wife were doubtful for these reasons:

1. Ted was very close to the Bush administration, and he had previously stated that there are many situations in which "government officials might quite legitimately have reasons to give false information out";

2. His conversations with Barbara were both vague and self-contradictory. On the other flights, several passengers and flight attendants made telephone calls, but Ted Olson was the only person who reported receiving a call from Flight 77; and

3.  A report of an interview conducted by the FBI with Ted
    Olson on 9/11 indicated that no such calls occurred.
    Furthermore, Ted Olson's story was "rejected by the
    historians who wrote *Pentagon 9/11*, a treatment of the
    Pentagon attack put out by the Department of Defense.[9]

[AC] An additional reason, as discussed more fully in chapter
17, is that such cell phone calls from an airliner at flight altitude
and speed were technically impossible in 2001 as established by
the FBI and a Canadian pilot. Without these conversations, there
is no proof that Flight 77 even turned around from its westward
flight. If Flight 77 did continue westward, the large aircraft that
flew toward the west wall of the Pentagon that morning at a low
altitude, passing north of the Citgo gas station, was probably a
suitably painted military drone.

[AC]An additional observation that is pertinent is that Flight
77 never took off; its passengers were flown to Newark Airport on
a charter jet and then walked on the tarmac to the waiting Flight
93 which took off 41 minutes late, as described in Chapter 3.
[AC]

## Two Aircraft Converging Toward the Pentagon at Low Levels

Dick Eastman of Yakima, Washington, however, has located
several witnesses who were sure that they had seen two planes
heading toward the Pentagon. Eastman's theory was that an
American Airlines plane was making an attention-getting move
to draw all eyes to itself as it flew toward the Pentagon while a

military plane or a winged missile, flying too low to be seen by most witnesses, flew on a converging path toward the same target spot. The airliner passed north of a Citgo gas station on Washington Boulevard, but the military plane passed south of it. Then the airliner climbed over the Pentagon at the last second and disappeared behind the immense cloud of smoke produced by the crash of the military plane or winged missile. The airliner, probably being operated as a drone, landed unnoticed at Reagan National Airport, having a runway which is only a mile away in the same direction, or possibly crashed into the Atlantic Ocean.

Eastman has pointed out that when Flight 77 passed over the Naval Annex and headed perpendicularly toward the west wall of the Pentagon at a very low level, its landing gear was up. Sgt. William Lagasse was filling up his car at the Citgo gas station when the jetliner flew north of him on its way to the Pentagon. Two other witnesses were also at the station.

The other plane, which Eastman believed had a single engine, knocked over a lamppost at the west end of a bridge or overpass, which is a considerable distance southwest of the gas station, and then knocked over four other lampposts on its way to the west wall of the Pentagon. The first lamppost allegedly broke the windshield of a black taxi being driven by Michael England.[10]

## Identity of Flying Object That Hit the Pentagon

American Airlines Flight 77 could not have hit the Pentagon. American 77 was a Boeing 757-200, which is 155 feet long and has a wingspan of 125 feet. When the landing gear is retracted in flight, the distance from the bottom of its engines to the top of its fuselage is 18 feet. The height of the plane from the bottom of its engines to the top of its tail is 45 feet. The fuselage is 13 feet in diameter. The bottoms of the engines are 5 feet below the fuselage so that the engines would have dug a pair of furrows into the lawn if the nose had struck the first floor of the Pentagon, as indicated by initial photographs of the hole in the first floor of wedge one.

The hole made by the attacking object in the west wall of wedge 1 was estimated to be 15 feet high by 18-20 feet wide, and the width of the wall after collapse of the facade is 62 feet wide, half of 757's wingspan. The intact wall above the hole is about 20 feet too low to accommodate the 757 tail.

> The overall impression of a rather maladroit coverup is increased by the behavior of the FBI at and around the crime scene. First, all available video tape from surveillance cameras which might have captured the flying object was confiscated with the speed of lightning. This included video tape from the gas station that was directly under the flight path of the object, and from another gas station a hundred yards or so to the west. It also included video tape from a camera maintained by the Sheraton Washington Hotel. It included every business in the area. The FBI has never released these tapes, and they were not made public by the 9/11 Commission.[11]

As one of five proofs that the killer jet was not Flight 77 but was either a smaller remote-controlled jet or a missile, Mr. Eastman cited the security camera pictures released in March 2002 and officially released in May 2006, which "establish that the aircraft or missile that attacked the Pentagon was no more than half the length of a Boeing 757."

A small jet engine was found inside the Pentagon. According to this evidence and a series of five released pictures from a video made by a security camera that showed the "tail fin of the attacking object sticking up behind a parking-pass machine," the plane could have been a remotely controlled single-engine F-16 fighter jet that fired a missile having an explosive shaped charge to allow the remotely operated fighter jet to enter the hole that it had created.[12]

The Pentagon's five extremely sophisticated antimissile batteries did not function. If they had, "a missile should normally be unable to pass. As for a big Boeing 757-200, it would have strictly no chance." The photographic evidence, plus the fact that the antimissile systems of the Pentagon did not shoot down the plane plus the additional fact that "[e]ach military aircraft in fact possesses a transponder which permit[s] it to declare itself in the eyes of its possessor as friendly or hostile" indicates that the Pentagon was not hit by a Boeing passenger plane but was instead hit by a drone fighter jet or a military missile.

Another bit of evidence as to the flying object which hit the Pentagon is the red flame shown in photographs of the attack. One of the latest generation of AGM-type missiles, armed with a hollow charge and a depleted uranium BLU tip, causes such an instantaneous fire with red flames and gives off heat in excess of 3,600°F. It withdraws just as quickly, leaving behind a cloud of black smoke. This evidence reinforces the conclusion that the Pentagon was pierced by a missile, not smashed by an airplane, which would have produced yellow flames mixed with black smoke.

"The nose of a Boeing, which contains the electronic navigation system, is made of carbon fiber rather than metal." It is consequently "extremely fragile" and "could not have gone through three rings of the Pentagon, creating a seven-foot exit hole in the inside wall of the third ring." What could have created such a hole is the head of a missile "weighted with depleted uranium, an extremely dense meal that heats with slightest friction and renders piercing easier."[13]

A photograph taken by Tom Horan of the Associated Press, who happened to be in the vicinity at the time, showed that the Pentagon lawn was untouched, the hole in the west wing facade was between fifteen and eighteen feet in diameter, the west wing's facade had not yet collapsed, and there was no damage above the hole or to either side of it. The inside wall of the third of the Pentagon's five rings, identified as the C-ring, was penetrated to produce a hole about seven feet in diameter. If all of this damage had been done to three of the Pentagon's rings by a missile, it had to have penetrated six concrete walls, the first being reinforced. If Flight 77 had struck the Pentagon as told by witnesses, its nose would have crumpled against the wall and its two steel engines would have greatly damaged the facade on either side of the hole. So whatever hit the Pentagon made a clean hit from the air and went completely inside the C ring.[14]

### *A Conspiratorial Theory: Horizontal Lampposts Cut to Provide a Path for the Attacking Aircraft*

It has been pointed out that if a winged missile or fighter jet had struck and knocked down from one to five lampposts as alleged, the fighter jet or missile would have been wrecked.

Furthermore, after suggesting that a 450-500 mph plane would have thrown the lampposts hundreds of feet from where they were and writing that "some poles even fall to rest *underneath the lamppost base*," Peter Tiradera wondered why "if the top was sheared off, why would the lower portion have been broken off at the base and knocked down?"(A fatal accident to a twin-engine Gulfstream jet in Dallas resulted from clipping a light pole and causing the top one-fourth to be broken off.) Then he made this conspiratorial suggestion:

> Look at the bolts, they are not popped out, they were cut just cut under the base, notice there is very little, or no other trauma/stress related effect at the base. No poles were bent nor remained in their upright positions. If the supposed aircraft hit the pole near their uppermost sections why would all the posts been cut off at the base? Literally cut!

> Could someone have cut a lamppost path the preceding evening and laid them in the grass on the side of the highway or thrown them out of a truck that morning? Would anyone have noticed or even cared?

(A construction site was in the close vicinity so that the operation would have been very inconspicuous.)

Next Tiradera proposed "a theory that would explain things well—*lampposts were cut down in advance to allow a path for a UAV or remote jet.*" The possible path was "*just short of* being wide enough to accommodate a 125-foot wingspan of a 757."[15]

Three lampposts near Pentagon having cut bolts

## *Stand-Down Order on 9/11*

Charles E. Lewis had worked on security systems at Los
Angeles International Airport (LAX) on 9/11. He has provided
a written statement that he overheard LAX security officials at
guard post II discussing a stand-down order on the morning of
9/11. This statement included the following:

> At first, LAX Security was very upset because it seemed
> to Security that none of the controllers (ATCs) tracking
> the hijacked airliners had notified NORAD as required.
> More chatter revealed that ATCs had notified NORAD
> but that NORAD had not responded because it had
> been "ordered to stand down."

> This report made Security even more upset, so they tried
> to find out who had issued that order. A short time later,
> the word came down that the order had come "from the
> highest level of the White House." Security was puzzled
> and very upset by this and made attempts to get more
> details and clarification.

—

Because President Bush was away, Vice President Cheney was clearly in charge and was the "highest level of the White House," who must have given that stand-down order. Lewis had a private conversation in 2006 with Captain LaPonda Fitchpatrick of the Los Angeles Airport Police (LAWAPD), head of security in the Airport Operations Area. She said that "LAX security was well aware that 9/11 was an inside job."

> Lewis's testimony about what he heard LAX Security officials saying provides support for the most natural inference to draw from Mineta's statement about the conversation that he heard between Cheney and the young man, namely, that although Washington officials knew that an aircraft was approaching the capital, there were orders, confirmed by Cheney, not to shoot it down.[16]

## Three Side Effects of the Pentagon Attack

In contrast to strict flight control immediately after the WTC and Pentagon attacks, the bin Laden family were granted extraordinary White House privileges to fly out of U.S. airspace following the attacks of September 11, 2001. With the help of the FBI, the Saudis and the bin Laden family chartered an aircraft to pick up family members in Los Angeles, Orlando, and Washington, D.C. The bin Laden plane then flew the relatives to Boston, where—one week after the attacks—the group left Logan Airport bound for Jeddah.[17]

Joseph P. Firmage (http://firmage.org) noted that Vice President Cheney was rarely seen for weeks after the 9/11 attacks "and was reported to be shifting among undisclosed locations as a contingency in case further attacks took out President Bush . . ." Mr. Firmage also commented that if "one of the complicity theories is true, then Cheney was almost certainly the key leader of the operation" so that several weeks might pass "before he would have felt sufficiently informed of the aftershocks and information tributaries from 9/11 to come back into administrative routine."[18]

Clear Channel Communications, which owns and operates 1,225 radio stations and 39 TV stations, terminated Howard "Shock Jock" Stern after Stern came out against Bush. "Stern even had 9/11 skeptics as guests on his show and 'told his 13 million listeners that he did not believe a commercial airliner hit the Pentagon; a cruise missile, he said, was a far more plausible explanation.'"[19]

## The E-4B, a Substitute Pentagon, over Washington, D.C.

The E-4B is a modified Boeing 747-200, having a white color, the U.S. flag painted on the tail, and blue stripes and insignia on the fuselage. The blue stripes on the sides come together to form a blue spot at the rear of the aircraft which is visible from below. Its distinguishing feature, not on any other airplane, is a bump or pod directly behind the bulging 747 cockpit. The E-4B is 230 feet long with a wingspan of 195 feet and four jet engines. It has advanced radar and state-of-the-art communications equipment and everything needed to detect the approach of Flight 77 from many miles away.[20]

The E-4B plane (a Boeing 747) can be refueled in flight and consequently has essentially unlimited range so that it can remain aloft for days at a time. An E-4B usually follows Air Force One when the president is aboard and stays close at hand for reasons of national security. This protocol was not followed on September 11, 2001, however, although the Air Force has a fleet of four E-4Bs. One E-4B is always on alert. Each E-4B has a crew of 64. The plane can accommodate an additional 50 passengers, for a total of 114. Its spacious 747 fuselage includes command and work areas, conference and briefing rooms, and an operations center or battle station. In addition, the plane has a rest area, bunks for sleeping, and a galley stocked with a week's provisions.

"If the presidential plane, Air Force One, is a flying White House, then the E-4B is a substitute Pentagon. Its electronics cover the full radio spectrum, from extremely low frequency (ELF) to ultra high frequency (UHF)." The plane is outfitted with as many as 48 different antennae and is thereby able "to communicate worldwide with all U.S. military commands, including tactical and strategic forces, naval ships, planes, nuclear-armed missiles, even submarines." The E-4B is thereby "a state-of-the-art communications platform and can serve as an airborne command center for all U.S. military forces in a national or world crisis."[21]

According to at least three accounts, the E-4B was in the skies over Washington *before* the Pentagon strike. It could have seen Flight 77's approach when it was many miles away, long before it "executed

a 330-degree looping turn over Alexandria, Virginia, before making
its final approach, a downward spiral that took just over 3 minutes."
If the three observers of the E-4B over Washington were correct,
the "9/11 Commission's claim that the military had only 'one or two
minutes' notice of an approaching aircraft would become implausible."
In other words, how could the military have been surprised?

Gaffney includes photographs of the white airplane with four
jet engines as it circled at a low altitude over the White House
and shows, in comparative photographs, how different the E-4B
(230 feet long with a wingspan of 195 feet and four jet engines)
was in size and appearance from the Lockheed C-130H (100 feet
long with a wingspan of 130 feet and four propellers) that other
writers have described as following the approaching alleged Flight
77 and thereby providing "only 'one or two minutes' notice of an
approaching aircraft" as maintained by the 9/11 Commission. In
other words, Gaffney nails down the government story as a *lie and
a deception* about the length and detail of such notice.[22]

[AC]It could have alerted the Pentagon and/or ordered
ground-to-air missiles into action. Instead, it passed low over the
White House without causing any reaction and then simply flew
away.

[AC] The E4-B must have had the job of coordinating the
converging flights of the missile or fighter jet and the alleged Flight
77, both of which had to arrive at the outer wall of wedge 1 of the
Pentagon at the same instant. [AC]

## *Explosives inside the Pentagon*

Michael Meyer, a mechanical engineer with experience in high-speed impacts and how shaped charges are used to cut through materials, concluded that a Boeing 757 did not cause the damage at the Pentagon. He said to the members of the Scientific Panel Investigating Nine-Eleven that nearly all of the energy from impact of a complex structure like an aircraft into a discontinuous wall with windows, etc., would be dissipated in the initial impact and subsequent buckling of the aircraft. Meyer reminded his audience that we are led to believe that not only did the 757 penetrate the outer wall of ring E but continued on to penetrate five separate internal walls totaling 9 feet of reinforced concrete, the final breach of concrete being a nearly perfectly cut circular hole with no damage to the rest of the wall. In general, an explosive shaped charge is designed so that a focused line of energy is created. In a missile, the explosive shaped charge is designed to be circular in order to allow the payload behind the initial shaped charge to enter whatever has been penetrated.[23]

[AC] Because there was no aircraft wreckage on the pristine lawn in front of wedge 1, a missile must have created the initial opening in that reinforced wall. Also because a missile can explode only once, several internal bombs must have blown openings in subsequent walls, including the inner wall of Ring C. These six blast-resistant concrete walls had a total of nine feet of reinforced concrete. [AC]

Photo of exit hole #1 in inner wall
of Ring C of Pentagon on 9/11/2001

However, "three exit holes *or three blast holes*" are in the inner wall of Ring C, indicating that bombs must have blasted all three holes. And Tiradera observed that the exit hole is really a blast hole, evidenced by the abundant amount of Pentagon junk that went hurling through it.

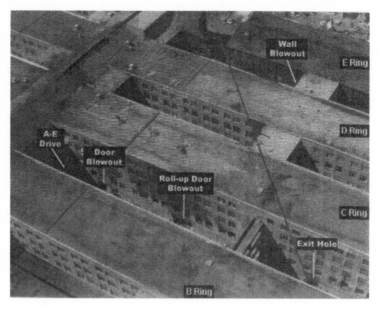

Photo of blast damage from initial impact
to three exit holes in Ring C

A photograph of the Pentagon roof shows a very-square-shaped opening, where the airliner allegedly hit wedge 1, a destruction that could only be rationally explained by use of detonated explosives.

"The upward envelope of the explosion—where the reinforcing rods are blown upwards—" provide dramatic evidence.[24]

Equally circumcised damage from wrapped around
and detonated blast charges within the Pentagon

This photograph of a column shows evidence of an attempt to bring down the column with explosives. Charges must have been wrapped around the column and then detonated remotely, producing equally circumcised damage around the column. "The upward envelope of the explosion—*where the reinforcing rods are blown upwards*—" provide dramatic evidence.[24]

Multiple explosions may have been an important indication of what happened. For example, "Tom Seibert, a network engineer at the Pentagon, mentioned, 'We heard what sounded like a missile, then we heard a loud boom . . . and five minutes later, *boom*." Lisa Burgess also heard multiple explosions. "I heard two loud booms—one large, one smaller, and the shockwave threw me against the wall."

Many people came right out and said, "I knew it was a bomb." Many of these people were combat veterans, who would know exactly what they were hearing and feeling and talking about. Lt. Col. Brian Birdwell was knocked down. When he stood up, he realized he was on fire. Peggy Mencl said, "It blew me ten feet."

Moreover, cordite has a fireworks-like smell, like gunpowder, but there is no cordite in an airliner. In contrast, jet fuel is not at all similar in smell to cordite; its powerful chemical odor is very nauseating. If both are present, the jet fuel smell easily overpowers the gun smoke smell.[25]

## No Initial Fire at Wedge 1 Impact Area

*April Gallop's Testimony:* Gallop, who was a U.S. Army executive administrative assistant with top security clearance, had just returned to work on the morning of September 11 after a two-month maternity leave. Having brought her baby son, Elisha, with her, she was planning to take him to the day-care center. She was told, however, that there was some paper work she needed to take care of immediately and she was allowed to take him with her to her work station, which was in the secure area, without getting him cleared.

Her work station was in the Army administrative offices in the E ring of Wedge 2. Her desk, she was later told,

was only 35 to 45 feet from the impact site. (According
to the government story, "Flight 77 entered Wedge 1 at
an angle, so that it quickly entered Wedge 2.) As soon as
she pushed the button to start her computer, she heard a
huge "boom" which "sounded like a bomb." The ceiling
caved in, covering her and her son with debris, which
caused several injuries to them.

After she regained consciousness and found her son, she
brought him outside, with help from others, by leaving through
the "so-called impact hole. She found no evidence that a plane had
hit the Pentagon."

> I had no jet fuel on me . . . I didn't see any airplane seats.
> I didn't see any plane parts . . . I didn't see anything that
> would give me any idea that there was a plane . . . I didn't
> see anything on the lawn . . . I didn't see luggage, metal
> pieces. and no bodies, arms, legs etc?

Gallop was certain that there had been no fire on the floor
because she had lost one of her shoes and did not feel anything hot
with her bare foot. She added, "I have not talked to anyone yet who
said that [they saw evidence of a plane."[26]

Another account of April Gallop's experience is as follows:

> She was getting ready to take her son to his day care
> when the impact occurred. I thought it was a bomb,"
> she recounted later. "I was buried in rubble and my first
> thought was for my son. I crawled around until I found
> his stroller. It was all crumpled up into a ball and I was

very afraid. But then I heard his voice and I managed to locate him. We crawled out through a hole in the side of the building. Outside they were treating survivors on the grassy lawn. But all the ambulances had left, so a man who was near the scene stepped up, put us in his private car, and drove us to the hospital. The images are burned into my brain.

While Gallop and her son were in the hospital, she received a series of visits from men in suits who never identified themselves or even said which agency they worked for. They told her "to take the [victim compensation fund] money and shut up. They also kept insisting that a plane hit the building. They repeated this over and over. But I was there and I never saw a plane or even debris from a plane. I figure the plane story is there to brainwash people."[27]

Adding support to Gallop's account of no all-consuming fire at the Pentagon are photographs taken at the scene that clearly show undamaged computers, chairs, tables and filing cabinets exposed at the location of the west wall's collapse. Yet, according to the official account, the fire was so intense that it completely melted the Boeing 757 aircraft, in an immense fireball, rising through the debris adjacent to this exposed office material.

An explosion destroyed the secretary of defense's hardened basement Counterterrorism Command Center. "'Did the attackers know where the [war game] exercises were being run and intentionally took it out?'

questioned Honegger. 'If so, they would have eliminated the one place frantic officials could call to ask details of the 'game' scenarios to try to find out what was real and what was just the games that morning."[28]

## Evidence for Bomb Explosions within the Pentagon

Others shared Gallop's belief that one or more bombs had gone off in the Pentagon. Army Lt. Colonel Victor Corea said, "We thought it was some kind of explosion. That somehow someone got in here and planted bombs because we saw these holes."

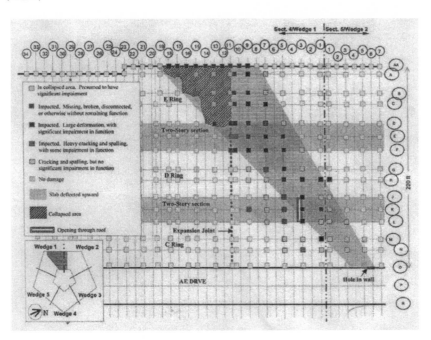

Diagram of damage from impact at
column 14 to exit hole in Ring C of the Pentagon

—

The conclusion that the explosions really were caused by bombs is supported by the fact that some witnesses said they smelled cordite, a substance that is used in bombs and has a very distinctive smell, completely different from that of jet fuel. One such witness was Gilah Goldsmith, an attorney at the Pentagon. After hearing an "incredible whomp noise," she saw a "huge black cloud of smoke," adding that it smelled like cordite or gun smoke. Don Perkal, the deputy general counsel for the secretary of defense, wrote:

> People shouted in the corridor outside [my office] that a bomb had gone off . . . Even before stepping outside I could smell the cordite. Then I knew explosives had been set off somewhere.

Dr. Griffin commented that the conclusion that bombs had gone off is also supported by reports of death and destruction in the B and A rings, which are farther inside the building than the C ring, beyond which the airliner reportedly did not go. A *Washington Post* story on 9/12 said, "The attack destroyed at least four of the five 'rings' that spiral around the massive office building . . . A 38-year-old Marine major . . . said he and dozens of his colleagues rushed to the area in the Pentagon that appeared most heavily damaged—the B ring between the 4th and 5th corridors."

Robert Andrews, the then acting assistant secretary of defense for special operations, said that he and his aide felt the effects of some violent event while they were in the counterterrorism center. They started rushing back to the other side of the Pentagon to join Rumsfeld. When they entered the corridor on the A ring, they found that they "had to walk over dead bodies."[29]

## *Winged Missile with Warhead Containing DU and Painted to Resemble American Airlines Plane*

Steve Riskus, a twenty-four-year-old computer worker, saw the craft pass over him and knock down a lamppost but not others nearby it within range of the plane's wingspan before plunging into the Pentagon. Using his digital camera, "[h]e immediately began snapping photographs from less than 200 yards away and later that day posted his photos on a newly acquired website." His photos showed a clean green lawn in front of the damaged wall. The hole in the wall, before the walls collapsed, was only between 15 and 20 feet wide and about 20 feet in height.

> Several photos of what appears to be part of a jet engine cannot be matched with the 757 engine, but more like that of a missile jet engine. *Isn't that special?*

The speed, maneuverability, and the high-pitched scream of the jet coupled with the smallness of the hole prompted many researchers to suggest that what struck the Pentagon was nothing less than some sort of winged missile painted to resemble an American Airlines plane.

Could this be why Defense Secretary Donald Rumsfeld *He wouldn't lie!* inadvertently mentioned a "missile" when describing the Pentagon attack to *Parade* magazine?

## NORAD Fighter Jet and Official Time of Attack upon the Pentagon

Honegger discovered that the "NORAD commander, Maj. Gen. Larry Arnold, had ordered one of his fighter jets to fly low over the west side of the Pentagon shortly the attack" at 9:32. Gen. Arnold reported that he had seen no evidence of a plane having struck the building.

> The likely reason the Pentagon has refused to lower the currently official time of Flight 77 impact from 9:37 to 9:32—the actual time of the first explosions there—is that they decided to pretend the blip represented by Arnold's surveillance jet approaching just before 9:37 was Flight 77," Honegger concluded. "As the Official Cover Story claims that the alleged 9:37 impact was the only Pentagon attack that morning, and by the time Arnold's surveillance jet arrived on the scene, the violent event had already happened, the Pentagon cannot acknowledge the earlier 9:32 attack time without revealing that there was an attack on the building prior to impact.

When Gallop touched her computer and a bomb exploded at 9:32, it left "undamaged computers, chairs, tables, and filing cabinets exposed at the location of the west wall's collapse" while destroying the area where Gallop worked. Her watch stopped at 9:32. However, the bomb did not cause a significant fire as evidenced by Gallop being able to go through the opening in the collapsed wall without noticing warmth on her bare foot. [30]

[AC] As a hypothesis, it is possible that an AGM-type missile reached the Pentagon west wall at 9:32, simultaneously with the alleged AA airliner, which skipped over the building, and created the opening in the west wall through which Gallop escaped over a floor which was at ambient temperature and then destroyed Gallop's office, leaving her and her baby son buried in debris. The missile, probably with assistance from bombs to destroy other walls, penetrated as far as the inner wall of ring C. Five minutes later, Gen. Arnold's surveillance fighter jet passed overhead without noticing the opening through which Gallop left the Pentagon. This missile fire produced much black smoke and a very hot red flame which lasted so briefly that it did not heat the floor over which Gallop walked to reach the impact opening. Two additional holes are visible in the inner wall of ring C. They suggest the use of additional bombs. [AC]

## Probable Identification of the Winged Missile

[AC] When Gallop and her son emerged onto a green lawn, having no plane parts or other evidence of an attacking plane, it was late enough after the 9:32 explosion that all of the ambulances had left. The conspicuous fire, which was noticed by numerous witnesses, must have occurred after Gallop and her infant son emerged from the opening in the E ring or it might have been produced by the burning construction trailer, described hereafter, which conspicuously created much black smoke. Because Gallop did not comment upon this burning trailer, which was parked close to the front of the impact hole,

—

279

it is likely that it burst into flame when the secondary explosion occurred later. [AC]

The Pentagon collapsed and burned shortly after the fire and rescue units pulled back! "Outside the Pentagon, witnesses noted, at 10:10, the mood abruptly changed when [a] *thunder-clapping sound echoed over the grounds*. Firefighter Russell Dodge noticed that there were two vehicles burning as well as a construction trailer that was the main producer of smoke on the outside of the building. The fire units concentrated on the trailer that was producing some severe fires and subsequent mini-explosions.

> If the trailer hadn't been on fire and producing all the thick black smoke, then there would only have been gray smoke coming from the crash site. Was the trailer loaded with fuel and/or chemicals that burn with black smoke, ignited at the time of the attack? This would give the illusion of an aircraft crash with its characteristic black smoke. From a distance, this "smoke" appeared to be coming from the Pentagon, but up close, the fraud was quite obvious.[31]

The multiple warhead penetrator version of the CALCM, called the AGM-86D, is the most advanced version of such a cruise missile. It "is the state of the art in killing."It has a 2,000 pound warhead that can shred through reinforced concrete with a hollow charge that blasts an entry hole and then broaches inside the depleted-uranium charge, which, in turn, explodes inside the target.

Like the navy's BQM/SSM, the BGM-34A was piloted by an operator watching a TV image transmitted from the drone's nose.

In tests during 1971/72, the BGM-34As successfully launched AGM-65 Maverick air-to-surface missiles and electro-optically guided glide bombs against simulated SAM sites.

The AGM-86D CALCM Block II is equipped with a new Lockheed Martin 540 kg (1,200 lb) AUP (Advanced Unitary Penetrator) penetrating warhead for use against deeply buried and/or hardened targets.

This missile is about 21 feet in length, has a wingspan of 12 feet, a diameter of 24.5 inches, and flies at high subsonic speed. Its warheads are a 2,000-pound class and a 1,300-pound class. It also has a conventional airplane tail.[32]

USAF AGM-86 "Cruise missile"in flight

### Blast Injuries to Pentagon Personnel

Captain Stephen S. Frost, Medical Corps, reported, "We saw many blast injuries." He commented that there is a big difference between blast and burn injuries. A fuel-air fire produces a fireball and fire that inflict thermal injuries on its victims. Blast waves cause injury because of rapid external loading on its victims' bodies and organs. Concussive effects of such shockwaves on victims may result in:

1. Injury to lung—cause of greatest morbidity and mortality. Pulmonary injuries— like pneumothorax and hemothorax;
2. Gastrointestinal blast injuries.
3. Secondary blast injury (propelled objects striking the victim.
4. Tertiary blast injury: (victim being propelled against structure by the blast wave or blast winds).
5. Burns.
6. Inhalational or toxic exposure.
7. Essentially all severely injured patients have TM perforations. Up to 30% of victims may have permanent hearing loss.

It appears consistently throughout that there was a blast, "shockwave," "bomb went off," "bright flash," getting thrown about, confusion, burns, multiple explosions, and smells of cordite. All proof that there were multiple high explosive devices planted and detonated within the Pentagon.[33]

## Inadequate Fire Suppression at Pentagon

There was an inferno at the point of impact on the Pentagon, obviously threatening the lives of those still in the building and also threatening to spread. Putting the fire out quickly was imperative. Foam is routinely used to extinguish fuel fires because it floats on the surface of fuel and cuts off its supply of oxygen. It should have been used immediately (assuming there had been an airplane crash and not solely an internal bomb and a missile). If water is used, the fuel floats on top of the water and continues to burn. Aviation fire-and-rescue personnel have only about two minutes to rescue people.

> So the top commanders of each of the services were on site. Each of the services uses aviators, each of the commanders HAD to know water does not extinguish aviation fuel fires, yet all of them let the farce continue.

Had the fire been put out quickly with foam, according to one theory, Rumsfeld would have lost valuable public relations mileage. The "stubborn" fire at the Pentagon was just one facet of a campaign designed to whip the American public and military into a bloodlust for a war on Islam. From a propaganda viewpoint, the higher the casualty list, the better.

Because the Arlington County Fire Department had an agreement with the Pentagon to handle fire emergencies (probably minor fires such as exploding coffee pots, not acts of war), the Arlington County police and fire departments arrived and started to ring the area and pump water on the blaze. The fire continued to spread and soon ignited the upper floors and roof. The floors collapsed.

However, three members of a Washington Hospital Center MedStar Transport helicopter team arrived among the very first at the scene, but they were told that another suicide plane was on the way, and they should leave. The MedStar people refused to leave and promptly helped eight victims to get out and took another to the hospital. They were prevented from returning. Area hospitals were surprised when few cases (totaling eighty) appeared for treatment. Flames were still erupting almost sixty hours after impact.[34]

Three site evacuations of the Pentagon were ordered on September 11, 2001. The first was at 0955 hours because of structural concerns. The second evacuation at 1015 hours was called by Chief Schwartz, and the "all clear" as given at 1038 hours, long after the plane crash in Pennsylvania had been reported. The third evacuation was at about 1400 hours on September 11.

Tiradera wondered why the firefighters were ordered to pull back and wait while people were being burned to death. He thought there was really no excuse for the inaction except that it was perpetrated for the following reasons:

- To make the situation look worse than it really was, curb the firefighting efforts, and sadly to increase the casualty count
- To arrange for setting the stage for another round of explosives—this happened at 10:10 a.m.
- To remove fire and rescue personnel so that they could not see agents planting debris and other evidence

Shortly after all fire and rescue units had been pulled back, about forty minutes after the attack, a portion of the Pentagon roof collapsed and burned. Witnesses who were outside the Pentagon noticed at 10:10 that a thunder-clapping sound echoed over the grounds. Tiradera commented that a collapse does not cause a "thunder-clapping sound," but high explosives do. Photos showed that the roof of the Pentagon was on fire and producing a grayish white smoke, but the office of the three floors just under the collapsing roof was unscathed.

Tiradera also wondered why the firefighters were spraying water onto the Pentagon because they surely knew that you do not fight fuel fires with water. Yet the water worked! He further noted that the fire, what little there was, came from the second-floor windows and wondered what had happened to all that fuel that was supposed to be spilled on the ground floor.[35]

## Navy Command Center (NCC)

Located in the first floor of the Pentagon, the Navy Command Center was a "powerhouse of information gathering, command control, and systems for monitoring 'all warfare mission areas.'" Indeed, the NCC was a very formidable command and control facility, with some overlapping capacities as compared to NORAD.

The strongest blast happened at 9:43 a.m. and was isolated at the NCC. Just above the location of the NCC, a "missing or broken" section of the ceiling with second floor beam damage was noted. This damage could only have been done by a powerful explosion deep inside D ring. This explosion was so strong that it destroyed columns and ceiling beams and blew through the slab of the second floor. The only U.S. Navy Command Center survivor, Lieutenant Kevin Shaeffer, said, "[At exactly 0943], the entire command center exploded in a gigantic orange fireball, and I felt myself being slammed to the deck by a massive and thunderous shockwave. It felt to me as if the blast started at the outer wall, blowing me forward toward Commander Dunn's desk. I never lost consciousness, and though the entire space was pitch-black, I sensed I was on fire."

Lt. Shaeffer claimed, "Had the Command Center not been destroyed, it surely would have been able to provide the highest levels of our navy leadership with updates as to exactly what was occurring."[36]

[AC] So if the NCC was not involved with the murderous group who had authorized access to the Pentagon and were planning the September 11, 2001, attacks on America, this group would have wanted to erase any evidence and silence any witnesses who had privy knowledge of what happened that day, thereby making the NCC a prime target. [AC]

## *Radiation at the Pentagon*

The "strongest blast" at the Navy Command Center occurred eleven minutes after the initial blast. High levels of radiation were detected near the Pentagon. A doctor with experience in radiation had detected elevated levels of radiation up to seven miles from the Pentagon shortly after the Pentagon attack, but his Geiger counter was able to detect only seven percent of the beta radiation and even less of the [very short-lived] alpha [radiation], being primarily a gamma ray detector, so that the actual radiation was undoubtedly significantly higher.

Dr. Sherman, a radiation expert, "alerted emergency responders to the risk from radiation at the Pentagon crash site. She also notified the NIRS, the Environmental Protection Agency (EPA), and the FBI. Radiation experts later *confirmed high radiation levels at the Pentagon crash site* possibly from the presence from (sic) depleted uranium or other unknown causes."

Boeing denied the use of depleted uranium in a 757 airliner, and the Pentagon was not known for having stored depleted uranium(DU) weapons. Tiradera concluded,"*The DU must have come from an outside source.*"

Another radiation expert, Major Rokke, who once headed the military's depleted uranium project, believed that the Pentagon was hit by a missile, not by a commercial jetliner. He insisted that high radiation readings after the strike reinforced the evidence that DU may have been used. Almost immediately after being notified, dirt and gravel were put over the entire Pentagon lawn near wedge 1, illustrated by a photograph of a dump truck laying dirt upon a layer of gravel in front of the damaged wedge 1. One week after 9/11, soil readings taken in a residential neighborhood in Leesburg, Virginia, 33 miles northwest of the Pentagon, were 75-83 cpm. Normal outdoor readings are between 12 and 20 cpm.[37]

Dirt being dumped onto the Pentagon lawn,
with impact damage being visible in background

[AC]It should be understood that if a wind blew over the Pentagon from the southeast, irradiated dust could have been blown toward the northwest and then fallen onto the Leesburg area, in this author's opinion. The Leesburg soil readings thereby confirmed the radiation readings closer to the Pentagon.[AC]

## *Lack of Alarms at the Pentagon on 9/11*

Steve Vogel pointed out that after people at the Pentagon learned about the New York attacks, they realized that "if there were more attacks, the Pentagon was an obvious target, but no steps were taken to alert Pentagon employees or evacuate the building."

Don Perkal, who testified about smelling cordite, said that even after people started shouting that a bomb had gone off, "[n]o alarms sounded." April Gallop also commented that there were "no alerts, no warnings, no alarms." She further observed that this was strange because prior to 9/11 there had been random "drill exercises utilizing an alarm for us to evacuate the building," which were so frequent that she became disgusted. Yet "on that particular day, no alarm." She added that it was especially odd, "Considering the fact of what had already taken place at the World Trade Center."[38]

Conclusions by Peter Tiradera (a partial list) from pages 325-328 of his book are as follows:

- The attacks on the Pentagon, as well as the WTC, were designed and planned by a group of top-level government insiders, not a hodge-podge band of Arabs. The neo-conservatives of the notorious PNAC had the *motive and means*, to carry out the attacks.

- The Navy Command Center was the target. More than likely they were monitoring the events that were happening that day. Therefore, if insiders were to attack the WTC then they would need to eliminate this command center as well.

- The government had rehearsed the events of 9/11 extensively as well as, setting into motion a series of *war games* that would bungle the nations [sic]air responses.

- Many agencies like the Secret Service, FBI, and fire rescue units were pre-positioned for a rapid response to the Pentagon attack.

- Dick Cheney assembled a shadow government in the PEOC on the morning of 9/11, and ran his own secret "command and control" operation.

- P-56 prohibited area was intentionally left unguarded on 9/11.

- Secretary of Defense Donald Rumsfeld changed the DoD directive that dealt with hijacked aircraft only months prior to the attacks. His changes resulted in the deliberate disabling of the air defense responses on 9/11.

- Further obstruction occurred at Andrews and Langley to delay their already delayed responses.

- Several first-timers were put in position of crucial authority, Sliney, Jellinek, Leidig, and others.

- The hijackers were CIA-sponsored assets that were just a "smoke screen" for the real events. They were patsies that the perpetrators would blame the 9/11 events on. Some of these supposed hijackers are still alive.

- The hijackers and their sponsors were put "off limits" to investigation by the Bush administration.

- The FAA grounding was orchestrated by the Cheney *shadow government* as to coincide with the attack on the Pentagon.

- The Pentagon explosions had all the characteristics of a "controlled demolition" operation. This could have only been done by insiders who had access to the secure facility. It would have taken weeks for setting up the "charges."

- Also at the probably *fake* highway construction area, (4) lampposts were cut at the bases to allow an unobstructed path.

- A remote controlled jet or drone similar to an MQM-107 or Gulfstream was painted with an AA color scheme, and filled with explosives, including a MWS "broach charge." This was the aircraft guided by the EC-130 toward the Pentagon.

- The drone attack had all the hallmarks of high explosives: brilliant white fireball (plasma), shockwave, blast injuries, multiple explosions, and evidence of blast damage.

- High levels of radiation were detected about the Pentagon. The only explanation was that the attacking object contained depleted uranium (i.e. MWS).

- The autopsy report with DNA testing was a fraud. There was not one hijacker on the official report. Nor were the government's results ever challenged.

- Massive profits were made on airline 'put' options—this was traced to *the top of the CIA*—Director 'Buzzy Krongard.'

- "The events would lead to two wars, seizure of strategic oil reserves, massive DoD profits, and essentially *everything the pro-Israeli PNAC neocons wanted, and more . . .*"[39]

[AC] Other references have involved the CIA with illegal drugs and cooperation with Mossad for installing explosives at the

World Trade Center. Such activity would certainly have enabled CIA top personnel to know what was planned to happen, so that money making on airline "put" options would have been very easy. [AC]

### Army's Financial Management Branch Personnel Killed in Pentagon Attack

[AC] This question also arises, based on Transportation Secretary Norman Mineta's testimony, why was the Pentagon not evacuated, considering that orders still stood as the airliner came within ten miles of the Pentagon? Specifically, why were 125 military and civilian workers in the west wing of the Pentagon allowed to be killed and why the specific personnel, mostly on the first floor?

[AC] One suggested answer puts together two facts: First, the day before September 11, Secretary of Defense Rumsfeld stated at a press conference that the Pentagon was missing $2.3 trillion dollars. Second, one of the most damaged areas was the army's financial management/audit area. This combination of facts led Barbara Honegger to ask, "Were the auditors who could 'follow the money' and the computers whose data could help them do it intentionally targeted?"

According to Honegger, this question was affirmatively answered by Michael Nielsen, civilian auditor for the army, who added that the records in the Operations Office of the Army's Financial Management Branch were, in fact, destroyed.[40]

[AC] The murderous group which attacked Americans on September 11 thereby killed two birds with one stone, that is, both the Navy Command Center and the Operations Office of the

Army's Financial Management Branch were destroyed. Results? No navy snooping on the group and no checking up on those missing trillions, much to the benefit of neocon Dov Zakheim. [AC}

Military affairs journalist Barbara Honegger pointed out that "if bombs were planted inside both the Pentagon and the WTC buildings, it would have been difficult—if not impossible—for foreign terrorists to have the opportunity to plant and detonate such bombs."

She also noted that "because the true *modus operandi* of the WTC and Pentagon attacks are so similar, a single group of US/domestic conspirators almost certainly planned both the WTC and Pentagon attacks and controlled both the approaching planes and inside-the-building explosions in real time on 9/11 and thus, neither attack could have been executed by al Qaeda."[41]

[AC] It appears that no other group but the top-level executives of the Defense Policy Board had the motivation, the concern, the knowledge, and the power to plan those attacks and perpetrate them upon both the WTC and the Pentagon and to control both the approaching planes and the inside-the-building explosions in real time on September 11. Those executives should be the primary objective of an unshackled federal grand jury about the 9/11 events. [AC]

# Chapter 12 Notes

1. The 9/11 Commission Report. Final Report of the National Commission on Terrorist Attacks Upon the United States: 9. Herorism and Horror, 314.

2. Marrs, Jim. *The Terror Conspiracy: Deception, 9/11 and the Loss of Liberty.* 2006. New York, NY 10003. The Disinformation Company Ltd., 163 Third Avenue, Suite 108, 30, 31.

3. Tiradera, Peter. *9-11: Coup Against America!: The Pentagon Analysis.* 2006. North Charleston, SC. BookSurge LLC, 45, 46.

4. Ibid., 135-146, 149.

5. Ibid., 69.

6. Ibid., 65-68.

7. Gaffney, Mark H. *The 9/11 Mystery Plane and the Vanishing of America.* Berkeley, California. 2007. University of California Press, 23.

8. Griffin, David Ray. *The New Pearl Harbor: Disturbing Questions about the Bush Administration and 9/11.* 2005. Northampton, Massachusetts. Olive Branch Press, 25-28.

9. Griffin, David Ray. *The New Pearl Harbor Revisited: 9/11, the Cover-up, and the Expose.* 2008. Northampton, Massachusetts 01060. Olive Branch Press, 60-62.

10. Eastman, Dick. "The Highest Treason Substantiated, Part 1." 6-25-9. Http://www.rense.com/general86/hight1.htm, 1-13.

11. Tarpley, Webster Griffin. *9/11 Synthetic Terror Made in USA.* 2005-2007. Joshua Tree, California 92252. Progressive Press, PO Box 126, 250-252.

12. Eastman, Dick. "The Highest Treason Substantiated, Part 2." 6-25-9. Http://www.rense.com/general86/hight2.htm, 1-7.

13. Griffin 2007, 30-32.

—

14. Ibid., 28, 29.

15. Tiradera, 188, 189.

16. Griffin, David Ray. 2008, 95, 96.

17. Marrs, 19.

18. Firmage, Joseph P. "Intersecting Facts and Theories on 9/11." *Journal of 9/11 Studies*. August 2006/Volume 2. No. 29. "Disappearance of Cheney for weeks. http://firmage.org. 2006-08-08, updated 2006-09-13.

19. Griffin, David Ray and Peter Dale Scott, Editors. *9/11 and America Empire: Intellectuals Speak Out*. 2006. Northampton, Massachusetts 01060. Olive Branch Press, 46 Crosby Street, 104, 105.

20. Gaffney, 37-39.

21. Ibid., 46-51.

22. Ibid., 72.

23. Meyer, Michael. "A Boeing 757 did not hit the Pentagon." *Scholars for 9/11 Truth*. http://www.scholarsfor911truth.org/ArticlesMeyer3March2006.html. 3/10/06.

24. Tiradera, 218.

25. Tiradera, 205-207.

26. Griffin 2008, 100-103.

27. Tarpley, 254, 255.

28. Marrs, 32.

29. Griffin, 102, 103.

30. Marrs, 34-36.

31. Tiradera, 212, 213.

32. Ibid., 307, 307, A43.

33. Ibid., 207, 208.

34. Valentine, Carol A. "Pentagon RESCUE? Open, Bloody, Questions . . ." (Parts I through IV of a five-part article.), 9-16. http://www.public-action.com/rescue.html.

35. Tiradera, 209-213.

36. Ibid., 220-222.

37. Ibid., 287-289.

38. Griffin 2008, 104, 105.

39. Tiradera, 325-328.

40. Griffin 2008, 104, 105.

41. Marrs, 70.

# PART V
## Disruption of Aircraft Attacks as Planned upon the Pentagon and Washington, D.C.

# CHAPTER 13

## United Airlines Flight 93 and its Needless Shootdown over Indian Lake, Pennnsylvania

### *Government Story for United Airlines Flight 93*

According to the government story, UA Flight 93 was the one airliner out of the four allegedly hijacked planes that should not have been shot down because the passengers were getting control of it, whereas the other three were being controlled by hijackers and were not shot down.

The passengers in Flight 93 included a professional pilot and a flight controller. United Airlines Flight 93 left Newark forty-one minutes late, at 8:42 a.m. Then at 9:27, Tom Burnett, one of the passengers, called his wife to tell her that the plane had been hijacked and for her to call the FBI. She did so, and the FBI was listening in. Then ground flight controllers heard sounds of screaming and scuffling. At 9:34, Tom Burnett again called his wife who told him about the WTC attacks so that he realized that Flight 93 was also on a "suicide mission."

A *Washington Post* story said that "passenger Jeremy Glick used a cell phone to tell his wife, Lyzbeth, . . . that the Boeing 757's cockpit had been taken over by three Middle Eastern-looking men wielding knives and a red box they claimed was a bomb. The terrorists, wearing red headbands, had ordered the pilots, flight attendants, and passengers to the rear of the plane. Glick said he and others aboard the plane had decided to rush the cockpit and try to subdue the terrorists."

A *Pittsburgh Post-Gazette* story about passenger Marion Britton said that she had called an old friend, Fred Fiumano, and told him that the plane had been hijacked, the throats of two people had been cut, and the plane had made a U-turn.

A flight attendant, Sandra Bradshaw, also made a cell phone call at about 9:30 a.m. and told her husband that the plane had been hijacked by three men with knives. One of them, she said, had an "an Islamic look."

Another passenger, Todd Beamer, began a long phone conversation with a Verizon representative, with the FBI listening in, as he described the situation. At 9:54, Tom Burnett called his wife again and said that three of them were planning to gain control of the plane over a rural area. Then at 9:58, Todd Beamer ended his phone call by saying that they planned "to jump" the hijacker in the back of the plane and asked, "Are you ready, guys? Let's roll."

Griffin concluded that, given the evidence that the passengers were successfully wresting control of the plane away from the hijackers, it seemed reasonable that this was the one plane that was likely to be landed safely, but that would also mean that there might be live hijackers to be interrogated. "Thus interpreted, the evidence about Flight 93 provides further reason to conclude the failure to shoot down the previous three flights was not due to incompetence. This evidence suggests that when the authorities wanted a flight shot down, they were not hindered by lack of either competence or coordination."[1]

[Author's Comment—AC]Instead of live hijackers to be interrogated, there would have been no hijackers to be seen; that would have blown the whole government story wide open.[AC]

## *Authenticity of Cell Phone Calls*

[AC]However, cell phone calls from 33,000 feet to the ground from a large airliner were not possible in September 2001. Cell phone calls from at least Flights 77 and 93 or any other airliner at such an altitude could not have been done for technological reasons.[AC]

This statement was proved by the research of Canadian mathematician and scientist A. K. Dewdney, who was a professor emeritus of computer science and adjunct professor of biology at the University of Western Ontario, as well as a professor of computer science at the University of Waterloo. He scientifically tested the US government's claim that imperiled passengers made such cell phone calls aboard the ill-fated flights of September 11, 2001. He made these tests by flying single-engine and two-engine aircraft at low altitudes in Canadian skies, which have a technological base that is identical to its US counterpart.

During these flights, Mr. Dewdney made repeated attempts to place successful cell phone calls at various positions and altitudes using several cell phones of varying brands and via multiple operating networks. These cell phones were on the market in 2001. Each call attempt was carefully monitored and documented as to the quality of transmission, if any call was achieved, and the success or failure thereof.

Mr. Dewdney "found that in a single-engine plane, successful calls could be counted on only under 2,000 feet. Above that altitude, they became increasingly unlikely." At 20,000 feet, Dewdney concluded, "the chance of a typical cell phone call making it to ground and engaging a cell site there is less than one in a hundred . . . [T]he probability that two callers will succeed is less than one in ten thousand." The probability that nine successful calls would be successful at that altitude, he concluded, would be "infinitesimal." And yet there had allegedly been, according to one count, nine cell phone calls from Flight 93 while it was above 30,000 feet."

In later experiments, Dewdney used a twin-engine plane, which had greater mass and provided greater insulation from electronic signals than a single-engine plane. He found that the "success rate decayed to 0 percent at 7,000 feet." Because large passenger jets have much greater mass and provide far more insulation, one loses contact during takeoff, frequently before the plane reaches an altitude of 1,000 feet. Dewdney concluded that numerous successful cell phone calls from airlines flying above 30,000 feet would have been "flat out impossible."

He added that any airliner, flying at its normal speed of about 500 miles per hour and at 2,000 feet or below, would encounter the "handoff problem." This term means that an aircraft traveling at this speed would not be over a first cell site long enough to complete the electronic "handshake" (requiring several seconds) before reaching the next cell site when the call has to be handed off from the first cell site to the next one (also requiring a few seconds). The result would have to have been at best, a series of broken transmissions ending, sooner or later, in failure.[2]

In other words, cell phone calls were increasingly impossible in 2001 at altitudes above 2,000 feet as speeds increased and were also impossible at altitudes below 2,000 feet when flying at high speed, such as 500 mph. Commercial airliners flew at high speeds shortly after take-off.

At least three separate official reports, including one by the FBI, have recently confirmed Mr. Dewdney's findings. "The evidence presented at the 2006 trial of the so-called 'twentieth hijacker' by the FBI included a report on phone calls from all four 9-11 flights." As to American Flight 77, the FBI believed that only one call came to Barbara Olson, and it was an "unconnected call," which lasted "0 seconds." Ted Olson consequently did not receive a single call from his wife using either a cell phone or an onboard phone, according to the FBI. But Ted Olson, her solicitor general husband, told the FBI that his wife had called him twice via her cell phone from Flight 77 before it allegedly crashed into the Pentagon. If that statement was false, Olson lied or he was duped by means of voice morphing technology by someone pretending to be his wife.

This was an amazing situation. The FBI is part of the Department of Justice (DOJ), and yet its report undermined the well-publicized claim of the DOJ's former solicitor general that he received two calls from his wife on 9/11. However, the number of self-contradictory reports by Ted Olson about phone calls from his wife justify the rejection of all of his stories and acceptance of the possibility that he lied to the FBI.[3]

Voice morphing technology could nevertheless explain the alleged cell phone calls from passengers and attendants to those persons on the ground who sincerely believed that they knew the callers by the sounds of their voices. For example, by taking just a ten-minute digital recording of someone's voice, voice morphing experts can "clone speech patterns and develop an accurate facsimile, causing people to appear to have said something that they would never otherwise have said."[4]

[AC] Someone (necessarily FBI agents) who were faking Barbara Olson's voice as well as the voices of Tom Burnett and Todd Beamer would have been part of the murderous conspiracy. If voice morphing had been used, listeners and one or more FBI agents, who were allegedly listening to the passenger conversations, could be exonerated. Because it had to be FBI or other government agents who were faking voices, the cell phone part of the Flight 93 story is false, thereby proving that the US government officially lied to the American people.

[AC] Barbara Olson's cell phone calls are of critical importance because these two calls from her are the sole basis for believing that Flight 77 (which had presumably reached Kentucky, near the Lawrence County Airport) had turned around toward Washington, heading for the Pentagon. If it had not turned around, the airliner could have landed at Groom Lake inside Nellis AFB, where it could have discharged its passengers for sequestering in a modern concentration camp inside the United States, as described in Chapter 3, provided that passengers were really aboard and provided that Flight 77 had actually taken off from Dulles Airport.

[AC]But as also described in that chapter, AA Flight 77 never took off from Dulles Airport in Virginia on September 11, 2001. Its passengers were brought to Newark Airport in New Jersey where they walked across the tarmac to board Flight 93 that landed in the Cleveland Hopkins International Airport in Ohio.

[AC]Without a single Muslim name being listed on any of the four flight manifestos and without a single cell phone call at flight altitudes from any of the four airliners being possible, there is no reason to blame anyone in Afghanistan or Iraq for the 9/11 crimes. There was no terrorism by Muslims involving the WTC or the Pentagon. The actual terrorists were powerful people in the U.S. government plus outsiders who were employed by these officials and probably agents of a certain foreign government. The U.S. attacks on Iraq and Afghanistan were consequently not justified and were in themselves criminal acts of terror against innocent people. The recently exposed torturing of men in Iraq and Afghanistan was accordingly unjustified, barbaric, and a reason for Americans to feel ashamed. Such torturing is typical Israeli behavior toward prisoners but is totally out of character for Christians. [AC]

## Alleged Crash of United Airlines Flight 93 at Shanksville, Pennsylvania

The flight path of Flight 93, from Cleveland to Washington, D.C., is a straight line that goes through Indian Lake and New Baltimore in Pennsylvania. Indian Lake is one to two miles northeast of Shanksville, and New Baltimore is southeast of Indian Lake. Shortly after 9:56 a.m. on September 11, fighter jets were finally given orders to intercept and shoot down any airplanes under the control of hijackers. Vice President Cheney authorized this shoot down three times.

Flight 93 was hit by a missile over Indian Lake, causing wreckage to come down over this body of water, and finally crashed near New Baltimore at 10:03 a.m. Debris, including seat pieces, melted plastic, checks, and a rib bone, began falling into Indian Lake before a mushroom cloud appeared at Shanksville. Flaming debris was seen falling onto New Baltimore, including in-flight magazines, a pilot's manual, and black webbing used for insulation along the belly of a jetliner.[5]

The government story concluded with Flight 93 crashing into the soft dirt of a filled-in strip mine near Shanksville, Pennsylvania. The 255,000-pound Boeing 757 airliner, 150 feet long and having a wing span of 124 feet, allegedly created a crater, an explosion, and a mushroom cloud rising 200 feet into the air. Everyone in the Shanksville area came to see the crater, which was eight to ten feet in diameter and about the same depth, but there was nothing there.

Pilots from Delta and Continental, when interviewed, said, "If you've ever seen a crash site, you'd never forget it . . . It's a rag and bone shop. It's foul, it's gross, and it's all over the place." In contrast, there was no tail sticking out of the ground, no large pieces of metal scattered everywhere, and no human remains at the crater. The coroner found nothing and went home.[6]

Apparently as a diversion, the controlling murderers had sent another plane to shoot a missile into the old strip mine near Shanksville at 10:06 a.m., creating not only the big mushroom cloud but also a big seismic event, according to several seismologists. It attracted the local people, thereby keeping them away from Indian Lake and New Baltimore, a town of less than 200 people.

Susan McElwain, a witness, saw a white object rocketing over her head without a sound and "said it was so close that when it passed over her van, she actually ducked because she thought it was going to hit her." It had no wings and was probably a Tomahawk or a cruise missile. Within seconds, the massive explosion and the mushroom cloud occurred.

A small white jet also flew at a low altitude over Shanksville. It was identified as an executive jet, which belonged to NetJet, a company under the umbrella of Berkshire Hathaway, owned by Warren Buffett, supposedly the second richest man in the world. The executive jet was tracking Flight 93 as it went down. Buffett was hosting a golf charity event during the morning of September 11 at Offutt Air Force Base. That was where Air Force One landed with President Bush after he left that Florida classroom that morning.[7]

The FBI, having cordoned off a huge area to the southeast of Indian Lake and extending to New Baltimore with the help of state police, began to carry away many bags of evidence from Indian Lake, the six-to-eight-mile area between Indian Lake and New Baltimore, and New Baltimore itself.[8]

## *Landing of United Airlines Flight 93 in Cleveland Hopkins International Airport in Ohio and Debarkation of Its Passengers*

As described in Chapter 3, Flights 93 and 175 were reported as having landed in the Cleveland airport and having been parked at opposite ends of the airport, whereupon the passengers were interrogated thoroughly.

## *Evaluation of the Government Story about UA 93*

Victor Thorn and Lisa Guliani cited different possibilities. They pointed out that the government's story, that Flight 93 crashed after the cell phone calls from passengers and the "Let's roll" from Todd Beamer, was essentially a conspiracy theory. "The government has stated that Flight 93 vaporized inside a crater at an abandoned strip mine in Shanksville," thereby explaining why there was no physical wreckage surrounding the ten-foot diameter crater. It's been calculated that a jetliner would have to be flying at Mach 4 (3,044 mph) for its aluminum and steel to be vaporized—an impossible speed for an airliner.

Thorn and Guliani quite reasonably concluded that the Flight 93 calls were a total ruse. As previously described, the technology for calls by passengers from 33,000 feet in the air was not even available in 2001. Qualcomm developed this new technology and first tested it in July 2004, using satellites instead of cell sites on the ground so that the "handoff problem" was avoided.

The plane believed to be Flight 93, according to the government story, crashed at 10:03. Three minutes later, at 10:06, the crater was made in Shanksville, creating a seismic event that "was recorded at two earthquake monitoring stations located in Millersville, Pa., and Standing Stone, Pa." and "an explosion and a 200 foot mushroom cloud rising up into the sky." The explosion and cloud attracted the local people and kept them away from Indian Lake and New Baltimore. "Then on September 12, the day after 9-11, crash debris started washing up on shore at Indian Lake Marina and people said they found seat pieces, melted plastic, checks and also a rib bone."[9]

Griffin noted that the White House was not evacuated until seven minutes after the Pentagon was struck at 9:32 a.m. even though Vice President Cheney and National Security Advisor Rice were taken to the White House's underground bunker by the Secret Service at about 9:03. He accordingly raised still another disturbing question: "Was there a plan to have deaths in the White House or the U.S. Capitol Building as well as the Pentagon and the World Trade Center?"[10]

# Chapter 13 Notes

1. Griffin, David Ray. *The New Pearl Harbor: Disturbing Questions about the Bush Administration and 9/11*. 2005. Olive Branch Press, 46 Crosby Street, Northampton, Massachusetts 01060, 49, 50, 53.

2. Griffin, David Ray. *The New Pearl Harbor Revisited: 9/11, The Cover-up, and the Expose*. 2008. Olive Branch Press, 46 Crosby Street, Northampton, Massachusetts 01060, 112-114.

3. Staff of *American Free Press*, "Studies Deny 9-11 Tall Tale."645 Pennsylvania Ave., SE, Suite 100, Washington, D.C. 20003, April 21, 2008, 6.

4. Griffin 2008, 114, 115.

5. Thorn, Victor and Lisa Guliani. *Phantom Flight 93: And Other Astounding September 11 Mysteries Explored*. 2007. American Free Press, 645 Pennsylvania Avenue SE, Suite 100, Washington, D.C. 20003, 64-67.

6. Ibid., 44, 48-50, 68, 69.

7. Ibid., 57, 58, 72, 73.

8. Ibid., 67-69.

9. Ibid., 64, 65.

10. Griffin 2005, 54, 55.

# CHAPTER 14

## The Six-Blunder Conspiracy Theory of Thorn and Guliani

### *The First Blunder*

Victor Thorn and Lisa Guliani (no relation to the former mayor of New York City) proposed that "the global-government organized crime syndicate who planned 9-11" made six blunders that were caused by the delayed take-off of Flight 93. Flight 11 was supposed to have taken off from Boston at 8:01 a.m., and Flight 77 was supposed to have taken off almost simultaneously at 7:59 a.m. from Dulles International Airport but was eleven minutes late. Flight 93 was supposed to have taken off at 8:01 a.m. from Newark International Airport but was delayed till 8:42. Failing to plan for this delay was the crime syndicate's *first blunder*.[1]

[Author's Comment—AC] A seventh blunder was vital; it was failing to remember that the airlines routinely change scheduling flights when the passenger load is so low that a flight will be a

311

business loss. The four transcontinental flights had an average load of 27.5 per cent. That is why Flight 11 did not take off from Boston Airport, why the Flight 11 passengers were loaded aboard Flight 175, why Flight 77 did not take off from Dulles Airport, and why the Flight 77 passengers were flown by a charter jet from Dulles Airport to Newark Airport where Flight 93 was waiting for them on the tarmac. [AC]

According to researcher Dave McGowan, the airplanes should have struck their targets in the Washington, D.C. Area (Flight 77 hitting the Pentagon and Flight 93 hitting the White House or the Capitol Building) before the Twin Towers were hit in Manhattan by Flights 11 and 175. There would naturally have been chaos and pandemonium at the Pentagon that would have given the government an ideal excuse for fighter jets being delayed in following SOP to intercept Flights 11 and 175. Moreover, if the Pentagon, the National Military Command Center (NMCC) being in its basement, had been hit at 8:40 a.m., the North Tower at 8:46 a.m., and the South Tower at 9:03 a.m., it would all have been over in a mere twenty-three minutes, assuming that Flight 93 had hit the Capitol Building or the White House during that time interval.[2]

## The Second Blunder

Thorn and Giuliani's theory was that the crime coordinators made their *second blunder* by having Flight 77 fly into Ohio and Kentucky simply to buy time until Flight 93 could take off and do its part. Then when Flight 77 finally turned around forty-one minutes later (at 9:01 a.m.), Lower Manhattan was already in a mess, caused by Flight 11 smashing into the North Tower (WTC-1) at 8:46 a.m.

## The Third Blunder

The *third blunder* was creating fires in the Twin Towers that were inadequate for making the collapses of these impressive buildings believable. That was especially true for the South Tower (WTC-2), which had been struck at an angle so that 90 percent of the plane's fuel spewed out from two sides, creating an impressive fireball, which lasted only a short time. Firemen reached the seventy-eighth floor and stated unequivocally that the flames could have been put out in an hour by a half dozen men.[3]

## The Fourth Blunder

The *fourth blunder* was not having Flight 77 smash into the Pentagon. The FBI immediately confiscated videotapes from a Citgo gas station, the Sheraton hotel, DMV, and from their own on-site cameras. After initially claiming that the airliner "vaporized" when it hit the Pentagon, the FBI later said that the wreckage had been collected and stored in a warehouse. The matter could have been settled by merely opening the warehouse and letting reporters with cameras examine the aircraft parts because all such parts have an identifying number. However, that has never happened.[4]

[AC] The size of a Boeing 757 airliner or even a drone military Boeing 737 plane would have necessitated a second-floor attack, whereby the prime targets, which the author believes were the

Navy Command Center and the Operations Office of the Army's Financial Management Branch, would have been missed, if indeed a passenger plane had hit Wedge One of the Pentagon. A missile from an AGM-86D winged cruise missile, as described in Chapter 12, would have been low enough, however, to penetrate the first-floor level. [AC]

## *The Fifth Blunder*

The *fifth blunder* was the shoot-down of Flight 93 because it was useless for the crime syndicate's purpose after it had gone as far as Cleveland before turning around and heading for Washington, D.C. Shooting it down over Washington would have been a public-relations disaster. So the same conspirators quickly manufactured the cell phone conversations and the "Let's roll" order so as to maintain the Arab hijacking scenario. Then they ordered a missile or two to be fired into the airliner over Indian Lake in Pennsylvania so that the airliner crashed about six miles to the southeast near New Baltimore. Three minutes later, they put a missile into an abandoned strip mine at Shanksville, Pennsylvania, to create a ten-foot diameter crater having about the same depth, an impressive noise, and a fast-rising plume, thereby attracting local attention. The FBI told the public the airliner had crashed into the crater while its agents collected and "carted away bags and bags of evidence" from the Indian Lake and the New Baltimore areas.[5]

[AC] Thorn and Guliani state that the mayor of Cleveland had retracted his television statement, made on September 11, 2001, about Flight 93 having landed at Cleveland Hopkins International Airport because of a bomb threat and then discharging its passengers. One wonders if such retraction was done under severe pressure. Although the airliner could have been flown as a pilotless drone, perhaps the pilots had been ordered to fly the empty plane to Washington. That would explain the rib bone found in Indian Lake. Alternatively, as discussed in Chapter 3, some of the 58 SSDI (to be dead) passengers were unloaded from UA Flight 175 and transferred to the Army drone substituting for UA Flight 93. [AC]

### The Sixth Blunder

The *sixth blunder* was the delayed destruction of WTC-7. Thorn and Giuliani surmised that the planners had "wanted it to come down much earlier . . . within an hour of when the first two towers were destroyed." Then they realized that the resulting fires in the towers were not large enough to bring them down and that the firemen could completely put the South Tower fires out within an hour. So the crime syndicate started the destruction of the South Tower with the implanted cutter charges and saw to their horror that the "cap" of the South Tower and the approximately 30 floors below it "suddenly began to topple from its base and actually fell 23 degrees past vertical."

Such a scenario was disastrous beyond comprehension for the 9/11 criminals because if the cap plunged down onto the streets of Manhattan, it would look entirely farcical for the rest of the tower—the lower section, which hadn't been struck by an airliner and wasn't on fire—to suddenly collapse in broad daylight for no apparent reason in front of millions of live TV viewers. If those eighty floors had alternatively been allowed to remain in place, the cutter charges and any connecting circuitry installed therein would have soon been found.

Believing that the crime syndicate planners were in Rudy Giuliani's twenty-third floor bunker, which had a perfect view of both Twin Towers, Thorn and Guliani surmised that the 9/11 planners immediately pushed the panic button for WTC-2 and dissolved that "cap" and the top thirty floors into upwardly and outwardly thrown dust and steel beams by firing one or more mininukes (i.e., mini-fission bombs or possibly micro-fusion bombs) that had been respectively disposed at various places within the three buildings and beneath the lobbies, thereby also pulverizing all of the approximately eighty floors beneath those toppling thirty floors, with the help of at least hundreds of cutter charges, and bringing the South Tower down in less than ten seconds. This collapse came only fifty-six minutes after Flight 175 had struck the South Tower. The same treatment came to the North Tower soon thereafter when the pre-planted cutter charges and mininukes therein were set off.

Naturally, all hell broke loose in Lower Manhattan, which was enveloped by enormous clouds of smoke, most of which came from the pulverized concrete in those 220 WTC floors. This time would have been ideal for the controllers to have destroyed their final bit of evidence—WTC-7 and the twenty-third-story bunker that served as their nerve center. After all, they could simply evacuate the building, then under the cover of concrete dust and smoke from the fires, simply perform their third and final controlled demolition. And with so much bedlam surrounding the towers—fire engines, police sirens, and screaming citizens fleeing in all directions—they could explain that falling debris from the other towers had struck WTC-7, and therefore it crashed to the ground. Best of all, at least from their perspective, due to thick cloud cover blanketing the area, there would have been no snooping cameras to record this obvious controlled demolition.

[AC] Another possible nerve center could have been that AWACS plane, hovering overhead, which could have handled the entire operation. Yet if the authors are correct about Mayor Giuliani's bunker being the nerve center, it means that he was at least an accessory during the fact of this murderous tragedy.[AC]

Anyway, something went wrong. "Once the psychopaths exited WTC-7 and hit the panic button, the building didn't fall! There had been some sort of malfunction." The crime syndicate had to send technicians back into the tower to figure out what went wrong and then do some rewiring. The 9/11 planners were in a quandary. Because of the damning evidence in that twenty-third-story bunker, plus the explosives and wiring in the building, in their opinion, they had to destroy this forty-seven-story skyscraper.

Another good reason was the two hundred or so cases being handled by the Securities and Exchange Commission on the twelfth floor that could have put so many powerful and wealthy people where they belonged—in prison!

So the 9/11 planners did implode WTC-7 at 5:20 p.m. within 6.6 seconds into its own footprint, exactly as in a conventional controlled demolition.

And worst of all, the government has not to this day offered any satisfactory explanation whatsoever for how it collapsed. Not only is this scenario the height of depraved arrogance, but it's incredible beyond words that they've gotten away with this crime for so long.[6]

Thorn and Guliani suspected that there had been a replacement with another plane because Flight 93 flew around for fifty-five minutes without a fighter jet coming alongside and saying, "Identify yourself!" when "everybody knew that this was a real-time event and not a drill."[7]

[AC] How badly U.S. citizens need an unshackled, independent federal grand jury! [AC]

# Chapter 14 Notes

1.  Thorn, Victor and Lisa Guliani. *Phantom Flight 93: And Other Astounding September 11 Mysteries Explored.* 2007. Washington, D.C. 20003 . American Free Press, 645 Pennsylvania Avenue SE, Suite 100, 92-103.

2.  Ibid., 60, 61.

# PART VI
## Joint Planning and Execution of 9/11 Attacks by U.S. Officials and A Foreign Agency

# CHAPTER 15

# Joint Operating Agreement (JOA) Possibilities

### *JOA Activities That Made 9/11 Feasible*

"When one group assists another group for a common goal, they work together under a joint operating agreement" (JOA). Douglas Herman concluded that 9/11 was both allowed to happen and made to happen under a JOA. He quoted Wayne Madsen, a former NSA insider, concerning the CIA and the FBI, as follows:

> The FBI refuses to cooperate due to the orders coming from people like (Tom) Lantos, (John) McCain, FBI Director Robert Mueller, and others who do the bidding of the Russian-Israeli mob.

Herman also alluded to the Mossad operatives (the Dancing Five, also identified as the Dancing Israelis), who were caught on September 11, 2001, after celebrating in Liberty State Park, New Jersey as the Twin Towers were struck, with explosives in their confiscated vans. After being detained by the FBI, they were released and returned to Israel.

Other indications of a JOA were the thwarting and subverting of patriotic FBI special agents, who tried to warn FBI headquarters of a terrorist plot prior to 9/11. This subversion was the work of top FBI terrorist officials such as David Frasca and Marion Bowman, the latter being promoted and given a decoration after the 9/11 and anthrax attacks.

Herman further noted that the USA PATRIOT Act had already been drafted and was sitting on Ashcroft's desk on September 10, according to law professor Dr. Francis Boyle, who drafted the Biological Weapons Anti-Terrorism Act of 1989. That would indicate pre-knowledge of a terrible crime, such as 9/11. But nobody was fired; nobody was brought before a grand jury, and the heads of all protective agencies, such as NORAD, the National Security Agency, the Pentagon, the CIA, and the FBI looked the other way. If 9/11 was the result of a JOA, planned months before, that would explain such behavior.

> Consider: Mossad—the best covert spy org in the world—likely did the dirty work right here in America and planted the charges in the recently purchased and highly insured Silverstein buildings. Plausible denial would allow U.S. intel orgs to deny any culpability.

Herman also commented that in programs such as Operation Mockingbird, the CIA long ago "covertly put major publishing, newspaper, and media outlets, as well as thousands of individual reporters under direct agency control, from where they have mostly remained."

Perhaps most disturbing: Why wasn't anyone fired after 911? Indeed, even more indicative: many of those involved in key positions received rewards. For allowing or permitting or enabling or conspiring, to kill 3,000 Americans. The ultimate question remains: WHO planned 911? WHO remains securely behind the scenes pulling the strings? Certainly someone living in a penthouse rather than a primitive cave.

Finally, the Iraq War, a war based on lies, greed, and genocide is itself a JOA. The US "all-voluntary" military, together with Mossad/IDF advisors and M16/SAS Brit forces, is clearly a joint operating agreement. The key to the entire imperialist venture was the false flag operation, 911.[1]

## A JOA That Disabled the Pilots of the Four 9/11 Airliners

The late Col. Donn de Grand Pre organized the marathon meeting of a group of dedicated U.S. civilian and military pilots, who issued a report concluding that the official story about what happened on September 11, 2001, was improbable and unlikely. That seventy-two-hour nonstop symposium concluded that the flight crews of the four passenger airliners involved in the 9/11 tragedy had no control over their aircraft.

The retired U.S. Army colonel subsequently wrote three books that identified 9/11 as an inside job. He also wrote:

The trigger for the 9/11 activity was the imminent and unstoppable worldwide financial collapse, which can only be prevented (temporarily) by a major war, perhaps to become known as World War III. To bring it off one more time, martial law will probably be imposed in the United States.

In each of the major wars of the 20th century, the financial manipulators (located in the City of London and New York City) had placed the U.S. (and much of the Western world) in a monetary expansion mode, followed by an ever-tightening vice of a gigantic credit squeeze.

## The Enemy Is within the Gates

The seventy-two-hour pilot group "determined that the enemy is within the gates, that he has infiltrated into the highest policymaking positions at the federal level, and has absolute control, not only of the purse strings, but of the troop buildup and deployment of our military forces, including active, reserve, and National Guard units."[2]

As discussed by Jeff Gates, Charles Keating served as counsel to Cincinnati's Carl Lindner before he led a $3.4 billion fraud from the Phoenix office of Lincoln Savings & Loan. Michael "Junk Bond King" Milken financed and controlled that fraud, the origin of which can be traced to the same network behind the political ascendancy of Ronald Reagan.

Gates further pointed out that no public record has "examined the geopolitical implications of the organized crime network that encouraged and financed" John McCain's political ambitions. That network "includes Canada's Bronfman clan, Prohibition-era bootleggers whose family fortune capitalized the World Jewish Congress. Barack Obama's political career shares that suspect network with roots in Chicago's organized crime."[3]

## JOA Plans for Imposing Martial Law on the USA

Peter Dale Scott describes this JOA in American history, which apparently is still hanging over the United States in February 2011:

> Once in power, Ronald Reagan, his CIA director William Casey, and vice president George H. W. Bush initiated emergency planning, building from the Garden Plot plan, for what Alfonso Chardy of the *Miami Herald* called "suspension of the Constitution, turning control of the government over to FEMA [the Federal Emergency Management Agency], emergency appointment of military commanders to run state and local governments and declaration of martial law." The plan also gave FEMA, which had been involved in drafting it, sweeping new powers, including the power "to surveil political dissenters and to arrange for the detention of hundreds of thousands of undocumented aliens in case of an unspecified national emergency."

What is most astonishing about this 1980s planning is that Congress was "completely bypassed." Once again, as in the early days of OPC, private power allied with the extreme wealth of the overworld was imposing policies and structures by secret procedures that radically redirected the course of the public state. It was doing so at a constitutional level. COG—more properly characterized as *change* of government rather than *continuity* of government—was not seeking to influence or assist constitutional authority, but to control it, and if necessary, to override it.

Public alarm was alleviated by the false assurance that this referred to a proposed executive order from FEMA and that this had already been "effectively killed" by the attorney general William French Smith. In fact, FEMA planning continued up to the day of September 11, 2001, when COG was first implemented. Worse, however, there are indications that COG planning may have helped set the stage for 9/11 to happen.

Two members of the ultra-secret private group drafting COG in the 1980s were Dick Cheney (then a congressman) and Donald Rumsfeld (then the CEO of G. D. Searle, a pharmaceutical company). In the fall of 2000, a year before 9/11, Cheney and Rumsfeld signed on to a major study, *Rebuilding America's Defenses*, by the lobbying group Project for the New American Century (PNAC). The study called for a major increase in the defense budget, the removal of Saddam Hussein from

Iraq, and the maintenance of U.S. troops in the Gulf area even after Saddam's disappearance.

The PNAC study was a blueprint for the George W. Bush foreign policy that has been and still is being carried out. It also reflected support from the private sector for the blueprint of full-spectrum dominance that had been articulated in the Pentagon's *Joint Vision 2020*. Every critical study of 9/11 has noted the PNAC report's frank assertion that the policy changes it advocated would be difficult to implement quickly, "absent some catastrophic and catalyzing event—like a new Pearl Harbor."

Scott noted that the high profile PNAC report was merely the public face of a high-level consensus that "America would need full-spectrum dominance to guarantee access to oil and other resources in the rest of the world." Such dominance was expected to require massive expenditures, up to a trillion dollars. Congress could not be expected to provide this much money, "except in response to an attack as massive and frightening as Pearl Harbor."[4]

[AC] This consensus was deliberately erroneous because vast amounts of oil and natural gas had been discovered about twenty-five years earlier in the Beaufort Sea, five miles north of the shore, but then capped on order of the U.S. government, with even publicity thereon being strictly forbidden, as discussed in detail in chapter 38. [AC]

# Chapter 15 Notes

1. Herman, Douglas. "911 = JOA," 1-3. http://www.rense.com/general74/9110.htm.
2. de Grand Pre, Donn. "The Enemy is Inside the Gates," 1, 2. http://www.apfn.net/Messageboard/8-10-03/discussion.cgi.64.html.
3. Gates, Jeff. *Guilt by Association: How Deception and Self-deceit Took America to War.* 2008. Santa Barbara, CA 93105. State Street Publications, 3408 State Street, Suite A, xvii.
4. de Grand Pre, 2.
5. Scott, Peter Dale. *The Road to 9/11: Wealth, Empire, and the Future of America.* 2007. Berkeley, CA. University of California Press, 23, 24.

Garden Plot P. 325

# CHAPTER 16

## The Wide Influence of the Neocons on US. Foreign Policy

### *Brief Historical Background*

Trotskyites were Communists and followers of Leon Trotsky, a Russian Jew, who was editor of a publication termed *Novy Mir* in New York City during World War I. But after the Russian czar had abdicated in 1917, Trotsky was sent from New York City by international bankers in a ship with about three hundred young Jews to St. Petersburg. Working with Lenin and using "substantial funding from a mystery Wall Street donor, widely thought to be Jacob Schiff of Kuhn Loeb," they did not overthrow the monarchy. "*They overthrew the first democratic society in Russian history, set up through a truly popular revolution in March, 1917*... They represented the smallest of the Russian radical movements."

When Lenin died, Trotsky was in line to be the new Soviet leader, but he became sick, and "Stalin grabbed the reins of power."

Trotsky was expelled from Soviet Russia in 1928, returned for a while to New York City, and then went into exile in Mexico, where he was assassinated by a Soviet agent.

## Children of Trotsky Followers Became Neoconservatives (Neocons)

During the Cold War, created by the international bankers in order to regain their control of Russia, the Trotsky followers became the Neocons (or New Conservatives) who had moved "from the paranoid left to the paranoid right." Their consistent aims "were to prevail over the Russian regime and dominate the world economically and militarily."

During the Cold War, the neocons were effective "Cold Warriors." Prior to September 11, 2001, a number of neocons had powerful positions in the U.S. government.[1]

[W]hen the major American media wanted to promote a particular idea or viewpoint, newspaper reporters and broadcast journalists turned to Irving Kristol, who had many devoted followers, for his neoconservative point of view—often to the exclusion of better-known, more respected, and more knowledgeable individuals. For example, then Education Secretary William Bennett was a protégé of Irving Kristol. Some say this is no coincidence, considering what is perceived to be a strong pro-Israel bias on the part of the major media.

Many of the people writing the official speeches and public statements for President Bush and Vice President Cheney, as well as other key foreign policy makers, owed their patronage to William Kristol, son of Irving Kristol.

## The Neocons' Team B and Its Influence on U.S. Foreign Policy

In the mid-1970s, Richard Perle, an influential neoconservative who had been the former Reagan-era assistant secretary of defense for international security policy, helped to select members of a formal body, officially known as Team B. This team "functioned as a purportedly 'independent' advisory council on intelligence estimates relating to Soviet aims and capabilities." Paul Wolfowitz and Paul Nitze were among these selected members. Team B was "headed by Harvard Professor Richard Pipes, a Russian-born devotee of the Zionist cause."

In fact, the members of Team B were bound by their determination to make every aspect of U.S. foreign policy geared toward policies that would prove beneficial to Israel.

To understand what is happening in our world today as a consequence of the rule of the neoconservatives in official Washington, it is critical to understand the geopolitical events surrounding the history of the group known as Team B. A former CIA deputy director for national intelligence, Robert Bowie, thought that Team B was fighting "for the soul of the Republican party, for getting control of foreign policy within one branch of the party."

> Perle and other pro-Israel activists on Capitol Hill and in official Washington began attacking the CIA and demanding additional inquiry into the CIA's analysis of Soviet strength.

## Team B's Forecast: The Soviet Union Had First-strike Capability But Would Run out of Oil and Then Attack the Oil-rich Gulf States

These pro-Israel activists were trying to alarm the American people about how dangerous the Soviets would be to the oil-rich Gulf States. However, U.S. intelligence analysts openly doubted the accuracy of their alarms. Senior analysts in the Office of National Estimates were leaders in reassuring the White House that, at least for the moment, the Soviets did not intend to attack Gulf States and indeed lacked the capability to do so.

By early 1978 the Israeli-influenced B Team had finished its review of the CIA's procedures and programs. The team issued a lengthy report that harshly criticized almost every finding that U.S. intelligence had made in previous years about Soviet military power and how they intended to use it.

The report said that the Soviets were secretly developing a so-called first-strike capability. The team asserted that "Soviet strategic doctrine assumed that such a sneak attack would make them the winners of a nuclear exchange with the United States." In doing so, the B Team ridiculed the estimates of analysts who believed that Moscow was unlikely to start a nuclear conflict unless attacked. Estimates provided by Israeli intelligence—the foundation of the B team's report—was the warning that the Soviet Union was fast running out of its petroleum supplies. These estimates were wildly in error as Russia's exportation of gas and oil to Europe in the twenty-first century amply prove.

B Team's consequent forecast was that, beginning in 1980, Soviet oil production would suffer such critical shortfalls that the Soviet Union would have to import as much as 4.5 million barrels a day for its essential needs. The Israeli disinformation claimed that the Soviets would be so starved for oil that they "would invade Iran or another oil-rich gulf state even if it meant a nuclear confrontation with the United States."

### *John Paisley's Planned Refutation of the Israeli-influenced Team B and His Consequent Murder*

In the meantime, John Paisley, recently retired from the CIA, was appointed by CIA Director Bush to act as the CIA's liaison between the CIA's own in-house Team A and the Israeli-influenced Team B. Paisley soon realized that "these cosmopolitan intellectuals were simply trying to discredit the CIA's recommendations" and replace them with Israel's alarmist view of Soviet intentions.

Team B's final report was secret, but John Paisley obtained a copy in the summer of 1978 and began to write a detailed critique that would destroy this Israeli disinformation. Unfortunately, Paisley was murdered before he could finish his critique.

According to Richard Clement, who headed the Interagency Committee on Counter-Terrorism during the Reagan administration, "The Israelis had no compunction about 'terminating' key American intelligence officials who threatened to blow the whistle on them. Those of us familiar with the case of Paisley know that he was killed by the Mossad. But no one, not even in Congress, wants to stand up and say so publicly."

In the end, *with vital help from the media*, the B Team findings prevailed. The direct consequence was that the arms race was virtually revived and U.S. military and other aid to Israel during the 1980s received a massive new infusion, exactly what the B Team wanted to happen.

## *Vice President Dick Cheney and His Importation of Neocons into the U.S. Government*

Vice President Dick Cheney was never formally identified as a neoconservative, but he "had been a member of the board of advisors of the Jewish Institute for National Security Affairs (JINSA), a member of the board of trustees of the American Enterprise Institute (AEI), and a founding member of the neoconservative Project for a New American Century (PNAC)" before becoming vice president. He played a key role in bringing such neoconservatives as Wolfowitz, Perle, Feith, Bolton, and Libby into the administration. These men boxed in Secretary of State Powell after the 2000 election. As stated earlier, Cheney was apparently a chief MIHOP on September 11, 2001.

Cheney has been identified as "the most powerful vice president in U.S. history." He "created a large national-security staff in his office, constituting a virtual National Security Council in miniature, which had a major effect in shaping American national policy." His neocons had "potential power or stealth power because they had significant numbers whose power was magnified by their notable networking skills" that were supported by Cheney's powerful position.

Douglas Feith coauthored the policy paper "A Clean Break," which was sent to then Prime Minister Netanyahu of Israel. This paper suggested that Israel destabilize the Middle East by making

—
334

an attack on Iraq. Feith was also a member of the advisory board of JINSA before joining the Bush administration.

## Pro-war Neocon Activities in the U.S. Government

Veteran diplomat Paul Nitze of Team B fame, former undersecretary of state Eugene Rostow, and former treasury secretary Charles Walker founded the Committee on the Present Danger. Ronald Reagan brought no less than sixty members of the committee into his administration, including its founders, who were placed in the most critical arms control positions.

Many of these people set up another blue-ribbon committee with similar motivations to the Committee on the Present Danger. It was the Committee for a Free World, founded by Midge Decter, wife of neocon Norman Podhoretz. Elliott Abrams, Gertrude Himmelfarb (wife of Irving Kristol and mother of William Kristol), and Michael Ledeen were other members. Donald Rumsfeld, who prosecuted the U.S. war against Iraq as defense secretary in the George W. Bush administration and was a 9/11 MIHOP, helped to raise funds for this committee.

When they were in the Defense Department during the Reagan administration, Stephen J. Bryen and Richard Perle became the two chief promoters of Israel's lucrative but little publicized export of arms to the People's Republic of China while the Reagan administration was trying to deny U.S. weapons technology to communist countries. Thereafter, the *Wall Street Journal* published an article titled, "Roles of Ex-Pentagon Officials at Jewish Group Show Clout of Cold-Warrior, Pro-Israel Network." The article identified a "tight little circle [that] illustrated an enduring network

—

of Cold War conservatives and pro-Israel interests in Washington" and discussed the activities of the group known as the Jewish Institute for National Security Affairs (JINSA).[2]

Other influential neoconservatives, as well as those whom Pat Buchanan termed "Israel's Amen Corner," were Gary Bauer, William J. Bennett, Eliot Cohen, Midge Decter, Thomas Donnelly, Hillel Fradkin, Frank Gaffney, Reuel Marc Gerecht, Michael Joyce, Donald Kagan, Robert Kagan, Charles Krauthammer, John Lehman, Martin Peretz, Norman Podhoretz, Stephen J. Solarz, Vin Weber, and Marshall Wittmann. Paul Wolfowitz, the deputy secretary of defense in Bush's first term, became "the intellectual godfather and fiercest advocate for toppling Saddam." Wolfowitz had been a founding member of PNAC. He had also been associated with the Jewish Institute of National Security Affairs (JINSA).

Richard Perle "has been affiliated with almost every major neoconservative think tank and organization: AEI, JINSA, PNAC, Center for Security Policy, Hudson Institute, Committee for the Liberation of Iraq, Committee on the Present Danger, and Foundation for the Defense of Democracies." Perle also "held the unpaid chairmanship of the Defense Policy Board, which afforded him access to classified documents and close contacts with the administration leadership" although he was not technically a member of the Bush II administration. The Defense Policy Board was stacked with unabashed Iraq hawks.

While the neocons were planning a war strategy for an attack on Iraq, a drastically different foreign policy was being contemplated by those who thought about American global hegemony and control of mid-Asian oil. An influential energy task force headed by Vice President Cheney suggested the lifting of some economic sanctions against Iran, Libya, and Iraq in order to increase America's oil supply, but the even more influential pro-Israel lobby scuttled the oil lobby's efforts because it would have allowed the U.S. to reestablish economic relationships with Israel's enemies.[3]

## 9/11 Was the Neocons' Pretext for Beginning War against Iraq, Not Just al Qaeda

For the neocons, the terrible tragedy of 9/11 provided a very convenient pretext to begin their war agenda for the United States. "Before 9/11, regime change by invasion was still just a fringe part of the debate about how to handle Saddam Hussein." Immediately thereafter, the neocons had the perfect opportunity to push publicly for a wider war on terrorism that would immediately weaken Israel's enemies, starting with Iraq. However, the anger of the American public made the punishment of the guilty criminals more important, and these criminals were identified as being in Afghanistan in the person of Osama bin Laden and his al Qaeda network.

Nevertheless, as early as September 12, 2001, "Secretary of Defense Donald Rumsfeld raised the question of attacking Iraq. Why shouldn't we go against Iraq, not just al Qaeda?" he asked. Rumsfeld was speaking not only for himself but also for his deputy, Paul D. Wolfowitz, who was committed to a policy that would make Iraq a principal target of the first round in the war on terrorism."

## Secretary of State Colin Powell Boxed In by Neocons

However, Secretary of State Colin Powell was strongly opposed to attacking Iraq in the belief that the war should focus on the actual perpetrators of 9/11 because that was what the American people expected.

Fighting back, Richard Perle, chairman of the Defense Policy Board, convened a lengthy, nineteen-hour meeting of the board to discuss the ramifications of the 9/11 attacks. The meeting was held in Rumsfeld's conference room in the Pentagon. "Notably excluded from the meeting were Secretary of State Powell and other members of the State Department, as well as National Security Advisor Condoleezza Rice." During the meeting, Newt Gingrich, the former speaker of the U.S. House of Representatives and a member of the board, advocated using 9/11 to replace Saddam after replacing the Taliban.

The attendees prepared a letter for President Bush that called for removing Saddam Hussein. It was dated on September 20, 2001, under the name of the Project for the New American Century (PNAC) and called for a determined effort to remove Saddam Hussein from power in Iraq, asserting that failure to make such an effort "will constitute an early and perhaps decisive surrender in the war on international terrorism."

Neocons signing the letter included William Kristol, Midge Decter, Eliot Cohen, Frank Gaffney, Robert Kagan, Jeane Kirkpatrick, Charles Krauthammer, Richard Perle, and Norman Podhoretz.[4]


## U.S. War against Iraq (Kristol's War)

On March 17, 2003, the day before the United States began the war against Iraq, Kristol bragged in a signed editorial in the *Weekly Standard* that "obviously, we are gratified that the Iraq strategy we have long advocated . . . has become the policy of the U.S. government."

The next day the *Washington Post* reminded its readers that its columnist, Richard Cohen, had once declared the looming conflict to be "Kristol's War."[5]

[AC]For the unfortunate people of Iraq and for the American and British soldiers who died or were wounded to gratify the neoconservative war aims and for the American taxpayers, it was not so wonderful.[AC]

# Chapter 16 Notes

1.  Brown, Ellen Hodgson. *Web of Debt: The Shocking Truth About Our Money System and How We Can Break Free.* 2008. Baton Rouge, Louisiana. Third Millennium Press, 226-229.
2.  Piper, Michael Collins. *The High Priests of War: The Secret History of How America's "Neo-Conservative" Trotskyites Came to Power and Orchestrated the War against Iraq as the First Step in Their Drive for Global Empire.* 2004. Washington, D.C. American Free Press, 22-39.
3.  Sniegoski, Stephen J. *The Transparent Cabal: The Neoconservative Agenda, War in the Middle East, and the National Interest of Israel.* 2008. Norfolk, Virginia. Enigma Editions, 113-121, 127.
4.  Ibid., 137-144.
5.  Piper, 39.

# CHAPTER 17

# Zionists in Power in the USA during 2001

## Planning and Lobbying for "A New Pearl Harbor"

Douglas Herman wondered if it was only a coincidence that so many rich and powerful Jewish Americans played a pivotal role or at least a supporting role in the alleged "terrorist attack" on September 11, 2001, and the war on terror that followed thereafter, culminating in the war on Iraq just eighteen months later.

## Neocons and Fellow Zionists in Power in the Pentagon

Douglas Feith, Paul Wolfowitz, Dov Zakheim, and Richard Perle, all fellow Zionists, ascended to power at the Pentagon to become top military strategists while holding dual passports, Israeli and U.S. They also held top secret U.S. security clearances. Colonel Karen Kwiatkowski commented about her superior, Douglas Feith,

341

head of the Pentagon's Office of Special Plans (OSP), that he served the interests of Likud, a right-wing Israeli party, and observed, "I just don't have any countervailing information that would suggest he has ever done anything for America."

Douglas Herman summarized the situation as follows: "Philosophically they all shared the same goal: Strengthen Israel; weaken the tyrannical Islamic states; hasten U.S. hegemony of scarce resources for key global players and multinationals."

### *A Stony Silence about 9/11 by Jewish-owned New York City Newspapers*

Herman noted that all the New York City newspapers maintained a stony silence and a powerful self-censorship, as well as editorial reluctance, about the probable connection of Israel to the 9/11 attack. Why? Just a glance at the mastheads of daily New York newspapers showed a preponderance of Jewish editors and publishers. Not a single Judeocentric newspaper launched the tiniest investigation of seven prominent NYC steel buildings being demolished or seriously damaged on the same day under exceedingly suspicious circumstances. Even periodicals like *Popular Mechanics,* edited by a cousin of Michael Chertoff, who was promoted to head of U.S. Homeland Security, supported the official (Zionist) version of these critically important events. The result: launching of the war on Iraq with wholehearted White House, U.S. media, and Congressional support on March 18, 2003, just eighteen months later—"on Purim, a significant Jewish holiday, a day signifying destruction of Israel's enemies."

The Israeli source, *Ari Shavit Ha'aretz News Service*, stated on April 5, 2003:

> The war in Iraq was conceived by 25 neoconservatives, most of them Jewish, who are pushing President Bush to change the course of history.

Herman speculated that after examining this enormous evil iceberg further and below its tip, one might find a monumental mass of icy intelligence-connected layers. "Very likely, the entire WTC operation was a combination of an insurance scam (Benefiting one wealthy Zionist), a false flag 'terrorist' operation (benefiting one Zionist nation), and a billion-dollar gold heist (Benefiting various operatives from many branches of intelligence possibly)."

Herman thought that it was difficult to believe that the CIA, the Secret Service, and Giuliani's Office of Emergency Management had no glimmer of "prior knowledge about the impending destruction of their offices" and their very valuable contents.

### *Gold and Silver Burglaries under the WTC*

With regard to the gold heist, the *London Times* reported as follows:

> The Comex metals trading division of the New York Mercantile Exchange kept 3,800 gold bars—weighing 12 tonnes and worth more than $100 million —in vaults in the building's basement. Comex also held almost 800,000 ounces of gold there on behalf of others,

with a value of about $220 million (worth more than $560,000,000 today). It also held more than 102 million ounces of silver, worth $430 million (Worth $1.5 billion today). The Bank of Nova Scotia, which kept gold in the Comex vault, reported $200 million of gold lost in the wreckage. (Lost-!) Comex also held precious metals for Chase Manhattan Bank, the Bank of New York and Hong Kong and Shanghai Banking.

However, one massive gold-filled truck that had been crushed in the tunnels below the WTC complex was discovered. In the eight hours between 9:00 a.m. and 5:20 p.m. while horrified Americans were staring at their television sets, the gold (except for this crushed truck) had evidently not been vaporized and was instead stolen before WTC-7 was demolished.[1]

[AC] Such a moving operation would have required much prior knowledge and planning. Whose truck was crushed? Was any effort made to identify the owner of the truck and to solve this massive theft? Was the driver killed when the truck was crushed? Who was he? To what warehouse, bank, or very large vault were the more than 4,000 tons of gold and silver moved? How many workers loaded that weight into other trucks within a mere eight hours? (Or was most of it done during the preceding night?) Who were those workers? An unshackled federal grand jury, able to return a presentment, should be able to shed much light on this matter. [AC]

Victor Thorn and Lisa Guliani were invited on the 5th anniversary of 9/11 "to appear as guests on George Noory's *Coast to Coast AM* radio show (which is owned by Clear Channel.)

For the first time ever on nationwide radio, the subject of Israel's involvement in 9-11 was discussed."

*Coast to Coast* was simulcast "on over 500 radio stations across the country" so that "approximately 8 million listeners were exposed to the most dangerous and taboo subject in the field of 9-11 research—Israel's key role in the attacks on America." Two days later, Thorn and Guliani "posted a link to this show (from an independent source)" on their website, thereby "making this information available to an even larger audience."

About two months later Thorn and Guliani received a letter from the corporate counsel for Clear Channel, informing them that they had to remove that link to the George Noory's radio show immediately. All efforts to arrange payment or to establish a franchise were refused by Clear Channel. Thorn wondered what had caused Clear Channel to react so strongly. He remembered that they had spoken about items discussed in their book *9-11 Evil,* such as:

> The "Dancing Israelis"; how the first suspects arrested after 9-11 were Israelis; Michael Chertoff's dual Israeli/American citizenship; Urban Moving System's role as a front for the Mossad; and WTC owner Larry Silverstein's links to Ariel Sharon and Benjamin Netanyahu.

Thorn also remembered "two other revelations never before made public on American radio:"

> First, Ehud Sprinzak, a terrorist expert at Hebrew University in Jerusalem, said that from Israel's perspective,

*It's them!*

9-11 was the most important public relations act ever committed in their favor.

Secondly, a man named Ami Ayalon, head of the Israeli military, disclosed that since Sept. 22, their leaders have been euphoric. Now ask yourself: how many other people anywhere on the globe were ecstatic about 9-11? These Israelis were because this joint neo-con/Mossad terrorist event laid the framework for our current war in Iraq, Afghanistan, and potentially Iran.[2]

*good for Corporations also.*

## The Ultimate Plan: A Global Police State

*July / August that's next along w/all the aborting Colorado, Wisconsin, Arizona*

Victor Thorn remembered talking to Jim Marrs who told him:

Every trail leads back to the federal government. September 11 was an inside job that makes the JFK assassination look like a [cakewalk]. Immediately after the strikes, you had all these guys from the Council on Foreign Relations like Gen. Wesley Clark, Henry Kissinger, and Al Haig telling us we had a new kind of warfare—international terrorism—that would bind the nations of the world together. It's like they were all reading from the same script, pushing the same agenda, saying how we'd have to give up some of our liberties.

The Bush's closest friends are the bin Ladens and the Saudi royal family On the other hand, it doesn't take Sherlock Holmes to figure out that 9-11 was a U.S.

operation—with Israeli assistance . . . . Soon, they were rushing through the Patriot Act, and Attorney General John Ashcroft was publicly calling for concentration camps. In no time, the US. waged two wars of aggression as the mainstream media blended with the government into what is commonly known as fascism.

The effect was Orwellian. War equals peace, and slavery equals freedom. The neo-cons behind 9-11 and our current wars are . . . socialists in real life who seek more central authority, higher deficits, and want to shred the Constitution. The same families and corporations that created communism . . . also created the neo-cons and Obamites.[3]

# Chapter 17 Notes

1. Herman, Douglas. "Connecting the Dots - Zionists & 911." *http:// www.rense/com/general72/connect.htm.*
2. Thorn, Victor. "Israel's Role in 9-11 Attacks Explored." September 11, 2001. The 9-11 Terror Tragedy Seen Years Later: an AFP Special Anniversary Report. B-1. *American Free Press.* September 2008.
3. Thorn, Victor. "The Ultimate Plan Behind the Attacks: Global Police State." September 11, 2001. The 9-11 Terror Tragedy Seen Years Later: an AFP Special Anniversary Report. B-1. *American Free Press.* September 2008.

# CHAPTER 18

---

# Dual Israeli-American Citizenship and Its Cost to the United States

### *Rabbi Dov Zakheim, Comptroller of the Pentagon*

Rabbi Dov S. Zakheim was initially with the Congressional Budget Office. Then he became corporate vice president of Systems Planning Corporation (SPC), a high-tech research, analysis, and manufacturing firm. Next he was chief executive officer and president of SPC International, Inc. In 1998, as an expert on ballistic missiles, Zakheim worked with the Rumsfeld Commission. In addition, he was a long-time Bush crony and a policy advisor to Governor Bush in the 2000 campaign for president.

Zakheim also coauthored the now infamous article, "Rebuilding America's Defenses: Strategy, Forces, and Resources for a New Century," which was published by the Project for a New American Century (PNAC) in September 2000. On page

51 is that famous comment "the process of transformation, even if it brings revolutionary change, is likely to be a long one, absent some catastrophic and catalyzing event, like a new Pearl Harbor."

SPC produced remote control airborne vehicle technologies, and Zakheim had the money from Pentagon funds to pay for them. More importantly, SPC marketed the technology called Flight Termination Systems to take over the controls of an airborne vehicle already in flight. "For example the Flight Termination System technology could literally hijack the hijackers and land the plane safely wherever it wanted—or crash it as desired."

Systems Planning Corporation was a defense contractor majoring in electronic warfare technologies, including remote-controlled aircraft systems. Zakheim had access to this remote control technology while working at Systems Planning Corporation, and he had access to Boeing aircraft technology through a lease deal that he brokered while working at the Pentagon.

An ordained rabbi and a dual Israeli-American citizen, Zakheim was also a member of the Council on Foreign Relations. Zakheim was chief executive officer of Systems Planning Corporation's International Division . . . till President George W. Bush made him undersecretary of defense and comptroller of the Pentagon.

He resigned on April 15, 2004 when he was unable to explain the disappearance of one trillion dollars. Surprisingly, *al Jazeera* reported a "General Accounting Office report found Defence inventory systems so lax that the U.S. Army lost track of 56 airplanes, 32 tanks, and 36 Javelin missile command launch-units."[1]

*Pocket money for loose change*

*good old, USA*

## *Dov Zakheim and the Disappearance of $2.3 Trillion Plus $1.0 Trillion*

Donald Rumsfeld announced on September 10, 2001, that an audit had discovered $2.3 trillion was missing from the Pentagon books. Rumsfeld commented that it equaled "$8,000 for every man, woman and child in America." The story disappeared while those three WTC building collapsed the next day.

Moreover, most of Israel's armaments were obtained thanks to Zakheim, such as squadrons of U.S. F-16 and F-15 jet fighters, which were classified military surplus and sold to Israel at a fraction of their value. Israel was thereby handed the country's finest fighter jets while 15 percent of U.S. jets were grounded for lack of parts.

In May 2001, Dov began to serve at the Pentagon. His firm, SPS, had a subsidiary, Tridata Corporation, that oversaw the investigation of the first "terrorist" attack on the World Trade Center in 1993. This investigation should have provided an intimate knowledge of the security systems and structural blueprints of the buildings in the World Trade Center and especially the Twin Towers, which were damaged by that attack. From the '90s through 2001, security for the WTC was handled by Securacom, a Kuwait-American firm. Marvin Bush, the president's brother, sat on its board. After 9/11, Securacom lost its contract, changed its name to Stratosec, and was then delisted from the Stock Exchange in 2002.[2]

The Department of Defense announced on March 24, 2004 "that Under Secretary of Defense (Comptroller) and Chief Financial Officer for the Department of Defense Dov S. Zakheim will resign from government on April 15, 2004.

—

In this position, Zakheim initiated an enterprise architecture to achieve a vision of simpler budget processes, activity-based costing, and a clear audit by 2007. He oversaw three Department of Defense budgets, each totaling more than $300 billion, and recently proposed a 2005 budget of $401.7 billion. He played a leading role in raising in excess of $13 billion for the reconstruction of Iraq, and walked through six wartime supplementals in support of operations in Afghanistan and Iraq. He further created the Defense Business Board and worked closely with the Office of Management and Budget and the Government Accounting Office on financial management affairs.[3]

Joshua Daniels wondered where the missing Pentagon trillions came from. He added up the entire U.S. defense budgets from 1996 to 2001 and found about 1.6 trillion. Yet Rumsfeld said that an additional $700 billion had disappeared. To get that much, all the defense budgets from about 1991 to 2001 would have to be added up. "We know that most of that money got properly accounted for, because the GAO and OMB have been checking figures, making recommendations for savings, etc., and would have spotted a gap of any real size." For all that money to disappear, the Pentagon would have had to spend nothing for those ten years. Yet the military personnel were unquestionably paid and ammunition, tanks, planes, and missiles were bought. So from where and from whom did all that money come?

Daniels decided that "not many people outside the Federal Reserve owners had access to that kind of money."[3]

[AC] Note the word, "owners." Who are they? That seems to be a secret, but a possible answer is that the Fed is or was owned by eight banks, one being a large U.S. bank and the others being European banks owned by closely related individuals. Again, what an opportunity for an independent federal grand jury to make a real difference![AC]

# Chapter 18 Notes

1. Mazza, Jerry. "Recherche du trillions perdu." http://www. onlinejournal.com/artman/publish/article_1015.shtml.
2. U.S. Department of Defense. Office of the Assistant Secretary of Defense (Public Affairs). News Release. "Dov S. Zakheim to Resign." *Http://www.defense.gov/utility/printitem.aspx?print=http:// www.defense.* gov/Releases/Rele . . .
3. Mazza, Jerry. "Following Zakheim and Pentagon trillions to Israel and 9-11." http://onlinejournal.com/artman/publish/printer_1047. shtml.
4. Daniels, Joshua. "Missing Pentagon Trillions - Where Did they Come From?" http://www.rense.com/general80/missing.htm.

# CHAPTER 19

# Control of the United States by the Jewish People

### *American Political Subordination to Israel*

Osama bin Laden made these initial statements about 9/11 on September 28, 2001, according to a BBC Monitoring Service/ Unmat Interview:

> I was not involved in the September 11 attacks in the United States nor did I have knowledge of the attacks. There exists a government within a government within the United States. The United States should try to trace the perpetrators of these attacks within itself; to the people who want to make the present century a century of conflict between Islam and Christianity. That secret government must be asked as to who carried out the attacks .... The American system is totally in the control of the Jews, whose first priority is Israel, not

No bidding!

the United States. [Source: BBC Monitoring Service/ Unmat Interview, Sept. 28, 2001][1]

As if to prove Osama bin Laden's claims, former Israeli Prime Minister Ariel Sharon made this bold statement to Shimon Peres on October 3, 2001, as reported on *Kil Yisrael Radio:*

> Every time we do something you tell me America will do this and will do that. I want to tell you something very clear: Don't worry about American pressure on Israel. We, the Jewish people, control America, and the Americans know it.[2]

A concurring opinion with reference to the U.S. Senate is this portion of a letter, dated December 4, 2006, to Jeff Blankfort from James Abourezk, a former U.S. Senator from South Dakota, about the Israel Lobby:

> I can tell you from personal experience that, at least in the Congress, the support Israel has in that body is based completely on political fear—fear of defeat by anyone who does not do what Israel wants done. I can tell you from personal experience that, at least in the Congress, that very few members of Congress—at least when I served there—have any affection for Israel or for its Lobby. What they have is contempt, but it is silenced by fear of being found out exactly how they feel. I've heard too many cloakroom conversations in which members of the Senate will voice their bitter feelings about how they're pushed round by the Lobby to think otherwise.

In private one hears the dislike of Israel and the tactics of the Lobby, but not one of them is willing to risk the Lobby's animosity by making their feelings public.

Secondly, the Lobby is quite clear in its efforts to suppress any congressional dissent from the policy of complete support for Israel which might hurt annual appropriations. Even one voice is attacked, as I was, on grounds that if Congress is completely silent on the issue, the press will have no one to quote, which effectively silences the press as well. Any journalists or editors who step out of line are quickly brought under control by well organized economic pressure against the newspaper caught sinning."[3]

Dr. Pastore commented that "the list of political 'scalps' that AIPAC has collected in this manner is impressive. It includes Senator William Fulbright of Arkansas and Senator Charles Percy of Illinois, both former Chairmen of the Senate Foreign Relations Committee, who tried to curb Israel's dominance over the US Senate."

Other AIPAC victims include Congressmen James Traficant (ousted by a "scandal" after he spoke out against Israel), Congresswoman Cynthia McKinney, Congressman Earl Hilliard, and Congressman Paul Findley. The majority of Congressmen from both political parties receive large donations from AIPAC.

AIPAC is widely regarded as the most powerful foreign-policy lobby in Washington. Its 60,000 members shower millions of dollars on hundreds of members of Congress on both sides of the aisle. Newspapers like the *New York Times* fear the Jewish lobby organizations as well. "It's very intimidating," said a correspondent at another large daily "The pressure from these groups is *relentless.*"[5]

Victor Thorn's conclusion as to who had the capacity to engineer the 9/11 terror attacks included:

> The Mossad; Zionist elements within the CIA (who were direct descendants of James Jesus Angleton and the Office of Strategic Services); defense contractors who employed operatives such as Dov Zakheim and his ilk; and rogue elements within the Pentagon-White House (i.e. Donald Rumsfeld, General Richard Myers, and Dick Cheney).[4]

> There have also been many published reports regarding Silverstein's ties to heroin trafficking, money laundering, and other shady endeavors (which means he didn't have any compunction about engaging in criminal behavior—a key component whenever the mass murder of 9/11 is involved.[5]

## *Zionist Control over the Entire Global Financial System*

[AC] It appears that almost all of the American people are blissfully ignorant of such Jewish control, but U.S. presidents are evidently well aware of it as indicated by (1) the appointment by President George W. Bush of Rabbi Dov Zakheim to be undersecretary of defense and Pentagon Comptroller (May 4, 2001 to April 15, 2004) and (2) the announcement by Donald Rumsfeld on September 10, 2001, that the Pentagon could not account for $2.3 trillion and the subsequent announcement that one trillion dollars was also missing during Rabbi Zakheim's tenure, as well as "56 airplanes, 32 tanks, and 36 Javelin missile command launch-units." There has evidently been no grand jury investigation and no explanation as to where or to whom this vast amount of money was paid. [AC]

Matthias Chang's review of the worldwide derivatives scam in 2006 is pertinent. His simple explanation as to why the regulatory authorities and central banks allowed it is that the Zionist-controlled banks and investment houses demanded that they remain unregulated in order that the derivatives could continue to be traded (the interest-rate derivatives amounted to $286 trillion in mid-2006.) He added, "No central bank dare challenge the financial might of the Zionist-controlled banks because they are ultimately protected by the U.S. Federal Reserve, once headed by Alan Greenspan and now by Robert Bernanke! This is the strangle hold which the Zionists have over the entire global financial system."[7]

[AC] The derivatives scam is a mechanism for pumping wealth from the developed world into the bank accounts of the super rich who are planning to force every nation into a world government which they plan to control.

[AC] If the Jewish people really do control America, they must be responsible for the flood of illegal immigrants who are overloading hospitals, welfare services, and prisons in the US. The Jewish people must also be responsible for the long-continued degradation of public school education in the United States. Further, the Jewish people must be behind NAFTA, GATT, and other governmental efforts to export wealth and jobs from the U.S., leading to the present figure of about 9.5 percent unemployment which excludes those who have given up looking for work. The Jewish people must further be responsible for the vast amount of money spent on foreign aid (one-fourth goes to Israel). Further, the Jewish people must have been behind the Cold War and the wars in Korea, Vietnam, Iraq, and Afghanistan, costing trillions, wasting valuable resources, and killing and wounding many, many people. The Jewish people accordingly must have been an enemy of the American people for many years, although the blame should realistically be placed on their leaders. [AC]

## *The Israeli Attack upon the USS* Liberty *on June 8, 1967*

[AC] There have been many references in newspapers and other printed materials about Israel being America's "best ally." However, the facts show the opposite. Israel is America's enemy. A vivid proof is the surprise attack upon the USS *Liberty* by Israeli military forces on June 8, 1967. [AC]

The USS *Liberty* was cruising off the coast of Israel on the night of June 7, 1967, and continued to cruise in international waters more than 12 miles off the coast of the Sinai Peninsula while monitoring communications by aircrews of Soviet bombers in Egypt. Because Egypt was a Soviet client state, the United States needed to know about any possible Egyptian attack on America's ally, Israel, that could involve the United States in a nuclear war.

—

Israel, however, was preparing to make an attack the next day, June 8, 1967, that would enable it to capture Syria's Golan Heights. Israel was not supposed to widen its attacks. Further, Israel planned to murder six hundred Egyptian POWs and did not want the United States to know this.

The crew of the USS *Liberty* was enjoying the pleasant breeze and bright sunshine by sunbathing on her decks as the ship cruised at five knots for eight hours, parallel to the shore. Israeli reconnaissance planes flew at such low levels—sometimes as close as 200 feet—that they rattled the ship's deck. "Sailors aboard the *Liberty*, seeing the Star of David prominently displayed on these surveillance aircraft and believing Israel was America's friend, waved to the Israeli pilots, as allies would normally do." The ship was equipped with forty special-purpose antennae, a large satellite dish, and a large American flag. Large white numbers and letters were freshly painted on its bow and hull so that the Israeli pilots easily identified the ship as being the USS *Liberty*.[8]

Then the jets began dropping bombs to destroy the antennae and dropping napalm onto the sailors while strafing the ship with cannon fire. Next came three motor torpedo boats that fired torpedoes at the ship. One struck the USS *Liberty* amidships, blowing a large hole in its side and killing the radio specialists. A total of 34 men were killed and 172 were wounded.

The skipper ordered the ship to be abandoned, but as the crew was lowering wounded men into inflated life rafts, the torpedo boats machine-gunned the life rafts so that there would be no survivors. Since the ship was at this time off the coast of Egypt, they apparently believed that Egypt would be blamed for the deaths of all 294 Americans aboard.

Radio operators aboard the *Liberty* tried to signal for help, but their SOS distress messages were not heard because "Israel had deliberately jammed all five of the *Liberty*'s emergency radio channels—reserved solely for American use—a phenomenon proving beyond doubt the Jewish state was aware of who their target was beforehand and had previously zeroed in on it. To jam a stranger's radio in such a rapid manner without planning is virtually impossible."

The radiomen foiled the Israeli plans, however, by rigging a small antenna while under fire and sending a "Mayday," which was picked up by the Sixth Fleet. The admiral ordered Navy fighter jets to be launched from nearby aircraft carriers USS *Saratoga* and USS *America*. "Defense Secretary McNamara had them recalled on Johnson's direct order. Never before in U.S. military history had a rescue mission been cancelled with a U.S. Navy ship under attack." The Israelis stopped their attacks when they found out that fighter jets had been launched.[9]

Jim McGonagle, the ship's skipper, although wounded, stayed on the bridge until help arrived eighteen hours later in the form of the USS *America* and a destroyer, which removed the wounded. The USS *Liberty* reached Malta in six days. He "received a promotion, command of a newly commissioned ship, and the Congressional Medal of Honor." However, it was presented not at the White House but at the Washington Navy Yard by the Secretary of the Navy, not by President Johnson.

Admiral Moorer described the U.S. Navy reaction to the attack on the USS *Liberty* as "the most disgraceful act I witnessed in my military career." He also asked, "Does our government continue to subordinate American interests to Israeli interests?"[10]

Vivid proof of Israel's control of the United States is the aftermath of Israel's lies and heinous behavior. Senators Goldwater, Adlai Stevenson, and McCloskey all wanted full investigations while a secret 1976 congressional inquiry report concluded that Israel's attack upon the *Liberty* had been deliberate, but nothing happened.

In addition, a recent Independent Commission of Inquiry declared that Israel had committed "an act of war" against the United States. "The Liberty incident also remains the only peacetime attack on a US Navy vessel not investigated by Congress."

The Israeli killing of Americans aboard the USS *Liberty* (a premeditated murder according to Admiral Moorer) marked a strategic milestone for the Jewish state. No one in the Israeli government or military received even a reprimand. Tel Aviv suffered no political repercussions either for its preemptive seizure and continued occupation of Arab lands or for the murder of Americans. Instead, Lyndon Johnson increased U.S. financial, military, and political support, and the Pentagon was directed to include security of the belligerent Zionist state as a strategic objective of U.S. national security.

For fifteen years, the gravestone inscriptions read simply, "Died in Eastern Mediterranean." Then the USS *Liberty* Veterans Association protested and were able to have the "inscriptions changed to name the USS *Liberty* as the ship on which Americans died in what the crew thought was a defense of American interests."[11]

[AC] The author attended a ceremony in the Arlington National Cemetery in June 1997 alongside the graves of several victims of the treacherous attack on the USS *Liberty*, which was conducted by Evangelist Dale Crowley, Jr. Six veterans of the attack were present. Crowley wrote to the author that Admiral Moorer had persevered for seventeen years to have the original stones removed and replaced with more accurate ones on which "died" was changed to "killed."

[AC] The USS *Liberty* story is pertinent to the murderous events of September 11, 2001, because of this evaluation of the Mossad from the sixty-eight-page report, issued on September 10, 2001, by the army's School of Advanced Military Studies (SAMS), which focused on external threats of terrorism: "Wildcard. Ruthless and cunning. Has capability to target U.S. forces and make it look like a Palestinian/Arab act." It is also pertinent that the Mossad motto is "By way of deception, we shall make war."[AC]

## *The Israeli Murder of Rachel Corrie, an American Citizen*

Another example of Israeli enmity to the United States is the Israeli murder of a young American woman. She was Rachel Corrie, who was so moved by the Palestinian freedom struggle that she took leave from Evergreen State College to join the International Solidarity Movement (ISM) in Palestine. On March 16, 2003, she stood with others in front of an Israeli bulldozer as it approached the house of Palestinian pharmacist Samir Nasrallah.

"Witnesses from the ISM, in a report compiled by the Palestinian Centre for Human Rights, testified that the IDF bulldozer driver could clearly see Corrie, who was dressed in the standard ISDM fluorescent vest, yet proceeded to crush her to death with the blade of the bulldozer."

Rachel said this in an email to her parents, "I am in the midst of a genocide, which I am also indirectly supporting, and for which my government is largely responsible."[12]

### *Unlikely Events, When Combined, Create Almost Certain Probability That Israelis and the Neocons in the Defense Policy Board Participated in Both the WTC and the Pentagon Attacks*

[AC] There is apparently no hard evidence that proves Israel took part in the 9/11 attacks, but there is certainly evidence that some people in Israel had dependable information as to the date and exact time at which the WTC attacks would begin as shown by the three Israeli camera crews having their TV cameras focused on the Twin Towers before Flight 11 struck the North Tower at 8:46 that terrible morning.

[AC] The fact that only three Israelis died in the Twin Towers as compared to the 4,000 frantic telephone calls to the Israeli embassy in Washington, D.C. that Tuesday morning also indicates widespread foreknowledge. So does Odigo receiving a warning two hours before the North Tower was struck. Only a warning of imminent and certain death could have caused Zim Israel Navigation Co. to move its U.S. headquarters suddenly and expensively from the North Tower to Norfolk, Virginia, a mere week before 9/11. The few Jewish New York City workers who died in the WTC, out of the large number of Jews who lived in two New York City boroughs and worked in the WTC, also demonstrates that there was foreknowledge in those counties among the Jews only.

—

[AC] These four indications of Jewish and especially Israeli foreknowledge of a deadly fate for people in the World Trade Center add up to a certainty that these people who gave warnings knew about the complicated, extremely unlikely, and murderous series of acts that were planned to occur within a span of about two hours on a certain Tuesday morning. None of these warnings was remotely likely to have been possible without foreknowledge; put together, they provide a certainty of foreknowledge and involvement in planning the mass murders.

[AC] All these warnings were about events that were extremely unlikely to occur in view of the care with which airliner flights were conducted and the great skill of their pilots, the highly competent fighter jet arrangements for intercepting wayward or hijacked airliners, and the careful design of the massively overbuilt towers for withstanding such airliner collisions.

[AC] Another instance of certain foreknowledge that began at least about six weeks before that Tuesday morning was Silverstein's ninety-nine-year lease of the WTC a mere six weeks before 9/11, even though the Twin Towers were known money losers, plus his strange insurance policy against terrorism and specifically against airliner collisions with the Twin Towers, events that were so unlikely to happen and to cause major losses that the insurance company probably charged a low rate. That policy cost him $14 million but brought in $4.6 billion, while saving $15 billion in demolition costs. A realistic comparison would be an owner of two houses asking an insurance company for insurance against meteorites striking both of his houses. [AC]

## *Routine Illegal Movements of Israeli Cargo Planes through European and New York City Airports*

The crash on October 4, 1992, of El Al Flight 1862, which was carrying 114 tons of weapons of mass destruction (WMD), brought to light the routine waiving of Israeli air cargo through Amsterdam's Schiphol airport and several other European airports. "The cause of the crash was the relentless schedule of overloaded flights, "causing two engines to fall off before the plane crashed into a high-rise apartment complex 10 miles east of Schiphol."

"It was one of the worst air disasters in Dutch history, but that didn't stop Holland's government from conspiring in a cover-up and lying to its citizens to conceal Israel's unlawful chemical weapons arsenal and the international network that supports it."

> The cargo documents show that the aircraft carried dimethyl methylphosphonate (DMMP) and two other substances needed to make the deadly nerve gas Sarin. The DMMP was destined for the Israel Institute for Biological Research (IIBR).

> Mysterious planes loaded with tons of illegal chemicals, bio-warfare agents and nuclear materials were flown from New York to Schiphol to Israel on a regular schedule on Sunday nights—in violation of American laws and international laws that the U.S. has vowed to uphold."[13]

[AC] If such planes were able to move illegal cargoes eastward without supervision, it should have been just as easy to move demolition materials, such as thermite and thermate cutter charges and mininukes, westward in the weeks and months before 9/11. (Israel is known to possess at least 200 nukes and as many as 400.) The two Israeli demolition experts could then have brought these materials to the WTC and supervised their installment in the WTC buildings so that U.S. paperwork for movement of nuclear explosives could have been avoided and the neocons in the Defense Policy Board could then have plausibly maintained their noninvolvement in all 9/11 activities if challenged. [AC]

### Intervention of U.S. Military Officials during All-Aircraft Grounding on September 11, 2011 to Facilitate Departure of Full El Al Plane from JFK Airport for Tel Aviv

Hours after the Federal Aviation Administration (FAA) grounded all civilian domestic and international incoming and outgoing flights to and from the United States on September 11, 2001, "a full El Al Boeing 747 took off from JFK bound for Tel Aviv's Ben Gurion International Airport."

> The flight departed JFK at 4:11 p.m., and its departure was, according to the El Al sources, authorized by the direct intervention of the U.S. Department of Defense. U.S. military officials were on the scene at JFK and were personally involved with the airport and *air traffic control* authorities to clear the *flight for* take-off.

> The El Al flight took off two days before *commercial* flights were permitted to *resume* on September 14.[14]

[AC] The four-engine Boeing 747-400 seated 416 passengers, and the newer 747-8 seated 467 passengers. The plane being full, many Israelis must have had very urgent reasons to leave the United States on the very day that the World Trade Center was demolished. Those reasons were so compelling, in fact, that the Pentagon set aside Secretary of Transportation Mineta's order that grounded all other planes, and even sent defense officials to JFK airport in person to see the plane off for Israel, which does not extradite criminals for trial in other countries. That was real control. The nineteen Muslims blamed for the 9/11 attacks could easily have been among those passengers, whereby their mysterious disappearance on September 11, 2001 could have been accomplished as discussed in chapter 21. [AC]

## *Jewish Racism, Based on Study of the Talmud.*

Jews have believed that they were humans and that all other people were subhumans or even animals for many generations. "A Jew alone is looked upon as a man; the whole world is his and all things should serve him, especially 'animals which have the form of men.'"[15]

[AC] This belief and their repressed hatred for Christianity have had a profound effect upon the relationship between Jews and the host peoples with whom they have been living. Understandably, Jews must have tended to feel contempt for the ethics, morality, and Christian-based habits of their hosts. Equally understandable, resentment by their hosts probably tended to boil up occasionally, causing the pogroms in past years that Jews find hard to forget.

Jews, in consequence, tend to feel, even in the United States, that Israel must be protected as it might be a last refuge in case of more pogroms. [AC]

## *[AC] A Personal Experience*

[AC] After the author had commented, some 30 years ago, to a younger Jewish friend and attorney about the eviction of Palestinians from their homes by Israelis, as well as their torture, imprisonment, and financial harassment, the Jewish friend exclaimed with sincere conviction, "Marion, you don't understand! Palestinians aren't humans, they're animals!" [AC]

# Chapter 19 Notes

1. Pastore, Albert D. *Stranger than fiction: an independent investigation of the true culprits behind 9-11.* 20003. *Dandelion Books, LLC,* Tempe, Arizona, 55.
2. Thorn, Victor. *9-11 Evil.* 2006. *Sisyphus Press,* State College, PA 16805-0495, 36, 37.
3. "Beyond Chomsky: Jim Abourezk on the Israel Lobby." *http:// fanonite.org/2006/12/04/beyond-chomsky-jim* abourezk-on-the.
4. Thorn, 28.
5. Pastore, 34.
6. Thorn, 20.
7. Chang, Matthias. *The Shadow Money Lenders and the Global Financial Tsunami: An expose of the secrets of the Shadow Money Lenders and how they amassed a $500 trillion empire! The End of the U.S. Dollar Hegemony.* 2008, 2009. *American Free Press,* Washington, D.C. 20003, 645 Pennsylvania Avenue SE, #100, 17.
8. Thorn, Victor and Mark Glenn. *Ship Without a Country: Eyewitness Accounts of the Attack on the USS Liberty.* 2009. *American Free Press,* 645 Pennsylvania Avenue SE, Suite 100, Washington, D.C. , 5, 6.
9. Ibid., 6-9.
10. Gates, Jeff. *Guilt by Association: How Deception and Self-deceit Took America to War.* 2008. *State Street Publications,* 3408 State Street, Suite A, Santa Barbara, CA 93105, 65, 66.
11. Conyers, John, Jr. "Findings of the Independent Commission of Inquiry into the Israeli Attack on the USS Liberty, the Recall of Military Rescue Support Aircraft while the Ship Was under Attack, and the Subsequent Cover-up by the United States Government."

Congressional Record, Proceedings and Debates of the 108th Congress. Second Session. October 11, 2004.

12. "Rachel Corrie: Seven Years ago Rachel Corrie was crushed by an Israeli bulldozer while peacefully protesting the demolition of Palestinian homes." *Rock Creek Free Press*. Vol. 4, No. 4, April 2010, 1, 2.

13. Forbes, Ralph. "Mossad Role in Airport Security Troubling." *American Free Press*, 645 Pennsylvania Avenue SE, Suite 100, Washington, D.C. January 18, 2010, Issue 3.

14. "Full El AL flight took off on 9/11 from JFK to Tel Aviv." TVNewslies, March 16, 2010. http://www.tvnewslies.org/tvnl/index.php/news/911-related/13473-full-el-al . . .

15. Pranaitis, I. B. *The Talmud Unmasked: The Secret Rabbinical Teachings Concerning Christians.* 1892. *Imperial Academy of Sciences.* St. Petersburg, Russia.

—

# Chapter 20

## Israel's Plans under the Likud Party for Territorial Expansion

### *Ariel Sharon's Brutal Attacks upon Palestinians*

When the Bush administration began in January 2001, Israeli press reports quoted Israeli government officials and politicians who were speaking openly of mass expulsion of the Palestinians into Jordan. Ariel Sharon was elected as prime minister of Israel in February 2001. He had confronted Arabs most of his life while in various positions of governmental and military leadership. He had commanded special operations that launched brutal cross-border raids against Israel's enemies in the 1950s. These raids included the notorious massacre of Palestinian villagers at Qibya in the then Jordanian-controlled West Bank in October 1953.

As Begin's defense minister, Sharon had masterminded Israel's invasion of Lebanon in 1982 and had been closely involved in the slaughter of Palestinians by Lebanese Christian militiamen at the Sabra and Shatila refugee camps outside Beirut. As minister of housing in the 1990s, he directed Israel's settlement expansion, earning the title "Bulldozer" by destroying whatever Palestinian possessions stood in the way. In September 1999, Sharon made a highly publicized and provocative visit to the Jewish Temple Mount compound, which was close to the Dome of the Rock, one of Islam's holiest shrines in Arab East Jerusalem. Predictably, his visit caused Palestinian riots and lethal Israeli responses that became the Second Intifada.

Sharon had helped to establish the Likud bloc in 1973. He was the embodiment of Jabotinsky's "iron wall" philosophy, but he was not so strongly on the right as those who were unwilling to make even a temporary sacrifice of any part of what they regarded as the "Land of Israel." He was more of a pragmatist than an ideologue regarding tactics, but he was firmly in support of Israeli settlement and control of the West Bank.

### Israeli Plans for a Massive Invasion of the Occupied Palestinian Territories Enabled by the 9/11 Tragedy

In summer 2001, the authoritative *Jane's Information Group* reported that Israel had completed planning for a massive and bloody invasion of the occupied territories, involving "air strikes by F-15 and F-16 fighter bombers, a heavy artillery bombardment, and then an attack by a combined force of 30,000 men . . . tank brigades and infantry." It would seem that such bold strikes aimed at far more than simply removing Arafat and the PLO leadership. But the U.S. opposed the plan, and Europe made equally plain its opposition to Sharon's strategy. As one close observer of the Israeli-Palestinian scene noted in August 2001,

[I]t is only in the current political climate that such expulsion plans cannot be put into operation. As hot as the political climate is at the moment, clearly the time is not yet ripe for drastic action. However, if the temperature were raised even higher, actions inconceivable at present might be possible.

"The September 11 atrocities created the white-hot climate in which Israel could undertake harsh measures unacceptable under normal conditions." When former Prime Minister Benjamin Netanyahu was asked about the effect of the terrorist attack upon U.S.-Israeli relations, he blurted out, "It's very good." Then he corrected himself, "Well, not very good, but it will generate immediate sympathy."

Israeli's leaders believed that 9/11 had joined the United States and Israeli together against a common enemy which was not in far-off Afghanistan but was geographically close to Israel. "Israel's traditional enemies would now become America's as well." "Conversely, America would make itself the enemy of those who previously had focused on Israel." Perle agreed that "Nine-eleven was the turning point with respect to leaving Saddam unmolested."

The terrible tragedy of 9/11 provided to the neocons the "extremely convenient pretext to implement their war agenda for the United States." Before 9/11, how to handle Saddam Hussein was just a fringe part of the debate, but thereafter, the neocons "found the perfect climate to publicly push for a wider war on terrorism" that would immediately bring Israel's enemies, starting with Iraq, into America's plans.[1]

# Chapter 20 Notes

1. Sniegoski, Stephen J. *The Transparent Cabal: The Neoconservative Agenda, War in the Middle East, and the National Interest of Israel.* 2008. *Enigma Editions.* Norfolk, Virginia, 137-140.

# CHAPTER 21

## The Dancing Five and Other Mossad Assets

### *Filming of Burning Twin Towers by Celebrating Israelis*

As reported in the October 1, 2001, issue of *American Free Press* by Christopher Bollyn:

> At least three different groups of Israelis—some of whom may have had ties to Israel's intelligence agency, the Mossad—were arrested after eyewitnesses reported seeing them celebrating in several locations across the river from lower Manhattan in New Jersey. In two cases, the men were reportedly videotaping the initial kamikaze attack on the World Trade Center in New York. All of the detained Israelis were connected to Israeli-owned moving companies operating out of New York and New Jersey.

One group was reported to have been in Liberty State Park in Jersey City, another was seen in Liberty Park in Union City, and a third was apprehended on the roof of an Israeli-owned moving company, Urban Moving Systems, which was "based in Weehawken, N.J. and from which there is a dead-on view of the site of the World Trade Center."[1]

The following detailed account refers to the events in Liberty State Park, where a New Jersey housewife, who had been telephoned by a friend in an adjacent apartment building just after the first strike on the Twin Towers, grabbed a pair of binoculars and watched the horror on the other side of the Hudson River. Then she noticed several men on the roof of a white van in her parking lot, who seemed to be making a movie of the Twin Towers as they burned. They were "laughing uproariously" while dancing on the van. She jotted down the license number of the van and called the police. The FBI was alerted, and it put out their statewide all points bulletin. Witnesses said it appeared that these young men knew what would happen before it happened.

A few different accounts of their behavior follow:

> They were videotaping the disaster with shouts of joy and mockery.

> They seemed to be taking a movie. They were like happy; you know . . . they didn't look shocked to me. I thought it was strange.

> They were jumping for joy after the initial impact.

They were seen by New Jersey residents on September 11 making fun of the World Trade Center ruins and going to extreme lengths to photograph themselves in front of the wreckage.

Still more witnesses saw them celebrating with high fives.

It looked like they were hooked in with this. It looked like they knew what was going to happen when they were at Liberty State Park.

The five young men in the van were arrested by the New Jersey police in midday on September 11. They were dressed as Arabs. Their van was inspected, and the following items were found therein: "$4,700 in cash, foreign passports, box cutters, maps of New York City with certain monuments highlighted, and recently taken photos of the men celebrating as the WTC towers burned in the background."

They worked for Urban Moving Systems, a household moving company in New Jersey. The FBI briefly questioned the owner, Dominik Otto Suter. When the FBI returned a few days later, Suter had left for Israel, leaving the moving company premises in wild disorder.

These young men were later identified as Israelis. Their names are Sivan Kurzberg, Yaron Shmuel, Omer Marmari, Paul Kurzberg, and Oded Ellner.

The Jewish newspaper called *The Forward* stated in March 2002 that American intelligence agencies concluded that "Urban

Moving Systems was a front for the Mossad and operatives employed by it."

After more than two months of detention, the Israelis arrested in the van were released and subsequently returned to Israel. They were released by Israeli dual citizen Michael Chertoff, who was then a member of the Department of Justice and was promoted to be head of Homeland Security. Three of the five men were interviewed on Israeli television a few months later. When asked what they were doing in New York, the answer was "Our purpose was to document the event."

[AC] That indicates that the Israelis who *sent* the film crew from Israel had *foreknowledge* of what was to happen on September 11—that is, "the event." Thus these Israelis might have been involved—perhaps as members of the Mossad—in planning 9/11. The logical question is "How did they *know* beforehand that 'the event' was going to happen at that place, on that day, and at that hour?" [AC]

## *Foreknowledge and Planning for 9/11 by Zionists and Israeli's Mossad*

Thorn makes it clear as to who had the capacity to engineer the 9/11 terror attacks. They are "the Mossad; Zionist elements within the CIA (who were direct descendents of James Jesus Angleton and the Office of Strategic Services); defense contractors who employed operatives such as Dov Zakheim and his ilk; and rogue elements within the Pentagon-White House (i.e. Donald Rumsfeld, General Richard Myers, and Dick Cheney)."[2]

Prior to September 11, 2001, another group of about 140 Israelis were detained in the USA during a widespread investigation into a suspected espionage ring run by Israel inside the USA. They were organized into cells of four to six people according to a sixty-one-page report drafted by the DEA and the U.S. Immigration Service. The significance of what the Israelis were doing emerged only after September 11, 2001, when a report by a French intelligence agency noted "according to the FBI, Arab terrorists and suspected terror cells lived in Phoenix, Arizona, as well as in Miami and Hollywood, Florida, from December 2000 to April 2001 in direct proximity to the Israeli spy cells."[3]

Among these 140 Israelis in the Israeli spy corps within the United States were not only experts in electronics but also explosive experts. As Dr. Stephen J. Sniegoski has pointed out, "What else but collusion, at least intended collusion, with the terrorists could account for the Israeli demolition experts? Those experts must have been secretly in the United States either to aid Islamic terrorists or to set off explosions that could be attributed to Islamic terrorists."

[AC] Dr. Sniegoski's second idea seems more likely to be correct. More specifically, the Mossad probably learned that Arabs who were in the United States had plans involving the criminal use of airplanes within the United States and sent the 140 Israelis and the "art students" to the U.S. to learn the Arabs' plans and for other espionage. Then, while living close to the Arabs, the Israelis learned what these plans were and realized how easily they could create a false flag attack and blame it on these Arabs. They made a deal with the Arabs that they would leave broad trails, as instructed and for generous payment, and then disappear, as described below.

[AC] Next the neocons and the Israelis made a JOA to plan and destroy the WTC and to attack the Pentagon and probably the Capitol or the White House in Washington, D.C., with the murderous results shown repeatedly on TV during and after

September 11. Thereby the government story about 9/11 became imprinted on the minds of people in the United States and all over the world. [AC]

Quoting the "ever-insightful" Justin Raimondo, Dr. Sniegoski wrote:

> At the very least, the mechanics of what is obviously a covert operation directed by Israel imply a certain degree of foreknowledge. At worst, the details of this complex and by-no-means completely uncovered spy ring may wind up pointing to active albeit one-sided Israeli collusion with the mass murderers of 9/11. While the first conclusion is a virtual certainty, the second is, admittedly, speculation. What's scary is that such theorizing is not without a certain basis in fact.

Sniegoski commented that there exists a symbiotic relationship between Israel and the U.S. government with respect to Israeli covert activities. As a result, the U.S. government allows and even encourages Israel to conduct covert operations here and elsewhere because Israeli agencies can perform certain tasks, considered helpful to American interests, more effectively that U.S. agencies can.

> Israel's greater latitude in this area owes very much to the established U.S. media, which programmatically underplay Israeli operations. It is simply taboo to show Israel in a negative light (and the owners and controllers of Big Media are themselves among the creators and enforcers of the taboo). Consequently, Israel enjoys much more leeway to engage in dirty work than the United States does.

The spying was tolerated to the extent it was because, overall, it served the interests of U.S. officials. Once the goal of the American officials had been reached—a casus belli—Washington actively moved to eliminate the spy ring because now its continued activity would be largely hostile to U.S. interests. Of course, since Israel has so much support in the media and in the government itself, the breaking up of the Israeli spy ring had to proceed in the gentlest manner possible, and with no publicity.[4]

[AC] It seems to this author that inserting a variety and large quantities of explosive materials and their detonation systems into the WTC buildings would be exactly the type of covert operation that certain US officials would have greatly preferred to have done by the Israelis. But as to the Pentagon, probably not. [AC]

## [AC] Feasible Method for Removing the Nineteen Alleged Hijackers from the United States on September 11, 2001

[AC] The publicity about the Israeli spy ring may have obscured another Israeli activity of greater importance. An interesting possibility is that the Israelis organized barbering and tailoring operations after about midnight on September 10 for those nineteen Muslims who were the alleged hijackers and who had to disappear from public view. With no facial hair, Western haircuts, Western business suits and shoes, plus some briefcases, the Muslims would have been inconspicuous as they boarded a bus for the El Al terminal in JFK Airport before the early morning rush in New York City.[AC]

—

When the full El Al Boeing 747, containing 416-467 passengers, prepared for take-off with the oversight of U.S. military officials that afternoon, there would surely have been no investigation of a certain nineteen passengers aboard the plane. So after the flight's departure at 4:11 p.m., regardless of Secretary of Transportation Mineta's and then the FAA's grounding of all flights, both domestic and international, throughout the United States that morning, the alleged hijackers would have vanished, leaving no trace. "This El Al flight was the first instance of Israelis departing the United States while commercial traffic was grounded."[5]

# Chapter 21 Notes

1. Piper, Michael Collins. "Evidence Says Some Had Foreknowledge of Impending Attacks of September 11." *Debunking 9-11: Includes 100 Unanswered Questions about Sept. 11. American Free Press*, 645 Pennsylvania Avenue, Suite 100, Washington, D.C., 17-20.

2. Thorn, Victor. *9-11 Evil: Israel's Central Role in the September 11, 2001 Terrorist Attacks*. 2006. *Sisyphus Press*. P.O. Box 10495, State College, Pa. 16805-0495, 28-32.

3. "Five Israelis were seen filming as jet liners ploughed into the Twin Towers on September 11, 2001." *The Sunday Herald 9/11 Investigative Report*. http://ww1.sundayherald.com/37707.

4. Sniegoski, Stephen J. "The Israeli spy ring and September 11." http://www.thornwalker.com/ditch/towers_5.htm.

5. Bigger is Better. "Full El Al flight took off on 9/11 from JFK to Tel Aviv." *http://www.tvnewslies.org/tvnl/index.php/news/911-related/13473-full-el-al . . .*

# CHAPTER 22

## The Urgent Neocon And Israeli Need For "A New Pearl Harbor" = Necessary Motivation

### *A Russian Prediction of the 9/11 Attacks*

On July 12, 2001, *Pravda* published a story about a prediction by Dr. Tatyana Koryagina, a senior research fellow for the Institute of Macroeconomic Research under the Russian Ministry of Economic Development and reportedly close to President Putin's inner circle. This prediction was that an "unusual catastrophe" would strike the United States in late August 2001.

> The United States has been chosen as the object of financial attack because the financial center of the planet is located there. The effect will be maximal. The strike waves of economic crisis will spread over the planet instantly and will remind us of the blast of a huge nuclear bomb.

After the 9/11 attacks, she commented that a significant part of the world financial network was paralyzed as a result of the strikes which were aimed at destabilization and destruction of America and (in domino fashion) all the countries making countless billions of dollars. She advised Russian citizens not to invest in American dollars.

Dr. Koryagina also said that the 9/11 attacks were not the work of nineteen terrorists but a group of extremely powerful private persons seeking to reshape the world. She added that this group had assets of about $300 trillion, which it intends to use to legitimize its power and create a new world government.[1]

### Key to U.S. Domination of Central Asian Oil and Gas Reserves Was "A Truly Massive and Widely Perceived Direct External Threat"

Zbigniew Brzezinski argued in his 1997 book, *The Grand Chessboard: American Primacy and Its Geostrategic Imperatives*, that the key to U.S. dominating the world in the twenty-first century was the control of Central Asian oil and gas reserves around the Caspian Sea. He acknowledged, however, that only "a truly massive and widely perceived direct external threat" could justify the kind of military deployment needed for establishing a U.S. presence there. So it happened; "thanks to the attacks of 9/11—the Bush administration was able to carry out its plan to attack Afghanistan—a plan that, we now know, had been formulated several months before 9/11." Moreover, "[N]ot long after the invasion, the U.S. military started building several bases in Iraq, intended to be permanent."[2]

The neoconservative think tank, Project for a New American Century (PNAC), issued its 2000 manifesto, "Rebuilding America's Defenses: Strategies, Forces, and Resources for a New Century," before the 2000 presidential election. It was written for George W. Bush's team and was "commissioned by future Vice President Cheney, future Defense Secretary Rumsfeld, future Deputy Defense Secretary Paul Wolfowitz, Florida Governor Jeb Bush (George Bush's brother), and future Vice President Cheney's Chief of Staff, Lewis Libby."

This document stated that such a rebuilding process would take time without "a catastrophic and catalyzing event—like a new Pearl Harbor." Then the central roles to be played by Afghanistan and Iraq in setting up a new world order would make American supremacy unchallengeable. These statements are strikingly accurate as to what was "fortuitously" made possible by 9/11.

> Few would argue that we would be in Afghanistan and Iraq today had the attacks of 9/11 never occurred. It is therefore reasonable to be suspicious of the spectacularly convenient conformance between the PNAC manifesto, the rise to power of those who wrote the document and 9/11's absolutely essential role in facilitating the implementation.[3]

# Chapter 22 Notes

1.  Marrs, Jim. *The Terror Conspiracy: Deception, 9/11 and the Loss of Liberty.* 2006. New York, NY 10003. The Disinformation Company Ltd., 163 Third Avenue, Suite 108, 78.

2.  Griffin, David Ray and Peter Dale Scott, editors. *9/11 and American Empire: Intellectuals Speak Out.* 2007. Northampton, Massachusetts 01060. Olive Branch Press, 46 Crosby Street, 16.

3.  Firmage, Joseph P. "Similarity between PNAC agenda and 9/11 aftermath." No. 5. "Intersecting Facts and Theories on 9/11" *Journal of 9/11 Studies*. August 2006/Volume 2, 23.

# CHAPTER 23

## Warnings of the WTC Attacks Indicating Israeli Foreknowledge

### *Odigo Warnings*

Two employees of the Israeli instant messaging company Odigo were anonymously informed of the WTC attacks two hours before they began.

### *Foreknowledge by the Zim American Israel Shipping Co., Inc.*

In a partial evacuation of the North Tower, the Zim American Israel Shipping Co., Inc., broke its lease on the sixteenth and seventeenth floors of WTC-1 in early September 2001 and suddenly moved its two hundred employees to Norfolk, Virginia, in order to save on rent. Breaking the lease cost $50,000. But Zim did not stay long in Norfolk. Several months later, Zim was back in New York.

Zim is one of the world's largest container shipping companies, operating an international network of shipping lines with over eighty vessels. The parent company, Zim Israel Navigation Co., is nearly half owned by the state of Israel, the other half being owned by Israel Corp.[1]

[AC] Suddenly moving the headquarters of a large company a distance of several hundred miles is an expensive and inconvenient undertaking. It certainly did not save money. Revising communications, delivery arrangements, and the lives of employees, necessarily separating their families, requires much planning, effort, and expense so that it is only done if urgently necessary.

[AC] Especially in view of the $50,000 payment for breaking its contract, the information received by Zim American Israel Shipping Co., Inc., which justified this sudden but temporary move and indeed made it urgently necessary, clearly indicates advance knowledge of 9/11 about a week before it happened. An independent federal grand jury could put that shipping company's officials on the witness stand and thereby learn who provided the warning. An independent New York City grand jury, comprising as many 9/11 veterans as possible, should be another ideal vehicle for obtaining this information and solving the murderous crime of September 11, 2001. [AC]

### Why Would Israel Withhold Foreknowledge of 9/11 from Its Ally?

But such stories raise the question: Would a staunch friend of the United States like Israel conduct activities detrimental to its ally?

Two academic observers of Middle Eastern politics, Professors John Mearsheimer of the University of Chicago and Stephen Walt of the John F. Kennedy School of Government at Harvard University, sought to answer this question in a controversial eighty-three-page study titled "The Israel Lobby and US Foreign Policy." First published in digest form in the *London Review of Books* on March 10, 2006, and originally published in full as a working paper of the John F. Kennedy School of Government at Harvard University, the paper quickly prompted a raging controversy between pro and anti-Zionists.

"The U.S. national interest should be the primary object of American foreign policy," the pair wrote. "For the past several decades, however, and especially since the Six Days' War in 1967, the centerpiece of U.S. Middle East policy has been its relationship with Israel. The combination of unwavering U.S. support for Israel and the related effort to spread democracy throughout the region has inflamed Arab and Islamic opinion and jeopardized U.S. security.

"This situation has no equal in American political history. Why has the United States been willing to set aside its own security in order to advance the interests of another state? One might assume that the bond between the two countries is based on shared strategic interests or compelling moral imperatives . . . However, neither of those explanations can account for the remarkable level of material and diplomatic support that the United States provides to Israel."

These sensible professors concluded that "a pro-Israel lobby in the United States has exercised pervasive influence in Washington and in the United States through its intimidation of the press, and by the use of powerful think tanks and influential positions in academia." An indication of extreme bias in favor of Israel is dual citizenship with Israel by some neocons who are very active in think tanks and government.[2]

### *Israelis Were Warned*

Nearly five hundred foreign nationals from over eighty different nations were killed in the World Trade Center, but the number of Israelis was nearly zero (the *New York Times* later wrote that three Israelis had been killed in the WTC) although the Israeli embassy in the United States was bombarded on 9/11 with 4,000 calls from worried Israelis.[3]

[AC] The successfully accomplished act of warning at least hundreds of Israelis of danger in the WTC on September 11, 2001 clearly indicates there was foreknowledge of the attack by someone in Israel. That foreknowledge indicates probable Israeli or neocon complicity or major participation in preparing the murderous 9/11 events. [AC]

# Chapter 23 Notes

1. "An independent investigation of 9-11: Stranger than fiction - The miracle of Passover." *The First Freedom*, April 2006.
2. Marrs, Jim. *The Terror Conspiracy: Deception, 9/11 and the Loss of Liberty.* 2006. The Disinformation Company Ltd., 163 Third Avenue, Suite 108, New York, NY 10003, 122, 123.

# Chapter 24

# The 9/11 Attacks Were an Inside Job

## *A Successful Coup d'État*

As analyzed by Dr. Webster Griffin Tarpley, a distinguished historian, the 9/11 disaster, from the American point of view, was a successful coup d'état by a rogue network within the United States that was designed to shift the United States into a war of civilizations mode against the Arab and Islamic worlds as the first targets, with China and Russia to be next, according to the Wolfowitz doctrine. It was this rogue network that sent President Bush an ultimatum on 9/11 as he was flying from that schoolroom just after the Twin Towers had been hit, with the words: "Angel is next." "Angel" was that day's very secret code word for President Bush himself. It meant this: "Launch the war on civilizations or be liquidated."

Bush did not hesitate and turned the U.S. government over to the rogues in that network. This was not unusual, for U.S. presidents have generally been puppets of this rogue network that acts according to the commands of Wall Street and the City of London.

Tarpley maintained that the "main premise of the war on terror is the myth of September 11." He defined this myth as three thousand people were allegedly killed by a group of nineteen hijackers including Mohammed Atta, who were all members of al Qaeda and were directed by Osama bin Laden with a laptop computer from a cave in Afghanistan. It was all a *lie and a web of deceptions*.

> The 9/11 events were a deliberate provocation carried out from within the U.S. military, security, and intelligence apparatus by a government, the parallel government, the rogue network, the secret team. This faction cuts across the CIA, the Pentagon, the NSA, the FBI, the Treasury Federal Reserve, and other key parts of government. It is a faction which has been operating for more than a century. It meshes with the British MI-6 and Defence Ministry.

[AC] "Wall Street and the City of London" is a term that commonly denotes the very rich and powerful Jewish banking and financial interests in the United States and in Britain, respectively. The "City of London" is a term that somewhat corresponds to Wall Street, but the Queen of England has to request permission to enter it.[AC]

## *al Qaeda*

In the terminology of intelligence work, bin Laden, Atta, and the rest are patsies. They are double agents, fanatics, dupes, agents provocateurs . They operate under the umbrella of al Qaeda, a group which can only be described as the Arab Legion of CIA and MI-6, a classic countergang or pseudogang against Arab nationalism. Their ethnic and religious background allows the Arab and Islamic world to be blamed for terrorist acts. They receive support from the CIA, as typified by bin Laden's famous kidney dialysis. These figures have criminal intent, but what they do not have is the physical and technical ability to produce the effects observed.

The patsies could operate freely and openly, without being arrested, because of the network of moles inside the U.S. government. These moles are loyal to the invisible government, not to the Constitution and the laws. They make sure the patsies are available to be scapegoated, and they destroy the evidence and organize the cover-up after the fact. The moles were responsible for paralyzing U.S. air defenses for one hour and forty-five minutes on 9/11, in comparison with average intercept times of 15-20 minutes at most both before and after. No outside force could have obtained this result.

## *Able Danger*

The terrorist controllers and case officers for Atta and the others were evidently Able Danger, a joint project of the Defense Intelligence Agency and the Special Forces Command. Since Able

Danger came to light, we have learned that Able Danger destroyed 2.5 terabytes of its own records, equal to about a quarter of the Library of Congress, the largest library in the world. Rumsfeld forbade Able Danger officers to testify to Congress.

## Technocrats of Death

Members of the third group are trained professionals who are also the technocrats of death. They have the physical and technical ability to take control of planes containing the necessary software and TV cameras and then to change their courses and to crash them into buildings, such as the Twin Towers of the WTC, and finally to destroy the World Trade Center buildings with controlled demolition. "Some of these professionals operate from inside government bureaucracies and others from private offices. They seek anonymity, not publicity."

## Air Force Exercises on 9/11

"Recent progress in 9/11 research has focused on the role of war games, military exercises, and terror drills," particularly by the U.S. Air Force, "in hiding and facilitating the destructive and murderous terror actions of 9/11." So far 9/11 truth seekers know of fourteen separate exercises related to aircraft on or related to 9/11. Some exercises were used to suppress air defenses by moving fighter planes to northern Canada and Alaska, where they were far from the 9/11 targets on that morning. "Others paralyzed air defenses by inserting false radar blips onto the radar screens of defense personnel so that flight controllers wondered what was real and what was an exercise." Still other exercises involved "commercial and military aircraft, which reported themselves as hijacked," thereby introducing more confusion on 9/11 that paralyzed defense activity.

## The National Reconnaissance Office as Controller for the Four 9/11 Aircrafts

Moreover, there was another dimension. A drill was staged at the National Reconnaissance Office in Chantilly, Virginia, that morning that was actually based on the idea of flying commercial airliners into office buildings. There is every reason to believe that the kamikaze aircraft smashing into the Twin Towers were controlled from that office, the U.S. spy satellite headquarters, as well as Flights 77 and 93. "Amalgam Virgo, another drill associated with 9/11, involved firing a cruise missile against a land target from a rogue freighter in the Gulf of Mexico." This terror drill could have taught how to make the cruise missile attack against the Pentagon "since it is clear that no commercial airliner ever hit that building."

## Plan for Launching Nuclear War on 9/11

Tarpley thought that the most ominous of all such exercises, war games, and terror drills was "Global Guardian, a 9/11 drill that simulated all-out thermonuclear war with bombers, missiles, and submarines." This drill included a "bad" outsider with access to a key command and control system that made an attempt to penetrate the U.S. nuclear command structure from the outside. This situation was the secret portal "through which the rogue network was prepared to launch nuclear war on 9/11."

On 9/11, Bush called Putin in Russia with an ultimatum: "the U.S. would seize Afghanistan, plus bases in ex-Soviet central Asia. If Putin had rejected this, the U.S. rogue network had the capability to set off World War III by ordering nuclear escalation."

> When state terrorists attack, they often do it under the cover of an announced, seemingly legal drill that closely resembles or mimics the terror operation. This helps camouflage the criminal intent of the coup plotters inside their own bureaucracy. The drill is just a drill, until it goes live.[5]

# Chapter 24 Notes

1. Raimondo, Justin. "The Terror Enigma: Israel and the September 11 Connection." *Chronicles Intelligence Assessment.* http://www.chroniclesmagaxzine.org/Chronicles/August 2003/0803CIA.html.

2. "The DEA Report." *Physics 911: Scientific Panel Investigating Nine-Eleven.* http://physics911.net/deareport.

3. Tarpley, Webster Griffin, *9/11 Synthetic Terror Made in USA.* Fourth Edition 2007. 469, Joshua Tree, California 92252, Progressive Press, PO Box 126, www.progressvepresscom

# CHAPTER 25

## Israeli and Neocon Activities Prior to and During 9/11

### *Israeli Spying within the United States*

On December 11, 2001, Fox News began the first in a series of investigative reports that blew the whistle on a vast Israeli spy network operating on American soil—and openly posed the question of whether the Israelis had foreknowledge of September 11. According to *Jane's*, what is striking about Fox News reporter Carl Cameron's portrait of Israel's spy network in the United States was the sheer vastness of his subject. The broad scope of the operation, with its many fronts and activities conducted from coast to coast, had all the aspects of a major military campaign. In the months leading up to 9/11, Cameron claimed, Israel was waging a covert war against its principal ally and benefactor, the United States of America.

Cameron's reports were shown on four nights. Among the myriad details, "some of the 60 detainees arrested in the wake of September 11 were active Israeli military officers. Some had failed

402

polygraph tests when they were asked about 'surveillance activities against and in the United States.'" *The Mossad had thoroughly penetrated top-secret communications systems.* Even more importantly, veteran law-enforcement agents were afraid for their jobs if they questioned Israel's role. Even prior to September 11, as many as 140 other Israelis had been detained or arrested in an investigation into suspected espionage by Israelis in the United States.

The National Counterintelligence Center—whose mandate empowers it to identify and assess possible threats to U.S. national security—warned that "two of the 'students' had been arrested for immigration violations: The suspects possessed counterfeit immigration papers and identification. Later, many more would be picked up—nearly 200—and summarily deported to their country of origin: Israel."

> It turns out that Israel has had a potential wiretap on every phone in America for years, along with the ability to monitor and record who any person is calling, anywhere in America; information of great value even if one does not listen to the calls themselves. Amdocs, Inc. the company which sub contracts billing and directory services for phone companies around the world, including 90 percent of American phone companies, is owned by Israeli interests.

With regard to the Israelis, a highly placed investigator said there were "tie-ins." "But when asked for details, he flatly refused to describe them, saying—quote—'evidence linking these Israelis to 9-11 is classified. I cannot tell you about evidence that has been gathered. It's classified information.'"[1]

An unknown author wrote about the "existence of a system used by law enforcement authorities" wherein "investigations ranging from drug running and money laundering to the events of 9/11 had been compromised by leaks from the company that operated the phone taps." Phone data from an associated company handling billing services for almost every phone in America had also been leaked. The author's focus was on a single question: "could Israel be blackmailing the entire US Government and media?"

> It turns out that Israel has had a potential wiretap on every phone in America for years, along with the ability to monitor and record who any person is calling, anywhere in America; information of great value even if one does not listen to the calls themselves. Amdocs, Inc. the company which sub contracts billing and directory services for phone companies, is owned by Israeli interests.

> There is one more aspect to this issue that needs to be looked at. If indeed Israel is blackmailing our officials and media icons, it is because those who are being blackmailed ARE blackmailable. If we elect a government of criminals, we elect a government subject to blackmail. Finally, given the fact that blackmail may be assumed to be as widespread as the collection system itself is, those who persist in trying to defend Israel may no longer be assumed to be operating from the purest of motives. After all, who will defend a blackmailer more staunchly than those who are the blackmailer's victims.[2]

# The DEA Report

In June 2001, the Office of Security of the Drug Enforcement Administration (the DEA) issued a long report (the DEA Report) describing precisely the attempts of about 125 foreign nationals, most posing as art students, "to penetrate several DEA Field Offices in the continental United States." Many of them visited the residences of numerous DEA officials and those of their employees. Most were living in or near Hollywood, Florida, close to the residences of Arabs taking flight training. An Israeli New Jersey group was located in the second most important area where all five alleged future hijackers of the Pentagon plane lived within about a four-mile radius. The FBI's conclusion was that the Israeli New Jersey Group were Mossad Intelligence Operatives spying on local Arabs in Hudson and Bergen Counties.[3]

[AC] It is likely that the Mossad agents posing as art students were watching the Arabs as they went through flight training and soon learned their plans. Then these agents arranged for the Arabs to be their patsies in their own plans. Because the Arabs' names or alleged names were not on the flight manifestos, and certainly, the Arabs had no reason to conceal their names after leaving a broad trail for the FBI, it seems probable that the Israelis told them to disappear with a generous payment. The Israelis then took over in collaboration with the neocons while knowing that they had arranged for an excellent cover. As previously discussed in Chapter 19, the alleged nineteen hijackers may have also been helped in leaving the United States on the afternoon of September 11, 2001, by Israelis with the assistance of US military officials. [AC]

—

# Chapter 25 Notes

1. Hume, Brit. "Carl Cameron Reports." Fox News. "Powerful on Politics." *Http://web.archive.org/web/20011213022226/http://www.foxnews.com/* sto . . .

2. Unknown author. Is Israel Blackmailing America? Fox News Spikes Four Part Story on Phone Tapping Scandal. What Really Happened. com. *http://whatreallyhappened.com/WRHARTICLES/blackmail.html?q=* black . . .

3. SPINE. "The DEA Report." Physics 911. Public Site. Http://physics911.net/deareport.

# PART VII
## Aircraft Defense, Aircraft Capacities, and Passenger Compensation

# CHAPTER 26

# Air Defense and the Pilots of Flights 11, 175, 77, and 93 on September 11, 2001

### *Standard Operating Procedures Used in Air Defense in the USA*

Under standard operating procedures (SOP), the pilots of every flight must file a flight plan before leaving an airport. This plan includes the exact altitude at which the plane is to be flown and the direction between precisely located points on the route to its destination. Pilots are expected to hit each point or fix with pinpoint accuracy.

When a plane deviates from this flight plan by fifteen degrees or two miles, the nearest flight controller considers it to be a real emergency and tries to make contact (4 1/2 minutes are allowed by the Federal Aviation Administration [FAA] for making contact with the plane). Then the North American Aerospace Defense Command (NORAD) is notified, and within 2 1/2 minutes after the "scramble order" from NORAD, two F-15 fighters or two F-16 fighters are at 29,000 feet, flying at up to 1,875 nmph (nautical miles per hour) or 1,500 nmph, respectively, to intercept the plane and escort it to a landing site. Such interceptions, which should involve no more than ten minutes from noticing a flight deviation, are essential to avoid midair collisions as well as hijacks. They normally occur more than one hundred times per year.

> More specifically, interceptors were scrambled sixty-seven times between September 2000 and June 2001. In the year 2000, jets were scrambled 129 times.

> In the case of Flight 11 that allegedly crashed into the WTC's North Tower (Tower No. 1), radio contact was lost at 8:14 a.m. and would normally have led the flight controller to begin emergency procedures. When the transponder signal was also lost, the situation would have become doubly suspect. The controller would have immediately contacted the National Military Command Center (NMCC) in the Pentagon and its North American Aerospace Defense Command (NORAD), which would have immediately scrambled fighter jets. The fighter jets typically make a graduated response, by rocking wingtips, making a pass in front of the airliner, and firing tracer rounds in the plane's path to attract the pilots' attention. If a plane fails to obey the standard signal to follow the fighter jets to an airport to land, it is shot down.

Flight 11 would have been intercepted by 8:24 and certainly no later than 8:30, well before its alleged crash into WTC-1, the North

Tower, at 8:46:30 a.m. The actual situation, however, was much different: standard operating procedures (SOPs) were completely and inexplicably dropped on September 11—something that had never occurred before.

[AC] The strangely unanswered question then is: who was responsible for ensuring that routine emergency response rules were *not* adhered to? [AC]

The sabotage of routine protective systems, controlled by strict hierarchies, would never have been contemplated let alone attempted absent the involvement of the supreme US military command. This includes at least U.S. President George Bush, U.S. Secretary of Defense Donald Rumsfeld, and then Acting Head of the Joint Chiefs of Staff, Air Force General Richard B. Myers.[1]

An alternative explanation is given by Victor Thorn. Quoting from The Seventh Fire Web site, he commented:

> There was no stand-down on 9-11. The USAF performed exactly as it should when a Field Training Exercise (FTX) is planned. On September 11, 2001 several war games were being staged. War games involved (a) Northern Guardian and (b) Vigilant Guardian (NORAD), (c) CIA/NRO, (d) MASCAL (Pentagon). The security of the United States was at its peak on 9-11—Threatcon Delta. There was absolutely no doubt regarding the readiness of NORAD, NRO, FAA, Military, CIA and FBI on that day. But the line staff did not know that the activity on their screens was real instead of the mock exercise. War games were used to trick the line staff into inaction.

Victor Thorn had this concluding comment:

> Only one entity would be in a position to create such an elaborately deceptive scenario—the Israeli-loyal Defense Policy Board which was manned at every top-level position by rabid pro-war Zionists who had no compunction whatsoever to spill blood or sacrifice human lives as collateral damage.[2]

In confirmation of Victor Thorn's belief is the fact that on September 11, 2001, the U.S. military was conducting between four and six war game exercises and operations involving aircraft from or in the northeastern United States, at least one being involved in simulating hijacked aircraft. Others required northeast fighters to be sent to Canada for scenarios involving invasion by Russian aircraft. As is sometimes done in such exercises, fake aircraft signals were "inserted" into the air traffic control systems of NORAD and FAA in order to test the response protocols of the air traffic and air defense networks.

These exercises degraded the response capacity of FAA and NORAD on 9/11 at least to some degree as indicated by transcripts on that day, asking if "this is real world or exercise," and "I've never seen so much real-world stuff happen during an exercise." Rather revealing is this quotation of a key figure in the air defense command on NORAD tapes: "The hijack's not supposed to be for another hour."

Some researchers have suggested that Vice President Cheney was the lead authority over these exercises on September 11, 2001.[3]

[AC] As stated at the end of Chapter 5, planes had flown over 1,000 times into the WTC restricted space since the WTC was erected, and every time they were intercepted.[AC]

## Defense Capabilities of the 9/11 Pilots

The pilots of the September 11 flights were highly experienced. John Ogonowski, who had been an Air Force fighter pilot in Vietnam, was captain of American Airlines Flight 11 with eighty-one passengers and eleven crew. He was big, burly, and physically strong. His copilot, Tom McGuinness, was also in excellent condition. LeRoy Homer was first officer of United Airlines Flight 93 with thirty-nine passengers and seven crew. Homer, a former Air Force pilot, was muscular and agile. Victor Saracini, a fighter pilot in Vietnam, was captain of UAL Flight 175 with fifty-six passengers and nine crew. He was in superb physical shape and had a quick and alert mind. Chic Burlingame, a graduate of the Naval Academy, flew F-4s in Vietnam; he was captain of American Airlines Flight 77. He was a health nut, a jogger, and an exceptionally competent pilot. Clearly, no alcohol-drinking Arabs, armed with razor or pistol, could take the controls away from any two of these men, much less overpower them.

Col. Donn de Grand Pre's summary of what these highly experienced pilots would have done if there had actually been hijackers aboard was as follows:

> Their absolute best defense would have been to roll the airplane over, using the eight-click "barrel roll." At

413

fourth click, you are inverted; at eighth click, you are once again upright and straight and level. The total maneuver time is 10 seconds. A forced takeover could never have happened inside one of their cockpits.[4]

[AC] Think about it. The would-be hijackers would have been successively slammed against the seated passengers on one side, then against windows, baggage racks, ceiling, baggage racks, windows, and the seated passengers on the other side who could have easily grabbed the box cutters and otherwise immobilized the dazed, if not unconscious, hijackers, assuming that they were actually aboard the planes. [AC]

# Chapter 26 Notes

1. Griffin, David Ray. *The New Pearl Harbor: Disturbing Questions about the Bush Administration and 9/11*. Updated edition. 2005. Olive Branch Press, 46 Crosby Street, Northampton, Massachusetts 01060, 4-11.

2. Thorn, Victor. *9-11 Evil: Israel's Central Role in the September 11, 2001 Terrorist Attacks*. 2006. Sisyphus Press. P.O. Box 10495, State College, Pa. 16805-0495, 102, 103.

3. Firmage, Joseph P. Journal of 9/11 Studies. August 2006/Volume, No. 19, 2, 29.

4. de Grand Pre, Donn. "Former Pentagon Man Has Doubts About 9-11: Former high-ranking Pentagon official Donn de Grand Pre has raised questions about the government's version of 9-11 hijackings." *Debunking 9-11: Includes 100 Unanswered Questions about Sept. 11*. American Free Press, 645 Pennsylvania Avenue, SE 20003, Washington, D.C. 20003, 86.

# CHAPTER 27

# Capacities of the Four Hijacked Planes, Actual Passenger Loads, and Warnings

### *Seating Capacities, Seated Passengers, Crews, and Departure Times*

Published figures for capacity and actual passengers of the four 9/11 planes vary. Using data provided by SeatGuru.com, these four transcontinental flights had a capacity of 694 passengers. They were usually filled to 71 percent of capacity (493), as an average. On September 11, these four planes carried a total of 198 passengers, excluding the alleged hijackers. This is 28.5 percent of capacity and 40 percent of the usual loading. The usual number (493) minus the actual number (198) is 295 passengers. These represented 60 per cent of the usual loading, a really strange departure from normal for a transcontinental flight. It indicates that there must have been an unusual reason for not flying that day, such as an ominous telephone call received by each of those 295 people who stayed home that morning.

[AC] It is common knowledge that commercial airlines cancel flights, combine flights, or make other re-arrangements when lengthy flights are greatly under loaded and consequently losing money.[AC]

The published information about the four flights were as follows:

Table 4
Airliner Capacities, Occupancies, and Take-off Times

| Flight Aircraft | Boeing | Aircraft Capacity | No. Crew | No. of Passengers | Occupancy, % | Expected Take-off a.m. | Actual Take-off a.m. |
|---|---|---|---|---|---|---|---|
| AA 11 | 767 | 158 | 11 | 76 | 48 | 7:59 | — |
| UA 175 | 767 | 166 | 9 | 46 | 28 | 8:14 | 8:24 |
| AA 77 | 757 | 188 | 6 | 50 | 27 | 8:20 | — |
| UA 93 | 757 | 182 | 7 | 26[1] | 14 | 8:01 | 8:42 |

[AC] The author believes that these low occupancies caused crucial difficulties for the plotters and perpetrators of 9/11 who were probably unaware that their many warnings to Israelis and NYC Jews working in the WTC would cause them to warn their friends that it would be dangerous to travel on the four AA and UA airliners that Tuesday morning, resulting in occupancies of 14-48 percent, as compared to an average occupancy of 71 percent. They did not anticipate that, in order to minimize losing money, AA and UA would consequently cancel two AA flights and combine their passengers with two UA flights so that UA 175 would carry 122 passengers (73 percent) and UA 93 would carry 76 passengers (42 percent), thereby causing UA 93's late take-off.

[AC]Their arrangements to swap Flights 11 and 77 with military drones were impossible because of their cancellations, and their arrangement to swap Flight 93 with a military drone was impractical because of its lateness. Allowing Flight 93 to fly around without being intercepted presumably occurred because of the confusion and delays needed to make new arrangements. If occupancies had been normal so that all four flights had taken off on time, all four targets could have been hit by 9:00, within a time span of merely 23 minutes, presumably by four military drones. [AC]

Five hijackers were alleged to have been on each of the first three flights and four on the last, Flight 93.

## *Knowledge of Danger Ahead*

Who knew of the approaching danger? How were 295 passengers, aggregating forty percent of the usual load, selected and notified of this danger to these early morning transcontinental flights on September 11, 2001?

One possibility is worth noting: *Newsweek* twice reported that top Pentagon officials were warned of the impending attack on September 10 and canceled their flights for the next morning. "Ashcroft used charter jets."

The mayor of San Francisco, Willie Brown, was planning to fly into New York on the morning of September 11 but received a call from what he described as his "airport security" late on September 10, advising against flying due to a security threat.[2]

[AC] These warnings indicate that at least several people knew the date, locations, and methods of the attacks before the attacks occurred because selecting and notifying at least about three hundred individuals would surely have required the attention of more than one person. Who is concealing this information? Who selected those to be warned? On what basis were the warned ones selected? On what basis were the actual passengers chosen? Were some chosen to be murdered, some chosen for permanent employment in a super secret project in Nevada, and some chosen for indefinite detainment? Clearly an unshackled federal grand jury can and should investigate the situation and obtain the answers, for they may lead to closer identification of the 9/11 criminals and more justice for some of those passengers. [AC]

# Chapter 27 Notes

1.  "Commandeered Flights: Passenger Jets Taken Over on September 11th." *9-11 Research. http://911research.wtc7.net/planes/attack/index.html.*

2.  Matier, Phillip and Andrew Ross. "Willie Brown got low-key early warning about air travel." SFGate/com. *http://sfgate.com/cgi-bin/*article.cgi?file=/c/a/2001/09/12/MN229389.

# CHAPTER 28

## Options Trading During At Least Ten Days Preceding 9/11

### *Put Options Extremely Numerous Before 9/11*

During the critical days just before 9/11, an extremely high number of "put options" were purchased for the stock of Morgan Stanley Dean Witter, which occupied twenty-two stories of the WTC, and for the stocks of American and United Airlines, the two airlines used in the attacks. For just these two airline stocks, "the level of these trades was up by 1,200 percent in the three days prior to the World Trade Center attacks."

Buying a put option is betting that the price of shares will go down. These bets were highly profitable because "the options multiplied a hundredfold in value, making millions of dollars in profit." The volume of these purchases "raises suspicions that the investors . . . had insider knowledge of the strikes."[1]

## *Trading Consistently Proved Innocuous*

Although enormous resources were used by the SEC and the FBI to investigate this issue, including the cooperation of many foreign governments, this "trading consistently proved innocuous." Dylan Ratigan of Bloomberg Business News commented, "This would be one of the most extraordinary coincidences in the history of mankind if it was a coincidence."[2]

[AC] Ratigan was saying that such a coincidence was almost certainly impossible. If Jews were involved in this short trading and those "enormous resources" were insufficient to detect their "insider knowledge of the strikes," it surely demonstrates their control over not only "America" but also over "many foreign governments."[AC]

## *Israeli Traders Sold Thirty-eight Stocks Short*

Government investigators knew the identities of the people placing these put options, but their names have never been revealed. The speculators were identified by the American Securities and Exchange Commission as Israeli citizens who sold "short" a list of thirty-eight stocks, which could be expected to fall because of the WTC attacks. These speculators operated out of the Toronto, Canada, and Frankfurt, Germany, stock exchanges. Their profits were in the millions of dollars.

The Chicago Board Options Exchange (CBOE), according to Lynne Howard, a spokeswoman for the CBOE, said that their automated system called "blue sheeting" is set up specifically to look into insider trading. It provides instant information on such trades, including the name and even the Social Security number on an account. This short selling, beginning three weeks before the WTC and Pentagon attacks, seemed to City of London broker and analyst Richard Crossley to be evidence of foreknowledge of the coming attacks.

On Sept. 6, 2001, 2,075 put options were recorded for United Airlines, and on Sept.10, 2,282 put options were recorded for American Airlines. As of 2005, the matter was still under investigation, but none of the government investigating bodies, including the FBI, the Securities and Exchange Commission (SEC), and DOJ were speaking to reporters about this insider trading. Moreover, other countries, such as Japan, Germany, the United Kingdom, France, Luxembourg, Hong Kong, Switzerland, and Spain, were investigating such insider trading. Strangely, as in the United States, all of these countries were treating their findings as if they were state secrets.[3]

[AC] Such high-volume put option purchases clearly indicate prior knowledge of the WTC disasters for days before they occurred. Why has the U.S. government not revealed the names of these put option traders? Why haven't the eight other countries also revealed the names of their insider traders? Who could be so powerful that a total of nine countries have been afraid to reveal the names of the traders? There were millions of dollars involved, and the governments of nine countries protected the guilty people. That is *corruption*. Again, an independent federal grand jury could unearth the names of those traders and why they were kept secret. The world needs honesty and the ability to trust others in business activities. It is time to uncover such evil. [AC]

# Chapter 28 Notes

1.  Griffin, David Ray. *The New Pearl Harbor: Disturbing Questions about the Bush Administration and 9/11*. 2005. Olive Branch Press, Northampton, Massachusetts, 71, 72.

2.  Firmage, Joseph P. "Options trading in days preceding 9/11." *Journal of 9/11 Studies*. August 2006/Vol. 2. No. 16, 27.

3.  Mossad watch. "Israelis were 9-11 short sale stock buyers, betting on WTC terror strikes, story killed . . ." http://portland.indymedia.org/en/2005/04/315296.shtml.

# PART VIII
## US GOVERNMENT ENABLING AND US GOVERNMENT COVERING UP OF 9/11 ATTACKS

# Chapter 29

# Lack of US Response to Warnings from Foreign Governments

## *Warnings from Eleven Countries*

A multitude of warnings, many high-level and urgent, came from the intelligence services of eleven countries. As an example,

The following document was published in June of 2002. If genuine, it must rank as one of the most remarkable documents in history. It purports to be a top-secret report from the German external intelligence agency, the Bundesnachrichtendienst (BND) prepared with assistance from an internal German intelligence agency, the BfV.

Among the most important claims it makes are the following: German intelligence detected plans for an attack by Arab extremists on the United States, to take place on September 10 or 11, 2001. Israel was aware of the plans and wished the attack to take place without hindrance. The German ambassador informed the President of the United States of the impending attacks. He thanked the ambassador and said that he already knew. Subsequently, his administration urgently requested the suppression of information on this warning. The report elaborates that among the various reasons for the attack being encouraged by the US administration was a desire to have a pretext to attack Afghanistan to secure a pipeline route for western oil companies to export oil from the Caspian basin.

Despite angry denunciations of the authenticity of the report from various quarters, the German government has to the best of our knowledge not issued a denial of its authenticity. Even if it were to do so, the alleged urgent request for secrecy could provide grounds for such a denial. No other effective refutation of the accuracy of the report has been seen by the editors of this website. Consequently, it is presented for what it is worth as a possibly genuine document of immense historical significance.

A four-part Fox News report on Israeli spying in and on the United States, shown on U.S. TV after September 11, 2001, corroborated certain parts of the BND report, particularly as to "the alleged Israeli tactic of supplying unusable warnings, links to drug-dealing organized crime, and failure to share information supposedly developed on terrorists with the FBI." The following information summarizes portions of that Fox News report on TV.

## *Background of Planned Oil Pipeline from Kazakhstan through Afghanistan*

Between 1991 and 1997, Texaco, Unocal, Shell, BP Amoco, Chevron, and Exxon-Mobil discussed oil rights with Kazakhstan, which has enormous oil reserves, and a pipeline to the Indian Ocean with Afghanistan. The Afghanistan pipeline could avoid the "exorbitant rates charged by the Russians to use their pipelines." These companies paid Kazakhstan over $3 billion for the oil rights and agreed to invest $35 billion for plant and equipment for Kazakhstan oil projects. These companies announced confidentially that the gas and oil reserves in Kazakhstan would amount to $4 trillion.

Official Taliban representatives attended a conference at Unocal headquarters in the U.S. in December 1997 to discuss the Afghanistan pipeline. They made what Unocal felt were excessive financial demands so that the talks failed. Unocal responded by offering the Taliban "a carpet of bombs or a carpet of gold."

Three U.S. officials met with Russian and Pakistani intelligence officers on July 11, 2001. The U.S. officials stated that "the United States planned to launch military strikes against Afghanistan in October" in order to topple the Afghanistan government and the Taliban" and replace them with a government "more sensitive to the needs of American oil interests."

Because 50 percent of the U.S. oil supply is imported from various foreign sources and some 80 percent of that amount comes from OPEC countries, there is a very strained relationship with these Arab governments as a result of the "unconditional support by American political leaders of the state of Israel."

## Specific Warnings from the German, Russian, and French Governments

On Monday, August 6, 2001, German Ambassador Ischinger personally notified President Bush that information from the German domestic secret service and the German foreign secret service indicated that an attack by a radical Arab group, partially based in Germany, was to occur on September 10-11, 2001. This warning "was specific as to date, time, and places of the attacks."

After the 9-11 attacks, the U.S. State Department "made an urgent request to the government of the Federal Republic of Germany that no reference whatsoever should be made to the official warning given by Ambassador Ischinger."

The president of the Russian Federation, Putin, ordered the American government officials to be warned of pending attacks on government buildings inside the United States. This warning was given in mid-August directly to President Bush.

On August 20, the French government, "through the American Embassy in Paris and their Embassy in Washington, issued a more specific warning that specified the exact date, time and places of the attacks."

## The Role of Israel's Mossad in the 9/11 Attacks

The government of Israel made an official, but very secret, request to President H. W. Bush to permit agents of the Mossad, Israel's Foreign Intelligence, "to enter the United States and conduct surveillance operations against various Arab groups residing" therein.

The stated purpose of this surveillance was to give Israel early warnings of terrorist plots against it. The United States granted this request "with the caveat that the Mossad would have a liaison with the FBI and report any and all finding to that agency."

However, the Mossad did not observe these conditions and "not only did not inform the FBI of any of its findings, it . . . engaged in commerce with several groups of Israeli criminals of Russian backgrounds." Moreover, "Mossad agents were able to subvert American criminal investigations through their knowledge of American telephone surveillance of such groups."

[AC] That seems to indicate that the Israeli agents protected the "Israeli criminals of Russian backgrounds" from FBI surveillance. [AC]

Investigations were made into Mossad penetration of various extremist groups in both Germany and the United States. They disclosed in late May of 2001 that "an attack was to be made against certain specified targets in American cities of Washington and New York. But it was apparent that the Mossad was not only fully aware of these attacks well in advance but actually, through their own agents inside these Arab groups, assisted in the planning and the eventual execution of the attacks."

It is "absolutely certain and proven" that "the Israeli government was fully aware of these attack." (sic) Based on diplomatic traffic between the Israeli embassy in Germany and the Israeli Foreign Office, "Minister President Sharon was fully aware of this pending attack and urgently wished that no attempt was made to prevent the attacks."[1]

## *The Role of the Christian Fundamentalists in American Politics*

*[handwritten: I used to like his sermons + but no more!]*

*[handwritten: He says that Jews don't need to confess Chri— they're already saved!]*

On July 21, 2010, reporters and editors from *American Free Press*, plus some like-minded friends, including this author, demonstrated before Washington's convention center where the "multimillionaire preacher for profit Pastor John Hagee" was having his annual Christians United for Israel's 2010 Summit.

"Some of the most powerful pro-Israel people in the United States" passed by, such as "rabidly pro-Israel legislators like Rep. Eric Cantor (R-Va.), Rep. Mike Pence (R-Ind.), and former Sen. Rick Santorum (R-Pa.), as well as neo-conservative mouthpieces Frank Gaffney and Michael Medved."[2]

AFP copy editor John Tiffany was holding a sign saying plainly and accurately, "ZIONISTS MURDER PALESTINIANS." "John Tiffany was physically attacked by a supporter of Christian Zionist leader John Hagee outside the Washington, D.C. Convention Center late on the afternoon of July 21," as he "was peacefully protesting Hagee's appearance at the convention center." Another person who was violently attacked was Ms. "Medea Benjamin, the leader of Code Pink, an anti-war, pro-peace organization that has been critical of Israel's behavior in the West Bank and Gaza."

"Although a police officer was present and witnessed the incidents, he refused to honor Ms. Benjamin's request that the Hagee supporter, who had fled into the convention center, be arrested." The assailant, Harold Lightstone from New Jersey according to his name tag, "was an older man, considerably taller and heavier than Ms. Benjamin, who is a slight, slender woman." Lightstone wielded a heavy carrying bag, "swinging it at Mr. Tiffany repeatedly, shouting angrily and loudly as he did so," but Mr. Tiffany did not strike back.[3]

# Chapter 29 Notes

1. "The German Intelligence Report." Physics 911—Scientific Panel Investigating Nine-Eleven (since June 9, 2003), 1, 3.
2. *American Free Press* Staff, "Hagee Worships Israel in D.C". American Free Press, 11, August 2, 2011, Issue 31.
3. *American Free Press Staff,* "Hagee Fanatic Attacks, Strikes AFP Writer." American Free Press, 11, August 2, 2010, Issue 31.

# CHAPTER 30

## Flight Training of Arabs and Their Use as Patsies Within the United States Until September 11, 2001

### *Arabs as Alleged Hijackers*

According to the *Washington Post* and *Newsweek* in stories published days after 9/11, three to five of the alleged hijackers may have been trained at U.S. military installations in the years leading up to 9/11. Specifically, three of the trainees had names matching alleged hijackers who used the same address at the Pensacola Naval Air Station. Other alleged hijackers trained at a Florida flight school which many in the region believed had been utilized by the CIA. Moreover, it has been alleged that Governor Jeb Bush ordered records removed from his offices within twenty-four hours of the 9/11 attacks.[1]

## *The Carousing Nineteen and the Broad Trail They Left*

Nineteen Arab hijackers were involved in 9/11 according to the official account of the Bush administration, but seven of these have been reported to be alive. These alleged Arab hijackers, who were using stolen identities, spent the night of September 10 getting drunk in bars while making noise, screaming insults at the "infidels," and attracting as much attention as possible. They used their driver's licenses and credit cards issued in their stolen names and even public library computers to send unencrypted emails about their plans to steal aircraft and crash them into buildings. "Whatever trail was left was left deliberately—for the FBI to chase."[2]

[AC] Such behavior does not agree with the official narrative in which the hijackers are described as devout Muslims preparing to meet Allah, but it is in agreement with belief that the alleged hijackers were not devout Muslims but were serving, in the beginning, as false flags and paid patsies for perhaps al Qaeda or another Muslim group.[AC]

[AC] Because at least some of these Arabs received flight training at the Pensacola Naval Air Station, certain U.S. officials apparently approved of their flight training and eventual use in 9/11, before Israel became involved. In other words, their behavior fits with the description of 9/11 as a long-planned "inside job" and a "false flag" operation that led to blaming Osama bin Laden and then justifying the attack on Afghanistan.[AC]

## Disappearance of the Nineteen Arabs from the US during the Afternoon of September11, 2001

[AC] Then when US military officials enabled the full El Al Boeing 747 aircraft to take off from JFK airport at 4:11 p.m. on September 11, 2001, bound for Tel Aviv's Ben Gurion International Airport two days before commercial flights were permitted to be resumed on September 14, the US government was also enabling the getaway of the accused hijackers and thereby covering up for the actual criminals.[AC]

# Chapter 30 Notes

1.  Firmage, Joseph P. "Intersecting Facts and Theories on 9/11." No. 8, 24.
2.  "At Least 7 of the 9/11 Hijackers are Still Alive." WHAT REALLY HAPPENED," 5.

# CHAPTER 31

## Ongoing Cover-up about the Secret Able Danger Operation

### *The Able Danger Team and Its al Qaeda Data-Mining Operations*

In the months prior to 9/11, a super secret Pentagon operation known as Able Danger was tracking and monitoring al-Qaeda. The Able Danger team under the command of U.S. Special Operations Command (SOCOM) had been conducting "data mining" with Orion (data mining is the computer processing of vast amounts of communications, focusing in this case on known members of al Qaeda). This data mining included intercepting and recording the telephone calls of numerous al Qaeda operatives, including Osama bin Laden himself. Former U.S. Army Major Eric Kleinsmith, who was in charge of the operations, testified about the Pentagon orders, but everyone on active duty was not allowed to testify.

When Army Lt. Col. Anthony Schaffer, a principal member of Able Danger, arranged one Able Danger/FBI meeting in the fall of 2000, it was canceled by orders from higher-ups in the Defense Department—as were all other efforts to inform the FBI. More significantly, Clinton administration officials ordered the main Able Danger files destroyed in 2000. Subsequently, Bush administration officials ordered Schafer's duplicate Able Danger files destroyed in 2004.

[AC] These two cover-ups, by ordered destruction of important information about al Qaeda operations during both Democratic and Republican administrations, is another example of high-level corruption. Its occurrence and continuation has only been possible by government and media cover-ups in a climate of tolerance for dishonesty and disregard of the need for truth and trust. [AC]

When Rep. Curt Weldon, who was vice chairman of the Armed Services Committee and the Homeland Security Committee, delivered a forty-five-minute speech on the House floor on June 27, 2005, about Able Danger and the data it had developed, it was the first major exposure of this operation, which has since then been the subject of growing controversy and intense international interest. After several schedulings and postponements, a U.S. Senate Judiciary Committee held a hearing on September 21, 2005, but it was a letdown because the Pentagon blocked the star witnesses from testifying. That pattern has continued, and even worse, many U.S. decision makers have received promotions instead of being penalized for their failures regarding 9/11. In contrast, the agents who have tried to warn and protect the country have been muzzled.[1]

Able Danger's 2.5 terabytes is a small percentage of all available Internet data. A University of California Berkeley study showed that (1) "in 2002, 532,897 terabytes of new data flowed across the Internet, 440,606 terabytes of e-mail was sent, and the Web contained 167 terabytes of data that was accessible to all users, plus another 91,850 terabytes in the Deep web where access is controlled" and (2) data collected by data mining techniques, such as was used in Able Danger, could result in large amounts of data; thus the quality of the data in those 2.5 terabytes was much more relevant than the amount; the data-mining software enabled the data to be sifted into any chosen categories of significant data.

## Knowledge of al Qaeda Activities and Plans

As several 9/11 truth seekers have pointed out, if the Al-Qaeda operatives had simply been arrested prior to September 11, 2001, and kept in custody past that date, there would have been no possibility of plausibly staging 9/11. It was obviously not the desire of the administration to forestall 9/11, however.

According to statements by Lt. Col. Anthony Shaffer and those of four others, Able Danger had identified the September 11, 2001 attack leader Mohamed Atta and three of the 9/11 plot's other nineteen hijackers as possible members of an al Qaeda cell linked to the '93 World Trade Center bombing. This theory was heavily promoted by Rep. Curt Weldon, vice chairman of the House Armed Services and House Homeland Security committees.

In his book *Countdown to Terror* (2005, ISBN 0-89526-005-0), Weldon asserted that an Able Danger chart produced in 1999 identifying 9/11 hijackers Mohamed Atta, Marwan al-Shehhi, Khalid al-Mihdhar, and Nawaf al-Hazmi had been presented to then Deputy National Security Advisor Stephen Hadley in 2001, days after the 9/11 attacks. He later stated that he was no longer sure that Atta's name appeared on that document.

## *Government Interference with Able Danger Attempts to Inform the FBI*

After Congressman Weldon's information had been disputed by the media, Lt. Col. Anthony Shaffer, a member of the Able Danger team, identified himself as Weldon's source and claimed that he had alerted the FBI in September 2000 about the information uncovered by the secret military unit Able Danger but had been blocked by military lawyers after setting up three meetings with bureau officials. Congressman Weldon asked for a new probe into the efforts to silence Lt. Col. Shaffer from publicly commenting on Able Danger and its identification of the 9/11 hijackers. The congressman termed these efforts "a deliberate campaign of character assassination."[2]

# Chapter 31 Notes

1. Jasper, William F. "Able Danger" & 9/11 Foreknowledge: The ongoing cover-up concerning the secret Able Danger operation provides further evidence that the 'war on terror' is a farce." *The New American*. October 31, 2005, 12-14.
2. Complete 911 Timeline: The Able Danger program, 21-35.

# CHAPTER 32

## Fema-Enforced Cover-Up by Immediate Illegal Removal of Evidence

### *Planned Bioterror Exercise for September 12, 2001, in Lower Manhattan*

Conveniently, a bioterror exercise had been scheduled for September 12 in Lower Manhattan, which meant that officials from various agencies had arrived earlier. They were then put to work at WTC on September 11. As Mayor Rudolph Giuliani later testified, "Hundreds of people . . . from FEMA, from the federal government, from the state, from the State Emergency Management Office" had come to New York to take part in the exercise. Giuliani stated that the equipment for the exercise was in place on September 11 so that when he was told that his emergency operations center (in WTC-7) would collapse, he moved to the center set up for the planned bioterror exercise.[1]

[AC] Who told Mayor Giuliani that WTC-7 would collapse? That forty-seven-story building was very strongly built over an electrical power station; it had not been hit by a plane. Its fires were small, and it had not been seriously damaged by flying debris. Who had such foreknowledge? From whom was it obtained? How? The ready answer to these questions is the Office of Emergency Management (OEM), which was directly under Mayor Giuliani, as described in Chapter 6.[AC]

## Hasty and Criminal Removal of Steel from the World Trade Center

Immediately after the collapse of the towers, federal agents and police secured the WTC area. Contrary to federal and state laws concerning crime scenes, the debris from WTC was never subjected to a forensic investigation. Over subsequent weeks and months, thousands of tons of steel beams were evacuated from the site to the port in secured conveys—with GPS devices tracking every vehicle—and then shipped to Asia to be melted and reused for other construction. Thus, the most crucial physical evidence to reveal the causes of the collapses of the towers was intentionally and illegally destroyed without public examination. Each such removal was a felony. At least one of the few pieces of once-molten metal that somehow got around this process has been examined. Residue was discovered consistent with the use of the kind of explosive used in controlled demolition.

The journal *Fire Engineering* had this to say in an editorial:

Comprehensive disaster investigations mean increased safety. They mean positive change. NASA knows it. The NTSB knows it. Does FEMA know it?

No. *Fire Engineering* has good reason to believe that the "official investigation" blessed by FEMA and run by the American Society of Civil Engineers is a half-baked farce that may already have been commandeered by political forces whose primary interests, to put it mildly, lie far afield of full disclosure. Except for the marginal benefit obtained from a three-day, visual walk-through of evidence sites conducted by ASCE investigation committee members—described by one close source as a "tourist trip"—no one's checking the evidence for anything.

Maybe we should live and work in planes. That way, if disaster strikes, we will at least be sure that a thorough investigation will help find ways to increase safety for our survivors.

As things stand and if they continue in such fashion, the investigation into the World Trade Center fire and collapse will amount to paper—and computer-generated hypotheticals.

However, respected members of the fire protection engineering community are beginning to raise red flags, and a resonating theory has emerged: The structural damage from the planes and the explosive ignition of jet fuel in themselves were not enough to bring down the towers.

Clearly, there are burning questions that need answers. Based on the incident's magnitude alone, a full-throttle, fully resourced, forensic investigation is imperative. More important, from a moral standpoint, for the safety of present and future generations who live and work in tall buildings—and for firefighters, always first in and last out—the lessons about the buildings' design and behavior in this extraordinary event must be learned and applied in the real world.[2]

This strong statement from real experts was ignored by the 9/11 Commission, the Bush administration, and the mainstream media.

One of the main themes of hearings held by the House Science Committee on March 2, 2002, was the scandalous eradication of the WTC crime scene. Congressman Anthony D. Weiner, a New York Democrat, compared the "businesslike handling of the crash scene of Flight 186 on November 12, 2001 with the chaos and disdain for the integrity of evidence that had prevailed on the WTC pile under Giuliani's management."

Within literally moments of that plane crash, the National Transportation Safety Board was on the ground sequestering evidence, interviewing witnesses, subpoenaing information, if necessary, and since then, they have offered periodic reports. One month and a day earlier, when the World Trade Center collapsed, nothing could have been further from the truth. According to reports that we have heard since, there has been no comprehensive investigation. We haven't examined any aspects of the collapse that might have impacted rescue worker procedures even in this last month. Second, reports have emerged that crucial evidence has been mishandled. Over 80 percent of the steel from the World Trade Center site has already been sold for recycling, much of it, if not all of it, before investigators and scientists could analyze the information.

Even the National Science Foundation, which has awarded grants to several scientists to study the collapse, didn't coordinate these efforts with FEMA or the American Society of Civil Engineers.

The reality was even worse. FEMA's Building Performance Assessment Team (BPAT) investigation was carried out not by full-time government officials, but rather by a group of volunteer investigators, with a budget of just $600,000. (Ken Starr's budget for hounding Clinton: More than $40 million.) FEMA volunteers had no subpoena power, and could not stay the hand of steel recyclers or confiscate evidence if they required it. They were denied the blueprints of the buildings. They generally could not enter ground zero, apart from an early walking tour. They never saw a piece of steel wreckage until October. Out of millions of fragments, the FEMA BPAT was able to save only 156 from the recyclers.

—

Congressman Weiner was also amazed by the skinny budget for the investigation—less than a million dollars, "and the Bush Administration has refused to commit to release the full funding necessary." (House March 48) He knew that the "Giuliani administration, just like the Bush regime in Washington, was behaving with implacable hostility towards any and all investigations."[3]

[AC] Federal, state, and city personnel were present when the illegal removal of evidence from the WTC site began. If that had occurred after a typical fire in a restaurant, resulting in a few deaths, for example, such removal would have been considered to be evidence of guilt and would have been punished as a felony. So why did all federal, state, and city attorneys general keep mum about this major crime involving nearly three thousand deaths? Such a removal of important evidence was a cover-up and clearly was, and is, the product of a conspiracy, in the author's opinion. It is a type of covered up corruption that an independent grand jury can readily investigate so that truth can be uncovered and justice can be done. [AC]

# Chapter 32 Notes

1. Firmage, Joseph P. No. 27. *Immediate destruction of evidence at WTC sites. Journal of 9/11 Studies.* August 2006/Volume2, 34, 35.

2. Manning, Bill. "Burning Questions . . . Need Answers": *FE's* Bill Manning Calls for Comprehensive Investigation of WTC Collapse, 2, 3. *http://fe.pennet.com/*Articles/ Article_Display.cfm? Section=Online Articles&SubSection=Display&PUBLICATION_id=25&ARTICLE_ID =1.

3. Tarpley, Webster Griffin. *9/11 Synthetic Terror Made in USA.* Fourth *Edition.* 2005-2007. Progressive Press. PO Box 126, Joshua Tree, CA 92252, 232-234.

# CHAPTER 33

## Flight Victims Compensation

### *Did a Military Plane Hit the South Tower?*

Chapter 4, titled "Passenger List Oddities," of *Phantom Flight 93: And Other Astounding September 11 Mysteries Explored*, by Victor Thorn and Lisa Guliani, was written by Vincent Sammartino. He noticed that a Fox News Report had said that the airliner that crashed into the South Tower had no windows. Mr. Sammartino also remembered a few Web sites showing what appeared to be a pod under Flight 175 and an unexplained flash that was visible just before the airliner hit the South Tower on 9/11, thereby indicating that a military plane had been substituted for Flight 175 and that an explosion had occurred on the face of the building at the exact spot that the airliner fuselage was about to hit.[1]

[AC] Another indication that a substitution had taken place was the CFM-56 engine that landed at the corner of Church and Murray Streets in Manhattan from the plane that hit the South

Tower. That engine is not powerful enough to lift a Boeing 767, but it is used in a Boeing 735 plane, as discussed in Chapter 3.

## Discrepancies Among Listed Compensation Recipients

Sammartino also paid attention to Ellen Mariani who lost her husband, Louis, on Flight 175. Then he found Black Op Radio and an archived show (#156) on which Mrs. Mariani and her lawyer, Mr. Berg, appeared as guests. "During this broadcast, Mrs. Mariani said that she was the only relative of all the passengers that died on Flight 175," and Mr. Berg repeated this statement. Then it dawned on Sammartino that the US government might have lied not only about the physics of 9/11 but also about the number of people who died that day.

Sammartino next checked on the Social Security Death Index (SSDI), which is a privately owned Web site having no affiliation with Social Security. It believes it has an accuracy rate of about 83 percent. He further made use of the 9/11 Victims Compensation Fund, which was paid to relatives of people killed or wounded on 9/11. The minimum federal award to a relative was $250,000, and the average payout was about $1.8 million. The recipients had to agree not to sue the airlines. According to the *9-11 Victims Compensation Final Report*, 98 percent of all the people who suffered a loss took the fund money.

[AC] The author wonders why the federal government had any responsibility for the 9/11 tragedy that would justify spending so much taxpayer money to protect the airlines. Upon reflection, perhaps the reason was the government's stand down order and its scheduling of so many war games that morning that fighter jets were not available. If so, it would have been Vice President Cheney's responsibility. [AC]

Sammartino's results are shown in the following table which is strange because of the discrepancies among lists in the table and because human nature is truly greedy for money.

Table 3

Passenger and Crew Deaths and Victims Compensation Recipients for all 9/11 Flights

| Airline & Flight No. | Boeing Model | No. Dead in Pass. & Crew | No. Acc. Fund $ | No. Acc. $ as % of No. Dead | SSDI | No. in SSDI as % of No. Dead | No. in SSDI Who Accepted Fund $ |
|---|---|---|---|---|---|---|---|
| AA 11 | 767 | 92 | 65 | 71 | 20 | 22 | 3 |
| AA 77 | 757 | 64 | 33 | 52 | 14 | 22 | 5 |
| UA 175 | 767 | 65 | 46 | 71 | 18 | 28 | 3 |
| UA 93 | 757 | 45 | 25 | 56 | 6 | 13 | 0 |
| Totals | | 266 | 169 | | 58 | | 11 |

According to columns 2 and 3, which are government data, a total of 169 relatives (64 percent of 266 dead people on the four flights) accepted fund money. According to the last column, of the 266 people who died according to the government story, only 11 relatives of the 58 people who were dead according to the Social Security Death Index applied for compensation under the 9/11 Victims Compensation Fund. More than one deception is surely involved in those numbers![2]

[AC] And what about the discrepancy between the total number of people who died (266) compared to the number who died according to the SSDI List (58), which believes it has an accuracy of 83 percent? An accuracy of 83 percent is not 100 percent; 83

—

percent is five sixths; the remaining one sixth of 58 is about 10 passengers. So the number of SSDI dead can vary from 48 to 68.

[AC]As described in Chapter 3, "Above Stuart air force base,— flights 11 and 175 nearly collided they got so close." However, Flight 11 did not take off from Logan Airport that morning. Probably the other plane which nearly collided with Flight 175 was one of the "2 military drones which were to strike to (sic) world trade centers" and which took off from that air force base.

[AC]That seems to indicate that the theory of airliners swapping with military drones while transponders were off was accurate for two of the airliners, UA Flights 175 and 93. Then these airliners could have continued on their westward flights from Cleveland. [AC]

[AC] Another possibility is that Flight 175 landed at Stuart Air Force Base and discharged approximately 58 selected passengers who were loaded (with their luggage) onto the remaining military plane that took off and hit the north face of the North Tower. As described in chapter 3, these passengers and their luggage became the "bouncy" objects that rebounded, because of the explosion on the face of the North Tower, onto the corner of Vesey Street and West Broadway. Flight175 then took off again from Stuart AFB and landed at the Cleveland Hopkins International Airport.

[AC]Next both Flights 175 and 93, after extensive questioning of the passengers, were flown to Nellis AFB in Nevada, as also described in chapter 3. Subtracting the 58 SSDI dead from the 266 total dead gives 208 as either mysteriously dead or the passengers and crews who were disembarked into one of the detention centers in the western states. [AC]

## *Alternative Disposal Theories for Crews, Passengers, and Airliners*

Referring to Chapter 27, the number of passengers is 198 and the number of crew members is 33. These figures were published by *CNN.com*. The total of 231 is quite different from 266.

Carol Valentine provided an alternative theory in "Flight of the Bumble Planes" in 2002, and A. K. Dewdney wrote a similar theory in 2003, titled "Operation Pearl," referring to Pearl Harbor. Dewdney's synthesis is as follows:

1. Four commercial passenger jets (American Airlines Flights 11 and 77 and United Airlines Flights 93 and 175) take off and shortly after the pilots are ordered to land at a designated airport with a military presence.

2. Two previously-prepared planes (one a Boeing 767, painted up to look like a United Airlines jet and loaded with extra jet fuel) take off and are flown by remote control to intercept the flight paths of AA 11 and UA 175 so as to deceive the air traffic controllers.

3. These (substituted) jets then fly toward Manhattan; the first crashes into the North Tower and (eighteen minutes later) the second crashes into the South Tower.

4. A fighter jet (under remote control), or a cruise missile, crashes into the Pentagon.

5. Back at the airport the (innocent) passengers from three of the Boeings are transferred to the fourth (UA 93).

6. This plane takes off, flies toward Washington, and is shot down by a U.S. Air Force jet over Pennsylvania, eliminating the innocent witnesses to the diversion of the passenger planes.

7. Under cover of darkness later that evening the other three Boeings are flown by remote control out over the Atlantic, are scuttled and end up in pieces at the bottom of the ocean.

Mr. Dewdney pointed out that "the appearance of a terrorist attack on the United States" can be done "by the simple substitution of one aircraft for another, particularly when the transponders are turned off. The only people who need to be deceived by such an operation are the radar operators at air traffic control (ATC) centers." He described in detail how two planes to be swapped come within a half kilometer of each other, one above the other, whereby the radar operator sees only one aircraft. As the blips merge, both planes swerve, each taking the other's former direction. The radar operator simply sees the aircraft cross and has no way to realize that a swap has occurred.[3]

[AC] The author believes that Flight 93 did not crash at Shanksville but over a large area of several square miles near New Baltimore, Pennsylvania. The author prefers the detention center theory because a detention center was available within a large air force base in the West, Flight 175 landed in the Cleveland airport, Flight 77 is known to have flown as far west as Kentucky before allegedly turning around, and Flight 93 was reported to have flown as far west as Cleveland, Ohio, and unloaded its passengers there before turning around toward Washington, D.C.

[AC] The time difference between the Flight 11 and Flight 93 crashes is one hour and 20 minutes. Surely that was enough time for the plane swappings and the Flight 175 landing at Stuart AFB, where those passengers whom the 9/11 planners wanted to eliminate (presumably 58 people) were loaded onto the military drones substituting for Flights 11 and 93 during that time. When those drones crashed onto the north face of the North Tower and onto the area near New Baltimore, Penn., respectively, their bodies and luggage would have been what was found, as described in Chapter 3. [AC]

# Chapter 33 Notes

1. Griffin, David Ray. *The New Pearl Harbor: Disturbing Questions about the Bush Administration and 9/11, Updated Edition.* 2005. Northampton, Massachusetts, 208, 209.

2. Thorn, Victor and Lisa Guliani. *Phantom Flight 93: And Other Astounding September 11 Mysteries Explored.* American Free Press, 645 Pennsylvania Avenue SE, Suite 100, Washington, D.C. 20003, 105-111.

3. Dewdney, A. K., "Operation Pearl." August 2003. http:www.serendipity.li/wot/operation_pearl.htm, 1, 4, 5.

# PART IX
## Origins and Numbers of Dead People at Ground Zero, Missing People at Ground Zero, and Dead People in WTC-7 and in Corridor A of Pentagon

# CHAPTER 34

## Identified and Missing Human Bodies

### *Identifications of Found Bodies and Parts Thereof and Numbering of Missing Bodies*

**Six weeks** after 9/11, only 425 people had been identified. A year later, only 1,401 of the approximately 2,780 victims had been identified, 673 being based on DNA alone. Of the 19,906 remains recovered from Ground Zero, 4,735 were identified. Of these, up to 200 were linked to a single person, meaning that some people were shredded but not vaporized. Only 293 intact bodies were found, and only 12 of them could be identified by sight.

Victim identification statistics, reported in an *Associated Press* article on February 23, 2005, are listed in the following table and are about the same as those reported in articles published a year after the attack.

nearly 2,800 victims

fewer than 300 whole bodies found

fewer than 1,600 victims identified

over 1,100 victims remain unidentified

over 800 victims identified by DNA alone

nearly 20,000 pieces of bodies found

over 6,000 pieces small enough to fit in test tubes

over 200 pieces matched to single person

nearly 10,000 unidentified pieces frozen for future analysis

## *Typical Damages to Human Bodies during Previous Destructions of Large Buildings*

Significantly, the "aircraft impacts and fires in all probability would not have destroyed a single body beyond positive identification," and building collapses in the past have never been known to destroy human remains beyond recognition. Dental records, for example, have alone been sufficient for such identification. This article points out that "the buildings were destroyed in a manner that converted most of their non-metallic contents to homogeneous dust, including the bodies." The effective cremation of the bodies, within the towers and allegedly within the airliners, eliminated most of the evidence that could have undermined the official story of multiple hijackings, by finding that the people on board Flights 11 and 175 had been killed by some means before reaching the towers.[1]

[Author's Comment—AC] Since aircraft impacts and fires would surely not have destroyed a single body so badly that it could not have been positively identified, there must have been something different and far more powerful than all known reasons for such massive buildings to collapse, like a house of playing cards, that could have caused the victim identification statistics reported in the February 23, 2005 AP article. The government story that attempts to ignore the existence of this different and powerful reason is thereby proved to be deceptive and false. [AC]

Five years later, according to the *Washington Times* of October 24, 2006, more human remains were being found while Ground Zero construction continued. As of Tuesday, October 24, 2006, searchers had "yet to open more than half the underground spaces apparently overlooked during the initial excavation of Ground Zero. Already they have found more than 100 pieces of human remains, ranging in size from tiny fragments to leg bones."

The medical examiner's office said, "18 new pieces were found Sunday." For about 40 percent of the victims, no remains have been identified. "Their actions say, 'Remains are not a priority. They're secondary to the rebuilding,'" said Charles Wolf, who lost his wife and has never received any of her identified remains. "This is bringing up all the gnawing, gut-wrenching stuff inside us again." "Hundreds of bone fragments were recently discovered on the roof of a nearby skyscraper that was badly damaged in the attack and had been condemned."[2]

[AC] It seems probable that when living bodies within a tower were touched by an intensely hot heat wave, death came in a millisecond if not sooner as the bodies were instantly brought to the boiling point and exploded. Fragments hurled beyond the heat wave were retrievable. Fragments within the heat wave were instantly cremated into talcum-like dust. [AC]

—

## Psychological Warfare upon the WTC Firefighters and Police by Mayor Rudolf Giuliani

By the end of October, Mayor Rudolf Giuliani was filled with humanitarian concern about the danger of accidents to the firefighters who were seeking the bodies or other remains of their hundreds of fallen comrades in the pile at Ground Zero. On October 31, Giuliani decreed, without any meaningful consultation, that these rescue workers would be limited, on each shift, to twenty-five firefighters, twenty-five New York City policemen, and twenty-five Port Authority patrolmen. Soon "the rescue workers were up in arms" and believed that Giuliani had simply given up on finding bodies and "wanted to speed up the cleanup so it would be finished before he left office."

Giuliani reaped the harvest of his provocations on November 2 when more than one thousand firemen came together at the WTC, chanting, "Bring the brothers home! Bring the brothers home!" "Do the right thing!" "Rudy must go!" and "Tom must go!" (Tom was Fire Commissioner Thomas Van Essen, a Giuliani appointee.) The firefighters and the police guarding the site soon began to argue, and then a full-scale riot began. Twelve firefighters were taken to jail while five policemen were injured. "Giuliani had gladly sacrificed the 9/11 myth of national solidarity to the needs of his campaign of psychological warfare and provocations against the firemen."

On Monday, November 11, 2001, Mayor Giuliani and his officials were confronted by two hundred angry firefighters and bereaved families at a meeting. Giuliani was accused again and again of running a "scoop and dump" operation. One widow protested, "Last week, my husband was memorialized as a hero, and this week he's thought of as landfill?" When Van Essen stammered that the department had been overwhelmed, a widow replied, "Stop saying you are overwhelmed! I am overwhelmed! I have three children and my husband is dead!" Dr. Charles S. Hirsch's theory tried to defend Giuliani by arguing that nothing resembling an intact body was being found any longer, but he was shouted down by firemen who knew from their experience on the pile that this was not so. Van Essen was forced to concede that, based on photographic evidence he personally examined, remains were indeed still being found that had to be "considered intact bodies."[3]

Giuliani's rush to eradicate the crime scene without regard to the preservation of human remains thus served two important goals. He was able to destroy much pertinent evidence, and he succeeded in throwing the firefighters on the defensive and playing them off against the police, the construction workers, and other groups. He was able to split the firefighters themselves. The firefighters were tied into knots emotionally and were left with no time or energy to pursue the issue of justice for their heroic fallen comrades, which could only have been served by directly raising the issue of controlled demolition as indicated in numerous points of the World Trade Center complex.

The firemen, it should be remembered, were those who knew most about the controlled demolition of the World Trade Center, and they were also the group most likely to tell what they knew. In this sense, the firemen posed perhaps the greatest immediate threat to the 9/11 myth upon which the oligarchy had staked so much.

## *Significance of Giuliani's Psychological Warfare and Its Effects upon the Bereaved Men.*

The obvious campaign of psychological warfare against the firemen, therefore, was of world-historical importance. The situation was described by the *New York Post* in an article by Susan Edelman titled "WTC $wine dining: Honchos bill heroes' fund for pricey meals."[4]

A brief article on page 2 of the *New York Post* for Sunday, November 11, 2007, titled "Tragic cop told of 9/11 landfill toil," by Susan Edelman, describes Mayor Giuliani's treatment of such "intact bodies." NYPD Sgt. Michael Ryan remembered his first assignment at the Fresh Kills landfill on September 13, 2001. "There were no contamination suits, no masks. I was just handed a rake and told, 'There's your pile, see what you can find.' That first day we found personal effects, credit cards, and some small body parts. Ryan said [he] sifted for remains for more than eighty hours at the Staten Island dump during twelve-hour shifts over the next six months.

Ryan, a twenty-year-year NYPD veteran and father of four, died at age 41 on November 5, 2007, of non-Hodgkin's lymphoma. This cancer was one of the blood-cell cancers that Dr. Robin Herbert of the WTC Medical Monitoring Program had warned in the previous May that could begin a "third wave" of illnesses caused by toxic exposure at Ground Zero.[5]

## Government-concealed Deaths in WTC 7 and in Corridor A of the Pentagon

[AC] As previously noted, dead bodies were seen and stepped over in the ruined lobby of WTC 7, but the US government maintained that no one had died in that building. People also had to step over bodies in the A corridor of the Pentagon, beyond the C Ring where Flight 77 had officially penetrated. Officials in the federal government have simply created a deceptive myth while ignoring facts about known deaths. Lying about and concealing facts about these murders is aiding the criminals and is itself a crime. [AC]

# Chapter 34 Notes

1. "Missing Bodies: More Than 1000 Bodies Are Unaccounted For." http://911research.wtc7.net/wtc/evidence/bodies.html.

2. "More remains found near World Trade Center: Ground Zero construction goes on despite families' pleas to stop." The Washington Times. October 24, 2006, A3.

3. Tarpley, Webster Griffin. *9/11 Synthetic Terror Made in USA*. Joshua Tree, California 92252. Progressive Press, PO Box 126, 230-232.

4. Edelman, Susan. "WTC $wine dining - Honchos bill heroes' fund for pricey meals." New York Post, November 11, 2007, 2.

5. Edelman, Susan. "Tragic cop told of 9/11 landfill toil." New York Post, November 11, 2007, 2.

# CHAPTER 35

## Unusual Health Hazards at Ground Zero and Resultant Illnesses and Deaths from Numerous Unusual Cancers Among WTC Searchers

### *Deficiency of Health Safeguards at Ground Zero*

Mayor Rudolph W. Giuliani presided over Ground Zero in the days after 9/11 with his usual decisiveness, determination, and self-confidence. His handling of the extraordinary recovery operation "shows that he seized control and largely limited the influence of experienced federal agencies." "While the city had a safety plan for workers, it never meaningfully enforced federal requirements that those at the site wear respirators." The administration also warned companies working on the site that they would face penalties or be fired if work slowed. On some occasions, officials gave flawed public representations of the nature of the health threat even while they privately worried about lawsuits by sickened workers.

David Newman, an industrial hygienist with the New York Committee on Occupational Safety and Health, a labor group, concluded, "The city ran a generally slipshod, haphazard, uncoordinated, unfocused response to environmental concerns."

> City officials and a range of medical experts are now convinced that the dust and toxic materials in the air around the site were a menace. More than 2,000 New York City firefighters have been treated for serious respiratory problems. Seventy percent of nearly 10,000 recovery workers screened at Mount Sinai Medical Center have trouble breathing. City officials estimate that health care costs related to the air at ground zero have already run into the hundreds of millions of dollars, and no one knows whether other illnesses, like cancers, will emerge.[1]

## Extreme Heat Underfoot, Dust Hazards, and Toxic, Ultrafine, and Nanosize Particles

When the Twin Towers fell at 9:59 a.m. and 10:29 a.m. on September 11, 2001, vast dust clouds rose over 1,000 feet, each time plunging the surrounding streets into a pitch-black gloom that lasted for minutes. The wind moved the clouds south over Brooklyn and Staten Island as their fallout covered Lower Manhattan in a blanket of dust. Environmental Protection Agency test reports in 2002 and 2003 distorted the highly alkaline (pH level well above 7) nature of this dust as maintained by Dr. Cate Jenkins, an EPA chemist and whistleblower. The gray brown dust was found in some tests to be as caustic or corrosive as drain cleaner and capable of causing severe irritation and burns.

However, independent scientists at New York University School of Medicine found that whereas large particles of dust were highly alkaline, smaller dust particles, which would be most likely to enter the lower airways of the lungs, where they could cause serious illnesses, were less likely to be alkaline.

The EPA assured New Yorkers in the days and weeks following 9/11 that the dust saturating Lower Manhattan and the smoke still coming from Ground Zero were not a health risk. The EPA issued five press releases within ten days of the disaster that assured people that the air was safe to breathe even though the EPA had no supporting data. However, in August 2003, EPA Inspector General Nikki Tinsley admitted that the reassurances were unfounded because of muzzling by the Bush administration. The EPA was also influenced to "add reassuring statements and delete cautionary ones."

A 2004 report by the Sierra Club indicated gross malfeasance by EPA, FEMA, and OSHA. Specifically, the Sierra Club charged that the government was not poorly informed about the Ground Zero health risk because it had its own long-standing body of knowledge about pollution from incineration and demolition. "EPA should have issued a health warning, based on its own knowledge of pollution before any test data came in."

## Illnesses and Deaths from Exposure to Health Hazards at Ground Zero

Deaths from exposure to the Ground Zero environment began to be reported in early 2006. Three men who had searched for victims in the ruins of WTC died within a seven-month period, according to an *AP* report of January 17, 2006. The *New York Post* reported in April that six 9/11 responders had developed brain cancer, and three of them had died. This paper also "reported in June that 283 World Trade Center rescue and recovery workers had been diagnosed with cancer."

Moreover, EPA's own Web site reported that it found no polycyclic aromatic hydrocarbons (PAHs) "in any 9-11 air samples." (PAHs are cancer-causing chemicals generally released by combustion of mixed materials.) However, PAHs were found at elevated levels in four independent tests and remained a health hazard into 2003. Even after it became clear that people were getting ill and that federal employees of a sister agency in the same building as EPA at 290 Broadway were suffering health impacts, the federal government did not release this information to the public.

Many Ground Zero workers did not have proper protection, especially in the early weeks. The 2004 Sierra Club report explained that federal assurances of safety gave workers conflicting messages about need for respirator masks, which are difficult and exhausting to wear. OSHA also refused to enforce worker safety standards at Ground Zero and wrongly claimed that it had no authority in national emergencies.

EPA and FEMA, cooperating with New York City's own health department, told families to clean up the contaminated dust themselves with wet rags and even discouraged area residents from wearing safety masks.

In a November 2005 meeting of the American College of Chest Physicians, Dr. David Pezant, of the Albert Einstein College of Medicine, gave the findings of a study on the lung function of 12,079 firefighters. Many of them had been active at Ground Zero. According to the study, the rates of pulmonary function declined up to twelve times higher than normal in firefighters exposed to the dust-filled air after the September 11, 2009. The *New York News Day* said that the study "showed that the average decline in lung function experienced by Ground Zero workers was equivalent to 12 years of aging. As of April 2006, about 8,000 people were requiring treatment caused by injuries arising from exposure to Ground Zero air.

[AC] The gross malfeasance of EPA, FEMA, and OSHA, the concealment of Ground Zero hazards by EPA from people working on the site, and the criminal refusal of OSHA to enforce worker safety standards are examples of corruption in the federal government that an unshackled federal grand jury can investigate so that a jury trial can bring the guilty people to justice in a federal district court. [AC]

Dr. Thomas A. Cahill, a retired professor of physics and atmospheric science at the University of California, Davis, said, "When they would pull out a steel beam, the lower part would be glowing dull red, which indicates a temperature on the order of 500 to 600°C. And we know that people were turning over pieces of concrete in December that would flash into fire—which requires about 300°C. So the surface of the pile cooled rather rapidly, but the bulk of the pile stayed hot all the way to December."

After collapses of both Twin Towers, Lower Manhattan was enveloped by more than one million tons of dust, and fires that lingered at Ground Zero until December created a plume of smoke, which was initially detectable from space.

The WTC disaster was entirely unparalleled. Its dust "was unlike any dust and smoke mixture I had ever seen before," said

—

Paul J. Lioy, deputy director of government relations for the Environmental and Occupational Health Sciences Institute (EOHSI), Piscataway, New Jersey. "The fluffy pink and gray powder was basically a complex mixture of everything that makes up our workplaces and lives."

"Six million square feet of masonry, 5 million square feet of painted surfaces, 7 million square feet of flooring, 600,000 square feet of window glass, 200 elevators, and everything inside came down as dust," said Greg Meeker of USGS. "The only thing that didn't get pulverized was the WTC towers' 200,000 tons of structural steel. That was just bent," Meeker said.

"All the dust samples were very alkaline, and aqueous suspensions of dust samples ranged from pH 9 to 11.5. These high pH values surprised no one, for it was recognized that the dust was mainly from cement, plus wallboard and other construction materials.

Dust was "no longer part of the plume per se after about day three or four because the rains came and washed some of the dust and smoke away," but smoldering fires remained. These fires began at over 1,000°C but gradually cooled during September and October 2001.[3]

The RJ Lee Group submitted an expert report, dated May 2004, on behalf of the Deutsche Bank AG at 130 Liberty Street, titled "WTC Dust Signature." On page 20 is this statement: "The ultra fine fibers in WTC Dust are of particular concern because they also carry other toxins and have the potential to penetrate deep into the lungs. On page 21 is this statement: "In the Building, lead was found in the ultra fine fraction, (Table 4) and is as much as a million times more respirable than lead in other dust." The median diameter is given in its Table 4 to be 4.0 microns, with 35.5 percent being within 0-2 microns.

The presence of lead oxide on the surface of mineral wool indicates the existence of *extremely high temperatures* during the collapse that caused metallic lead to volatilize, oxidize, and finally condense on the surface of the mineral wool. The temperature required to volatilize or boil lead is 1,740°C or 3,164°F. This temperature is far higher than an office fire or a jet fuel fire can produce.

The source of dust constituents was specified as 1.2 million tons of building "materials, including an estimated 300 to 400 tons of asbestos, mainly from insulation and from fireproofing, all of which were pulverized. An estimated 50,000 personal computers, containing 200,000 pounds of lead, were destroyed. "Tens of thousands of fluorescent light bulbs, switches, and other mercury-containing items were destroyed, releasing thousands of grams of mercury into the surrounding environment."

On page 13 of this RJ Lee Group Report is this conclusion:

> The Building is contaminated with WTC Dust that
> contains WTC Hazardous Substances, including, but
> not limited to asbestos, lead, mercury, cadmium, PCBs,
> PNAs, quartz, beryllium, mineral wool and dioxins/furans,
> in concentrations substantially in excess of those found in
> dust in other buildings unaffected by the WTC Event.[4]

As of June 11, 2006, 283 WTC rescue and recovery workers were diagnosed with cancer, and 33 of these workers had died of cancer. "One in 150,000 white males under 40 would normally get the type of acute white blood-cell cancer that strikes a healthy detective" We have nearly 35 of these cancers in the family of 50,000 Ground Zero workers. The odds of that occurring are one in hundreds of millions.

"Others suffer tumors of the tongue, throat, testicles, breast, bladder, kidney, colon, intestines, and lung," said Worby, of Worby, Groner, Edelman, Napoli & Bern, which filed the class-action suit.[5]

## *Dangerous Levels of Volatile Organic Materials Detected at Ground Zero*

An article by Kevin R. Ryan, James R. Gourley, and Steven E. Jones, published on August 4, 2008, has this abstract:

Investigators monitoring air quality at the World Trade Center, after the September 11th attacks, found extremely high levels of volatile organic chemicals as well as unusual species that had never been seen before in structure fires. Data collected by the Environmental Protection Agency indicate striking spikes in levels of benzene, styrene, and several other products of combustion. These spikes occurred on specific dates in October and November 2001, and February 2002. Additionally, data collected by researchers at the University of California Davis showed similar spikes in the levels of sulfur and silicon compounds, and certain metals, in aerosols. To better explain these data, as well as the unusual detection of 1, 3-diphenypropane, the presence of energetic nanocomposites in the pile at Ground Zero is hypothesized.

—

The authors noted that the fires at Ground Zero (GZ) could not be put out for months after the destruction at the World Trade Center (WTC), despite the following facts:

Several inches of dust covered the entire area after the destruction of the WTC buildings.

Millions of gallons of water were sprayed onto the debris pile

Several rainfall events occurred at GZ, some heavy.

A chemical fire suppressant called Pyrocool was pumped into the piles. (Lipton and Revkin *2001*)

In addition to the extensive but failed efforts to extinguish the GZ fires, the investigators noted several other physical indicators of the presence of energetic chemical reactions in the GZ rubble, including the following:

Photographs and witness testimony evidencing molten metal and explosions accompanied by white dust clouds.

Extremely high temperatures in the fires at the WTC (Jones et al *2008a*)

Unusual spikes in volatile organic chemical (VOC) emissions, suggesting abrupt, violent fires on specific dates.

Unusual species in the environmental monitoring data, also corresponding to specific dates.

—

Explosions at GZ, which were followed by white dust clouds of aluminum oxide and molten metal, indicated the thermite reaction. Other indications of pyrotechnic materials at the WTC were benzene, styrene, toluene, ethylbenzene, and propylene, which were measured by the U.S. Environmental Protection Agency (EPA) and obtained by a Freedom of Information Act (FOIA) request.

In high-traffic urban areas, "serious health consequences are known to occur when breathing benzene at 100 ppb, and it is known to cause diseases such as leukemia." Although the benzene levels detected at GZ during the first few weeks after 9/11 were relatively low, "the maximum value detected in November 2001 was 180,000 ppb, and average daily detection for October and November 2001 was 18,000 ppb."[6]

Homicide detective James Zadroga of the New York Police Department died on January 5, 2006, from illnesses caused by his hundreds of hours of work at Ground Zero. The Ocean County Medical Examiner determined in April 2006 that his death was caused by his work at Ground Zero, "the first time that any government agency had directly linked a death to the toxic aftermath of the 9/11 attacks." On the second anniversary of his death, three members of Congress said that they planned to "redouble their efforts to pass the James Zadoga 9/11 Health and Compensation Act, which would provide medical monitoring to everyone exposed to Ground Zero toxins and treatment for anyone who is sick as a result."[7]

# Chapter 35 Notes

1. DePalma, Anthony. "Ground Zero Illnesses Clouding Giuliani's Legacy." *New York Times*. May 14, 2007. *http://www.nytimes.com/2007/05/14/nyregion/14giuliani.html.*

2. 9-11 Research. "Ground Zero Hazards: Environmenta*http://pubs.acs.org/cen/NCW/8142aerosols.html.*

4. RJ Lee Group, Inc., 350 Hochberg Road, Monroeville, PA 15146. Signature Assessment, 130 Liberty Street Property. Expert Report, *WTC Dust Signature*. Report Date: May 2004. Prepared for: Deutsche Bank.

5. Edelman, Susan. "Cancer Hits 283 Rescuers of 9/11." *New York Post—Online Edition*. *http://www.nypost.com/news/regionalnews/cancer_hits* 283 rescuers _of_9_11_regionalnews_susan_edel . . . 96. Ryan, Kein R., James R. Gourley, and Steven E. Jones. "Environmental anomalies at the World Trade Center: evidence for energetic materials." Energetic Nano Composites (Thermite Thermate). *http://www.energeticcnanocomposites.com/.*

7. Press Release. Representative Carolyn B. Maloney. "On 2nd Anniversary of Death of Detective James Zadroga, NY Reps. Pledge to Redouble Efforts to Provide Care for All 9/11 Heroes," January 4, 2008.

—

# CHAPTER 36

## International Distribution of Deaths in the WTC

### *Eighty Different Nations*

The WTC being a center of international trade and finance, it is not surprising that nearly five hundred foreign nationals from over eighty different nations were killed in the World Trade Center. "Granada, Bermuda, Ireland, and the Philippines all lost people in the WTC."[1]

### *Israel*

According to *The Jerusalem Post* on September 12, 2001, "The Foreign Ministry in Jerusalem has so far received the names of 4,000 Israelis believed to have been in the areas of the World Trade Center and the Pentagon at the time of the attack." This information is not surprising because "the international Jewish involvement in banking and finance is legendary. Two of the richest firms in New

York are Goldman Sachs and the Solomon Brothers; and both firms have offices in the Twin Towers. Many executives in these firms regularly commute back and forth to Israel. New York is the center of worldwide Jewish financial power, and the World Trade Center is at its epicenter." Surprisingly, however, only one Israeli national was killed in the WTC itself, and one Israeli died aboard each of the airliners that crashed into the WTC.[2]

## New York City

The names of *all* the victims from Monmouth and Ocean Counties were published by the *Asbury Park Press*. Both counties were heavily populated by Jews, many of whom commuted daily to the WTC. A local reporter found only two Jewish-sounding names in that list.[3]

[AC] The number of men and women living in Monmouth and Ocean counties who worked in the World Trade Center in Manhattan must have been at least in the hundreds. Only two Jewish deaths on 9/11 is indeed surprising and certainly indicates that very convincing warnings must have been sent out shortly before 9/11, probably all on Monday evening. If the warnings had been transmitted over a period of days, word of mouth would probably have spread the ominous news too widely. [AC]

## Warnings and Insider Trading Profits

An instant messaging service, known as Odigo, had its Research and Development (R&D) center in Herzliya, Israel, a small town

—

north of Tel Aviv. Mossad's headquarters was also there. Odigo had a feature called People Finder that allows users to seek out and contact others based on certain demographics, such as Israeli nationality.

At least two Israel-based employees of Odigo received warnings of an imminent attack in New York City more than two hours before the first plane hit the WTC. Odigo had its U.S. headquarters two blocks from the WTC. Odigo employees, however, did not pass the warning on to the authorities in New York City, a move that could have saved thousands of lives.

Shortly after 9/11, Comverse Technology, another Israeli company, took over Odigo. "Within a year, five executives from Comverse were reported to have profited by more than $267 million from 'insider trading.'"

Using Israeli "venture capital" (VC) investment funds, Mossad spawns and sponsors scores of software companies, which do business in the United States. These Israel-based companies are sponsored by Mossad-funding sources such as Cedar Fund, Stage One Ventures, and Veritas Venture Partners. These Israeli VC funds and their portfolio companies have strikingly similar Web sites. Their key "team" players are often veterans of various branches of the Israeli military, and most are graduates of Israel's Technion school in Haifa, Mossad's Interdisciplinary Center (IDC) in Herzliya, or a military program for software development.

The IDC has a Marc Rich Center for the Study of Commodities, Trading and Financial Markets and the Lauder School of Government, Diplomacy and Strategy.

Ronald S. Lauder, a cosmetics magnate, who supported Israel's Prime Minister Ariel Sharon and his far right Likud Party and founded the Lauder School, was president of the Jewish National

Fund and former chairman of New York Governor George Pataki's Commission on Privatization. He was also the key player in pushing the privatization of the WTC and the former Stewart Air Force Base, where the flight paths of Flights 11 and 175 were reported to have strangely converged at approximately 8:36 a.m. on September 11, 2001. He further played a significant but unreported role in preparing for 9/11.[4]

## *Software Having an Artificial Intelligence Core That Was Installed on All Government and Military Computer Systems and Could Override FAA Systems as of September 11, 2011*

Ptech, a mysterious software company, which has been "tied with the events of 9/11," "produced software that derived from PROMIS, had an artificial intelligence core, and was installed on virtually every computer system of the U.S. government and its military agencies on September 11, 2001," according Michael Ruppert's From the Wilderness (FTW) Web site.

FTW reported that "this included the White House, Treasury Dept. (Secret Service), Air Force, FAA, CIA, FBI, both houses of Congress, Navy, Dept. of Energy, IRS, Booz Allen Hamilton, IBM, Enron and more."

> "Whoever plotted 9/11 definitely viewed the FAA as the enemy that morning. Overriding FAA systems would be the most effective way to ensure the attacks were successful," FTW reported. To do this, the FAA needed an evolution of PROMIS software installed on

their systems and Ptech was just that; the White House and Secret Service had the same software on their systems—likely a superior modified version capable of 'surveillance and intervention' systems."

Yet Ptech was "supposedly connected to the 'Muslim Brotherhood' and Arab financiers of terrorism." So did the U.S. government unwittingly install software capable of Muslim "surveillance and intervention" operations onto its most sensitive computer networks or was Ptech just a Mossad "cut out" company having the power to order such installations? "The firm's suspected links with terrorism resulted in a consensual examination by the FBI in December 2002." Media reports of the FBI "raid" on Ptech "soon led to the demise of the company."[4]

[AC] Assuming that Ptech was such a Mossad "cut out" company, it means that Prime Minister Sharon knew what he was talking about when he said, "We, the Jewish people, control America, and the Americans know it," as described in chapter 19.[AC]

## Canadian Estimates of 9/11 Deaths

Another book, published in 2006, contains a dedication table to 24 fellow Canadians, plus those killed from as many as eighty-four other countries, including five from Israel. (The source is Wikipedia.) This table states that a total of approximately 2,973 died in the September 11, 2001 disaster, including plane crews and Pentagon casualties, and another twenty-four remain listed as missing and then says that the total includes the following victims:

| | | | |
|---|---|---|---|
| Firefighters & Paramedics | 343 | WTC casualties | 2,667 |
| NYPD Officers | 23 | Flight 77 passengers | 64 |
| Port Authority Officers | 37 | Flight 93 passengers | 45 |
| Flight 11 passengers | 92 | Pentagon casualties | 125[4] |
| Flight 175 passengers | 64 | | |

These figures add up to 3,460 deaths. Subtracting the Pentagon deaths and the passengers in the four airline flights produces 3,134 people who died in the WTC.[5]

[AC] It is evident that nearly all Israelis working in the Twin Towers must have been forewarned to stay away from their offices on September 11, 2001. Certain Israelis must therefore have had foreknowledge. The question to be answered to the satisfaction of all who want to know the truth about 9/11 is, how did they know? Once again, an independent federal grand jury is where to begin.[AC]

# Chapter 36 Notes

1. "An independent investigation of 9-11: Stranger than fiction, The miracle of Passover." *The First Freedom*, April 2006.
2. AR Action Report *online*. Evidence of Mossad Treachery in the WTC *http://www.publiceye.org/frontpage/911/Missing_Jews.htm*.
3. Ibid., 7, 8.
4. Bollyn, Christopher. "Mossad: The Israeli Connection to 911." *http://www.rense.com/general64/moss.htm*.
5. "9/11: The Greatest Crime of All Time: The Best of *Global Outlook* Vol. II," First Edition 2006. Oro, Ontario, Canada LOL 2XO, *Global Outlook*, P.O. Box 22

# PART X
## What Was Planned and What Might Have Been

# CHAPTER 37

## Afghanistan Invasion Plan Ready on September 10, 2001

### *Planned Control over Oil Production*

Between 1993 and 1997, American oil companies negotiated with officials in Kazakhstan, which has enormous oil reserves. Unocal Oil Company wanted to build an oil pipeline through Afghanistan and then through Pakistan to the Indian Ocean, thereby avoiding payment of the exorbitant rates charged by Russia to use their pipelines.

On October 27, 1997, a consortium, called CentGas, was formed to build a pipeline through Afghanistan. Its two main partners were Unocal and Delta Oil of Saudi Arabia. Unocal hoped that the Taliban would stabilize Afghanistan and allow its pipeline plans to go forward.

In December of 1997, official Taliban representatives were invited as guests to the Texas headquarters of Unocal to negotiate over the proposed Unocal Pipeline. However, these talks failed

—

because the Taliban made excessive financial demands. In May 2001, a U.S. official delivered this ultimatum to the Taliban: "Either you accept our offer of a carpet of gold, or we bury you under a carpet of bombs."

A plan "to remove al Qaeda from the face of the earth" was placed on President Bush's desk on September 9, 2001. The plan dealt with all aspects of a war against al Qaeda and was "essentially the same war plan put into action after the Sept. 11 attacks. The administration most likely was able to respond so quickly to the attacks because it simply had to pull the plans 'off the shelf.'"[1]

Former Pakistani Foreign Secretary Niaz Naik later said that he was told by senior American officials—again, prior to September 11—that military action to overthrow the Taliban was planned to "take place before the snows started falling in Afghanistan, by the middle of October at the latest."[2]

[AC] This information indicates that these senior American officials knew about a "new Pearl Harbor" being scheduled to take place before the middle of October because such military action, involving war against a foreign country, could not have been begun without a very strong reason that would appear to justify it. Again, foreknowledge of the 9/11 disaster, this time by "senior American officials," apparently meaning people in the U.S. government, was indicated. [AC]

In April 2002, British Prime Minister Tony Blair stated: "To be truthful about it, there was no way we could have got the public consent to have suddenly launched a campaign on Afghanistan but for what happened on September 11."[3]

Dr. Sniegoski wrote a four-part analysis of events in mid-Asia resulting from the 9/11 attacks:

Despite her preparations for war, the United States couldn't just launch an attack on Afghanistan; U.S. officials required a compelling pretext in order to mobilize the American public into supporting a war in that faraway, and, to most people, unknown land. As Brzezinski had acknowledged, American military expansion into Central Asia could not be undertaken "except in the circumstance of a truly massive and widely perceived direct external threat." Even more importantly, an irresistible provocation was needed to prevent strong opposition to such a war in Iran and Pakistan. Support—or, in the case of Iran, acquiescence—was seen as necessary to allow for the successful conduct of such a war.

### *Necessary Israeli Support for US Foreign Policy*

As important as the interest of Big Oil is, the success of America's foreign policy requires the backing of the supporters of Israel, who hold a dominant place in the official media. Israel's supporters in America unsurprisingly constitute the vanguard of those who are working to enlarge the war into one against Israel's enemies. But Israel is more than simply a beneficiary of the 9/11 attack. Considerable evidence exists that Israel had some connection to the attack, at least to the extent that her intelligence agents possessed prior knowledge of it and its Mossad could send enough personnel to the United States to establish a moving company having at least fifteen people in three camera crews who were ready to film the North Tower attack on September 11, 2001.

—

A study by the army's School of Advanced Military Studies (SAMS) concluded that Israel might engage in deceptive terrorism against the United States. The report was described in a front-page article in the *Washington Times* on September 10, 2001, one day before the horrific attacks. The article said, "Of the Mossad, the Israeli intelligence service, the SAMS officers say, 'Wildcard. Ruthless and cunning. Has capability to target U.S. forces and make it look like a Palestinian/Arab act.'"[4]

## US Control over Drug Production in Afghanistan

Another factor has involved drugs and CIA involvement in drug importation for financing its clandestine operations. Charges about such CIA activities have been made ever since the Vietnam War and have also involved CIA drug smuggling connected to the airport at Mena, Arkansas, which benefited Governor Bill Clinton's needs for cocaine. When the United States began to be involved in Afghanistan in 1979, a provocation that led to the Soviet invasion, Alfred McCoy, author of *The Politics of Heroin in Southeast Asia,* made the following comments:

> CIA assets again controlled this heroin trade. As the Mujahedeen guerrillas seized territory inside Afghanistan, they ordered peasants to plant opium as a revolutionary tax. Across the border in Pakistan, Afghan leaders and local syndicates under the protection of Pakistani Intelligence operated hundreds of heroin laboratories.

[AC] The ineffective war on drugs by the United States has apparently been a supplementary reason for the U.S. attack on Afghanistan in 2001. Drugs, especially heroin, had been introduced into the United States on a large scale by the Communist Chinese during the Vietnam War. They accomplished this objective by making the drug cheaply available on the streets of Saigon as a means of destroying the morale of U.S. troops in Vietnam and to accustom the American public to its use for future sales. This criminal drug importation by American officials indicates corruption on a large scale. Again, an unshackled federal grand jury can reliably straighten out this criminal mess, if the American people care enough. [AC]

In 1995, the former CIA director of the Afghan operation, Charles Cogan, admitted that the CIA had indeed sacrificed the drug war to fight the Cold War.

> There was fallout in terms of drugs, yes. But the main objective was accomplished. The Soviets left Afghanistan.

In contrast, the zealous Muslims within the Taliban government had banned the growth of poppies and had succeeded in destroying nearly 95 percent of the crop by the spring of 2001. According to U.S. estimates, Afghanistan produced 74 tons of opium in 2001, compared to 3,656 tons the previous year.

[AC] Powerful drug distributors, responsible for peddling heroin on the streets of LA or New York, must have viewed the poppy loss as a business disaster. [AC]

After the U.S. invasion of Afghanistan in 2002, opium production soared again so that by the end of 2002, opium production was estimated at 3,400 tons. At least five books and many Web sites have connected both President George W. Bush and his father with the drug trade.

It may come as less of a surprise to learn that—ever since the Vietnam War—it has been charged that the CIA has imported drugs to support its clandestine operations. Mounds of court papers and news stories attest to this criminal activity, yet no one in high authority seems capable of doing anything about it. One former British commando who operated in Afghanistan during the Soviet occupation has stated that both American and British military officers tolerated opium smuggling by the Mujahedeen as the profits were used to support their actions against the Russians.[5]

# Chapter 37 Notes

1.  Tar Paper Sky Reports. "September 11th—The Energy Connection." http://www.heartson.com/Politics/background.html, 1-8.
2.  Griffin, David Ray. *The New Pearl Harbor: Disturbing Questions about the Bush Administration and 9/11*. Northampton, Massachusetts 01060. Olive Branch Press, 46 Crosby Street, 89-92.
3.  Tar Paper Sky Reports, 8.
4.  Siegoski, Stephen J. "September 11 and the origins of the 'War on Terrorism.'" Part four. *http://www.thornwalker.com/ditch/towers_4.htm.*
5.  Marrs, Jim. *The Terror Conspiracy: Deception, 9/11 and the Loss of Liberty*. 2006. New York, NY 10003. The Disinformation Company Ltd., 163 Third Avenue, Suite 108, 218-223.

# CHAPTER 38

## Vast Amounts of US Oil and Natural Gas in the Beaufort Sea Near the North Slope of Alaska, Its Concealment from the Public for the Past Thirty Plus Years, and the Bloody Road to Oil Extraction from Central Asia as the Elitists' Alleged Necessity for World Empire

### *Published Information about Oil Production and Repeatedly Published Deceptions about Oil Availability*

In an article published in *The Washington Times* on December 22, 2010, entitled "How Much Oil Is Left?" by John R. Coyne, Jr., in which he reviewed a book by Kenneth S. Deffeyes, entitled *When Oil Peaked*, Professor Deffeyes is quoted as follows:

> On a spherical Earth, there is a fixed surface area that we
> can explore for oil. World oil production increased rapidly

from the first wells, around 1859, up to year 2005. From 2005 onward, oil production has shown no growth. This is the story that is unfolding before our eyes."[1]

This professor, whose previous book was *Huppert's Peak: The Impending World Oil Shortage* (reissue, with a new preface in 2009) has been trying hard to convince us that world oil production would and did peak in 2005, causing a bidding war for the remaining oil in the ground, so that "the price of crude oil shot upward from $45 per barrel to $140 per barrel. Yet Jeffeyes "was born in the middle of the Oklahoma City oil field" and "grew up in the oil patch." He graduated from the Colorado School of Mines and obtained a graduate degree from Princeton, then rejoined Shell at its research lab in Houston.[2]

This "peak oil" prediction was the foundation for the idea that "America would need full-spectrum dominance to guarantee access to oil and other resources in the rest of the world," essentially establishing a world-dominating empire, and would "require massive expenditures, perhaps as much as a trillion dollars, and this could not be expected from Congress—except in response to an attack as massive and frightening as Pearl Harbor."[3] That attack with mini-nukes was 9/11, "the use of terrorism to construct world order."

[AC] But was such complete dominance of the world's oil supplies really necessary? Was it necessary, for example, to block China's access to Central Asian oil and even Mid-East oil (after an attack on Iran, as is being frantically pushed by the neocons even as late as 2011), thereby potentially starting World War III?[AC]

In his article, Mr. Coyne wrote:

> And where national governments don't own the companies outright—namely, in the United States—the government has become an active managing partner, determining where oil can be explored for or produced, and declaring vast prospective tracts of land, both on and offshore, off-limits to both exploration and production, usually bending to the emotional demands of extreme environmentalists dedicated to ridding the world of the internal combustion engine or preserving an imagined pristine beauty.

> Thus, when areas such as the Arctic National Wildlife Reserve (ANWR), a vast flat mosquito-breeding ground where even the caribou have trouble surviving, are placed off-limits to exploration, when great tracts in the continental West, offshore Florida, the whole East Coast and offshore California are closed to exploration, there's simply no way to know how much oil there is or, therefore, how much can be produced.[4]

[AC]To put the matter bluntly, the professor, who is an emeritus professor of geology at Princeton University, was probably accurate as to *production* in both books, but he was practicing *deception* as to *production capacity*. He must have known what Mr. Coyne, a former White House speechwriter, commented upon as to the US government "determining where oil can be explored for or produced," and he must have been familiar with the book by Chaplain Lindsey Williams about US oil reserves in Alaska that have been available for many years, as described in the next section. An interesting question: If the US government has the power to dictate where drilling for oil and gas can be done in the US, are we not now in a fascist dictatorship?[AC]

Jeffeyes' book referred to oil reserves that were "a vital ingredient" in M. King Hubbert's 1956 prediction that US oil production would peak in the early 1970's. "Oil reserves are defined as future production, using existing technology, from wells that have already been drilled."[5]

## Immense Petroleum and Natural Gas Reserves Proven in Beaufort Sea, Five Miles from North Slope

Lindsey Williams was a chaplain during construction of the trans-Alaskan oil pipeline. He ministered among the pipeline workers so well that he made a favorable impression with top executives and "was asked to improve worker-company relations." Then "he was sitting at meetings of the World Bank, the International Monetary Fund and various meetings of oil executives over a three-year period." Williams said that the "IMF-World Bank acts as a middleman between oil producing nations and refineries. In so doing, they set oil prices."[6]

As early as 1977, hundreds of oil wells had been drilled in the Beaufort Sea (centered on Gull Island, about five miles offshore from Prudhoe Bay in Alaska) without having a single dry hole over a forty-mile expanse. The oil in the Gull Island find had a chemical structure and a pressure that were different from the chemical structure and pressure of the oil in the Prudhoe Bay field and the Kuparuk field, thereby demonstrating that the area contains as much oil as the whole of Saudi Arabia and enough natural gas to last the United States for another two hundred years. The sulfur content of the Gull Island field is 0.9 per cent, "low in comparison to oil from other sources in the U.S., as well as many foreign oils."After spending 2 1/2 years in the area, winter and summer, Chaplain Lindsey Williams wrote a book, *The Energy Non-Crisis*, to tell this story, and the second edition is available at *http://www.reformation.org/energy-non-crisis.html* or by using Google to search for <Lindsey Williams> or <Gull Island>, thereby also accessing several articles about the artificial petroleum situation that is now endured by citizens of the United States.[7]

While on the northern end of the Trans-Alaska Oil pipeline, Williams found out "about the incredible regulations that forced the costs of the Trans-Alaska oil pipeline up from a projected $2 billion dollars to beyond $12 billion dollars."

When Senator Hugh Chance of Colorado visited him on the pipeline, Williams arranged for him to have a tour of the Prudhoe Bay facility and to be given information by a number of highly-placed responsible executives of Atlantic Richfield. Senator Chance said:

> Lindsey, I was in the Senate of the State of Colorado when the federal briefers came to inform us as to why there is an energy crisis. Lindsey, what I have heard and seen today, compared with what I was told in the Senate of the State of Colorado, makes me realize that almost everything I was told by those Federal briefers was a downright lie."

Senator Chance asked one of the officials "how much crude oil is there under the North Slope of Alaska, in your estimation?" The answer was:

> In my estimation, from the seismographic work and the drillings we have already done, I am convinced that there is as much oil under the North Slope of Alaska as there is in all of Saudi Arabia."[8]

The chief operating officer of Atlantic Richfield (Arco) for Alaska, Ken Fromm, brought Williams to high-level company meetings and helped Williams by reviewing the second edition of his book to correct its technical details. Mr. Fromm was finally fired by Atlantic Richfield for this assistance.[9]

As revealed on *The Officer Jack McLamb Show*, June 5, 2008, Jack McLamb said that a multibillionaire whom Williams had known on the pipeline at Prudhoe Bay, Alaska, had "called him and very nicely told him, 'Lindsey, if you start talking about Gull Island right now . . . we're going to kill you, and we're going to kill your family too.'" Williams has understandably ceased his efforts to awaken the country and has returned to being a simple chaplain.[10]

It should be noted that strict US government rules and regulations had not only prevented production from these already drilled wells offshore from the northern slope of Alaska but had also prevented the oil companies from even publicizing their success. These rules and regulations, imposed by the US government, were so stiff that disclosure by Arco about finding this field having immense quantities of oil and natural gas would have created such huge fines that Arco could have been bankrupted within a year.

—

[AC] Williams's efforts with speeches, DVDs, and his book to awaken the American people to the true situation about oil and natural gas were the reason for the threat to him and his family. To the powers-that-be, disclosing the source and quantity of this oil and gas in Alaska could have exposed their merciless increases in the cost of gasoline and the futility and stupidity of their military adventures in Afghanistan and Iraq.

[AC] The author believes that Reagan, Casey, and Rumsfeld (a PNAC member and a member of the COG secret team) wanted an empire in 1980 for its own sake, not because of an actual need for oil and gas. Alternatively, they may have been obeying orders from the neocons and their Zionist allies in about 1977 because plans were being laid then, more than thirty years ago, to have the United States destroy both Iraq and Iran for Israel's benefit.

[AC] An alleged scarcity of oil (and consequently of gasoline) was consequently planned at that time to provide future incentives for having the United States begin military operations in the Mid East. Then, after the United States had set up military bases and moved troops, aircraft, and other military equipment into the Mid East area, 9/11 was arranged to happen. Nothing else was then needed but to arrange an almost total news blackout and control about 9/11.

[AC] It seems likely that two groups were cooperating on 9/11 under a JOA with different short-term objectives but the same long-term objective. The short-term objective for the neocons seems to have been the protection *and expansion of Israel, especially the destruction of two of Israel's enemies,* Iraq and Iran. The short-term objective for the internationalist empire builders was clearly the control and utilization of mid-Asian oil reserves. The long-term objective for both groups seems to have been world government, often termed the New World Order.

[AC] Opportunities for investigations by independent federal grand juries abound in the preceding five pages, such as: (1) the propaganda plan for convincing the world that oil production and oil availability had peaked as of 2005 so that future increases in production would have to come from central Asia; (2) the regulations that multiplied the cost of building the Trans-Alaska pipeline by six times; and (3) the orders not to disclose the wonderfully successful Gull Island finds that culminated in the death threat against Williams and his family. [AC]

## *Big Oil's End Game*

Lindsey Williams has revealed that Henry Kissinger arranged a deal with the Middle Eastern oil-rich nations that the USA would buy their oil, and "(i)n return, the oil sheiks would take a portion of their oil-sales income and buy US. debt, including Treasury securities and other paper," as Williams reported three decades ago. Williams now predicts that, "because of the ongoing crisis and the continued decline of the dollar, oil will go to $150 and then to $200 a barrel before the year is out." Then the USA will double cross those nations and OPEC by ceasing to purchase "oil from the Middle East" and beginning to "extract it from Gull Island in Alaska's Prudhoe Bay, from the nearby Arctic National Wildlife Refuge (ANWR) in Alaska, and from the Bakken formation where North Dakota meets Canada," plus the "2 trillion barrels of shale oil" lying untapped beneath the Rocky Mountains.

—

Williams believes that the "end game" is bringing the USA more fully into the New World Order, an objective partially accomplished by shipping U.S. jobs and factories overseas and by the decline of the dollar.

## What Might Have Been

What might have been was clearly envisioned by Governor Sarah Palin of Alaska when she was "jump-starting progress on a natural gas pipeline" from the North Slope, and perhaps Gull Island also, "to bring Alaska's gas to the U.S. Midwest." She and the Alaskan legislature awarded the contract to TransCanada Corp. an independent pipeline company, not to an oil producing company, because "the producers having complete control of the oil pipeline has cost the state of Alaska billions of dollars over the years; that's a fact."[11]

[AC]Building the pipeline could have provided many good jobs for US and Canadian workers. That two-hundred-year supply of gas could have begun to provide clean, inexpensive energy to the Midwest and to eliminate the importation of much oil from the Mideast, thereby saving billions of dollars. Building a second pipeline for oil, alongside the gas pipeline, could have avoided more importation and saved much more money. Money spent on "green" energy and bio fuels could have been saved.

# Chapter 38 Notes

1. Coyne, John R., Jr. "How Much Oil Is Left?" *The Washington Times*, December 20, 2010, 30.

2. Deffeyes, Kenneth S. *Hubbert's Peak: The Impending World Oil Shortage.* 2009. Princeton University Press, 41 William Street, Princeton, New Jersey 08540, 1x, 12.

3. Scott, Peter Dale. *The Road to 9/11: Wealth, Empire, and the Future of America.* University of California Press, Berkeley, California, 24.

4. Coyne.

5. Deffeyes, 6.

6. Anderson, Mark. "Alaska's Gull Island Oil Fields Could Power U.S. for 200 years." *http://www.americanfreepress.net/html/gull_island_oil. html*

7. Skousen, Joel. "Gas Price Manipulation and Gull Island Oil." Rense. com. *http://www.rense.com/general82/gull.htm*, 2,3.

8. Williams, Lindsey. *The Energy Non-crisis.* Chapter 1. "The Great Oil Deception." http:www.reformatiomn.org/energy-non-crisis-. html.

9. Skousen, 2.

10. TBL.

11. Forgey, Pat. "Democrats join defense of Palin, natural gas pipeline." Juneau Empire. Http://juneauempire.com/stories/102908/ loc_349549309.shtml.

12. Shannon, Pat. Former Insider Reveals Big Oil's End Game: Lindsey Williams tells why the global elite will finally allow extraction of U.S. oil and how." *American Free Press.* March 28, 2011. Issue 13. www.americanfreepress.net.

# INDEX

## O

## P

Pataki, George, 483

Paul, Ron, 71

Pearle, Richard, 60

Pensacola Naval Air Station, 23, 435-36

Pentagon

controlled demolition of, 290

evidence for bomb explosions, 275

Peres, Shimon, 356

Peretz, Martin, 336

Perkal, Don, 276, 288

Perle, Richard, 331, 335-36, 338, 341

Pezant, David, 472

Pfeifer, Joseph, 84

Picciotto, Joseph, 115

pneumothorax, 282

Podhoretz, Norman, 335-36, 338

*Politics of Heroin in Southeast Asia, The* (McCoy), 492

polycyclic aromatic hydrocarbons (PAHs), 472

Port Authority Police Department (PAPD), 104

Powell, Colin, 337

Praimnath, Stanley, 89, 183

Pravda, 386

Predators, 61

Project for a New American Century (PNAC), 326-27, 334, 336, 338, 349, 388

Prudhoe Bay, 499, 501

Ptech, 483-84

Putin, Vladimir, 386, 400, 430

## R

Raimondo, Justin, 382

Rains, Lon, 255

RDX, 99, 194

Reagan, Ronald, 324-25, 335

Reynolds, Morgan, 54, 117, 168, 173

Rice, Condoleezza, 338

Richfield, Atlantic, 500-501

Riskus, Steve, 277

RJ Lee Group, 474-75, 479

Robertson, Leslie E., 139, 219

Rockefeller, Nelson, 27

Rodriguez, William, 134, 170, 228

Rokke (radiation expert), 287

Ross, Gordon, 172

Rostow, Eugene, 335

Rothmund, John, 105

Rumsfeld, Donald, 39, 73, 277, 289, 335, 337, 351, 359, 411

Russian Ministry of Economic Development, 386

Ryan, Michael, 466

—

Texaco, 429

Thorn, Victor, 71, 308, 311-12,
    314-17, 358, 380, 411-12,
    451

Tinsley, Nikki, 471

Tiradera, Peter, 253, 262, 288

*Towers of Deception* (Zwicker),
    144, 148, 187

Traficant, James, 357

Tridata Corporation, 351

Trotsky, Leon, 329-30

Trotskyites, 329, 340

Tully, Peter, 101, 166

Tully Construction, 101, 166

## U

Ucciardo, Frank, 129

Unocal, 429, 489

Urban Moving Systems, 378-79

USA PATRIOT Act, 322

U.S. Federal Reserve, 359

U.S. Geological Survey, 138

USS *America*, 362

U.S. Senate Judiciary Committee,
    440

USS *Liberty*, 360-64

## V

Valentine, Carol, 455

Van Essen, Thomas, 464

venture capital (VC), 482

Veritas Venture Partners, 482

Vialls, Joe, 60-62

Visual Flight Rules (VFR), 90

Vogel, Steve, 288

volatile organic chemical (VOC),
    476-77

von Buelow, 62

## W

Walker, Charles, 335

Walker, Wirt III, 32

Ward, Chester, 124

Ward, Ed, 199

war on terror, 145-46, 341, 396.
    *See also* Kristol's War

weapons of mass destruction
    (WMDs), 243, 251, 367

Weber, Vin, 336

Weldon, Curt, 440-41
    *Countdown to Terror*, 441

Westfield America, Inc., 31

White House, 176, 264

Garden Plot Plan   P. 325
also in news 7-24-12 New Oleans
corrupt police dept using government
to control the dept using US military

What is agenda 21 ?

J2B/1/P

9 781453 57561